ART CAPITAL

CULTURE AND ECONOMIC LIFE

ART CAPITAL

Museum Politics and the Making
of the Louvre Abu Dhabi

BETH DERDERIAN

STANFORD UNIVERSITY PRESS
Stanford, California

Stanford University Press
Stanford, California

Library of Congress Cataloging-in-Publication Data

Names: Derderian, Elizabeth, author.
https://id.oclc.org/worldcat/entity/E39PCjFDVt6DGRjPfDCQffjHYd
Title: Art capital : museum politics and the making of the Louvre Abu Dhabi / Beth Derderian.
Other titles: Culture and economic life.
Description: Stanford, California : Stanford University Press, 2026. | Series: Culture and economic life | Includes bibliographical references and index.
Identifiers: LCCN 2025022385 (print) | LCCN 2025022386 (ebook) | ISBN 9781503644779 (ebook) | ISBN 9781503644182 (cloth) | ISBN 9781503644762 (paperback)
Subjects: LCSH: Louvre Abu Dhabi. | Art museums–United Arab Emirates. | Museums–Political aspects–United Arab Emirates. | Art–Political aspects–United Arab Emirates. | Museum finance–United Arab Emirates.
Classification: LCC N3750.A24 (ebook) | LCC N3750.A24 D47 2026 (print) | DDC 708.95357 23/eng/20250–dc06
LC record available at https://lccn.loc.gov/2025022385

Cover design: Lee Friedman
Front cover art: Unsplash / Damian Kamp; back cover art: Raafat Ishak's artwork *Responses to an Immigration Request from One Hundred and Ninety-Four Governments* (2006–2009) at the Barjeel Art Foundation. Image courtesy the artist and Barjeel Art Foundation
Typeset by Newgen in 10/14 and Minion Pro

The authorized representative in the EU for product safety and compliance is: Mare Nostrum Group B.V. | Mauritskade 21D | 1091 GC Amsterdam | The Netherlands | Email address: gpsr@mare-nostrum.co.uk | KVK chamber of commerce number: 96249943

For PEK, who led the way,
and for H, for all the reasons I can articulate, and
the ones for which I lack the words. A7bish.

Contents

Acknowledgments

I first began this project in 2009 and have incurred many debts of gratitude in the ensuing fifteen years. My biggest debt of gratitude is to the community who hosted me in the Emirates—my interlocutors, who I cannot honor by name. *Alf, alf shukr.* I was once advised to "go where the generosity is" in conducting ethnographic fieldwork: It was advice that honors and foregrounds consent, which I appreciate. And I found overwhelming, humbling generosity in the Emirates. I am grateful to the artists, curators, gallerists, organizers, critics, bloggers, teachers, and art enthusiasts who welcomed me; shared their thoughts and worlds with me; invited me to openings, Pilates classes, weddings, and dinners; fed me; and trusted me with their experiences. It was a privilege to learn from you. This book, and I as a person, have been enriched by your generosity.

At NYU while earning my master's, Nadia Guessous and Jennifer Stampe converted me to anthropology and supported my fledgling project, for which I remain deeply grateful. Nadia's framing of what anthropology can be at its best—to take the lives of people seriously, on their own terms—has guided me ever since. Greta Scharnweber introduced me to Jessica Winegar; little did she know an email would so profoundly improve my life trajectory. When I moved to Chicago, I met Dr. Michael Aisenberg and his counsel has immeasurably improved my life, and I owe him a sizable debt of gratitude. At Northwestern, I found a supportive department and vibrant graduate cohort with Kat Catlin, Ruby Fried, Elisa Lanari, and Ryan Lash, whose engagement and support enriched my work. Thanks to Vanessa Watters Opalo, Nazlı Özkan, Jessica Pouchet, Livia Garofalo, and Kyle Craig, for their critical engagements as well as their support of me personally. The wider community, especially V Chaudhry, Foroogh Farhang, Hafsa Oubou, Mariam Taher, and Ella Wilhoit, contributed to making my years in Evanston stimulating, generative, and fun. In the department, Tracy Tohtz kept everything together, and I was humbled to learn from brilliant faculty. I aspire to the sharp wit, unapologetic tenacity, and fabulous style of Shalini Shankar. Helen Schwartzman sparked my interest in bureaucracy and what organizations actually do, and I am also inspired by her warm generosity and empathy. Micaela di Leonardo constantly drew me back to political economy, and made me a better writer. Most of all, Jessica Winegar believed in my project and in me, and has patiently supported me in every possible way: reading innumerable drafts, pushing me to expand my thinking and trust my analyses, and helping me learn my way back to the center as a person and a scholar when school, ethnographic fieldwork, or life in general toppled my balance. Having such a fierce advocate has been a tremendous blessing, and I aspire to her sterling level of intellect and mentorship.

The Fulbright and the Al Qasimi Foundation supported my fieldwork, and I also benefited from a year as a postdoctoral fellow at the Council on Middle East Studies at the MacMillan Center at Yale University. I have given talks at Yale, Northwestern, and Brandeis on portions of the book to audiences that gave generous critical feedback. My writing group, Laura Goffman, Adeem Suhail, Aparna Kumar, and Vanessa Watters Opalo, has sustained me, encouraged me, and offered community during challenging times, politically and personally. Ahmed Kanna has long supported my work in formal and informal ways, and I am grateful for his sustained engagement. Neha Vora has offered important feedback and friendship, which I so appreciate. Kyle Craig, Laura Goffman, Vanessa Watters Opalo, and Jessica Winegar have read multiple versions of this book in various stages, and their insights have immeasurably improved it; in addition, Zareen Thomas and Lisa Monetti offered critical insights and validation in the final lead-up to publication. I am also grateful to two anonymous reviewers who saw what I was trying to do in this book and offered generous feedback to help me get there, and for a sabbatical from the College of Wooster to focus on revising the manuscript. At Stanford University Press, I'm grateful for Kate Wahl's keen insights as we found the right home for this book, and Marcela Cristina Maxfield's enthusiastic championing of this project. Justine Sargent, Bailey Odom, and the copyediting team have been extremely helpful in the editorial process, and I appreciate their patience with all my questions. I also thank Rafaat Ishak; Anya Shaw; Mary Ellen Carroll and Alserkal Avenue; Maya Allison and Alaa Edris at NYU Abu Dhabi Art Gallery; Jalila Qattan and the Mirror House; 421 Arts Campus; Talin Hazbar and Hunna Art Gallery; Cristiana de Marchi and 1x1 Gallery; Mohamed Abdulraheem and the estate of Hassan Sharif; Abdulraheem Salim; and Dr. Mohamed Yousif, for generously allowing me to use images of their works, exhibitions, and archives in this book. A prior iteration of Chapter 3 was published in 2024 as "Visible Critique/Critical Visibility: Contemporary Artists and Conspicuous Omission in the UAE" in *American Ethnologist*.

When I joined the College of Wooster, I hired Anailah Funchess, Kayla Stevens, and Megan Conklin as sophomore research assistants, and their labor in cross-referencing and transcribing supported this book. Saeed Husain also assisted with UK-based research during the pandemic, for which I'm truly grateful. My first Independent Study (IS) advisees—Marloes Krabbe, Saeed Husain, and Tara Strauch—helped me integrate to Wooster and buoyed my spirits more than they know, and in subsequent years, I was lucky to advise Adam Hinden, Kate Read, Frankie Readshaw, Kayla Stevens, Oli Castañon Villa, and Emily Voneman, who each contributed to my thinking in different ways. At Wooster, Kara Morrow was a phenomenal mentor, and she consistently goes above and beyond in all she does. Zareen Thomas, Siavash Samei, Katie Farr, Denise Monbarren, Jim Bonk, Mark Graham, Heather Guarnera, Laura Sirot, Erum Haider, Joan Friedman, and Amber Garcia have been great colleagues and co-conspirators. Working on Pella at Wooster with Siavash Samei, Marianne Wardle, Olivia Navarro-Farr, Katie Farr, Denise Monbarren, Leo Daoud, and my students has been a truly pleasurable experience even if it did distract me from this book. The Soc-Anth Department was a welcoming and supportive community for a junior faculty member. Olivia Navarro-Farr has been an incredible support, and she inspires me in how she makes space for scholars of all ages to shine. As this book goes to press, I am joining the Crown Center for Middle East Studies and Department of Anthropology at Brandeis University, where I am delighted to have found a supportive and engaging community of scholars.

Anthropologists understand that we make kin networks just as we are born into them, and I have a wonderful kin network, by blood and by love. Bob and Nancy Lee Derderian have supported my work on this project, especially with childcare in recent years. James and Linda Tracy, Elda O'Brien,

Loren McWethy, and Christy Cox have long offered kind words, good food, and overall support. My grandparents Phyllis and Merlyn Krick are two of my favorite people, and I value my pilgrimages to their New Mexico home for their companionship, kindness, and imminently wise counsel. My parents, Daniel and Sylvia Harrington, were slightly disappointed that I strayed from their chosen field of history, but I appreciate how they have tolerated my "rebellion" by choosing anthropology. They instilled in me a love of reading and writing that I applied in a new direction. Rob Derderian has always believed in my work and offered many pep talks for various hurdles. I am thankful to Bayt Badri for unconditional love and unfailing kindness; to my sister and role model, Laura Harrington, for her brilliance, unflinching support, and clarity of purpose. I am so lucky to have her as a sister and friend.

Finally, I thank Julian for bringing joy to my life in challenging times. Seeing the world through his eyes has sustained me in very dark moments. Pablo Neruda wrote that experiencing love from our loved ones "is a fire that feeds our life," which I have found to be true. He also wrote that to feel kindness and affection from those we do not know "is something still greater and more beautiful because it widens out the boundaries of our being." Julian, I hope that as you grow you will experience, as I have in doing this work, kindness from those you do not yet know, and how transformative the gift of human connection can be.

A Note on Translation and Transliteration

For Arabic words, I have used the transliteration protocols and word list of *The International Journal for Middle East Studies*, except for individuals' names. For individuals and entities with official websites or web presences, I have preserved their spellings of their names.

ART CAPITAL

INTRODUCTION   Birth of a Twenty-First Century Museum

IN 2006, THE GOVERNMENT of the United Arab Emirates (UAE) announced plans to build a Louvre museum and a Guggenheim museum off the coast of their capital city, Abu Dhabi (Figure 0.1). These museums, alongside a national museum, maritime museum, and performing arts center, were part of a $27 billion development plan for a cultural district on Saadiyat Island (*Jazīrat al-Saʿdiyāt* in Arabic, or Happiness Island). *The New York Times* immediately labeled these plans a "cultural Xanadu" (Fattah 2007) and a group of French curators accused the Louvre of "selling its soul" (*vendre son âme*; Cachin et al. 2006). As the projects progressed, New York City–based labor activists staged protests, calling attention to the rampant abuse of migrant workers in the UAE and advocating for better treatment of those building the Guggenheim and Louvre. To say that the Louvre Abu Dhabi (opened in 2017) and Guggenheim Abu Dhabi (under construction in 2025) have been controversial is an understatement.

Despite the apparent novelty of franchising such iconic museums by constructing new satellite branches of them, the underlying tensions that inflamed these controversies have deep roots. Scholars exploring museums and art at the turn of the twenty-first century have identified two major phenomena causing drastic transformations in cultural practice, either separately or conjointly. The first is increasing capitalization in museum and art worlds, including the corporatization of museums and cultural organizations, and how these changes affect artists and art-making.[1] The second phenomenon is the

1

FIGURE 0.1. A 2007 model of Saadiyat Island, with the Guggenheim
Abu Dhabi in the back, Louvre Abu Dhabi in the top left,
and performing arts center and maritime museum in the
foreground. Photo by Imre Solt (WikiMedia Commons).

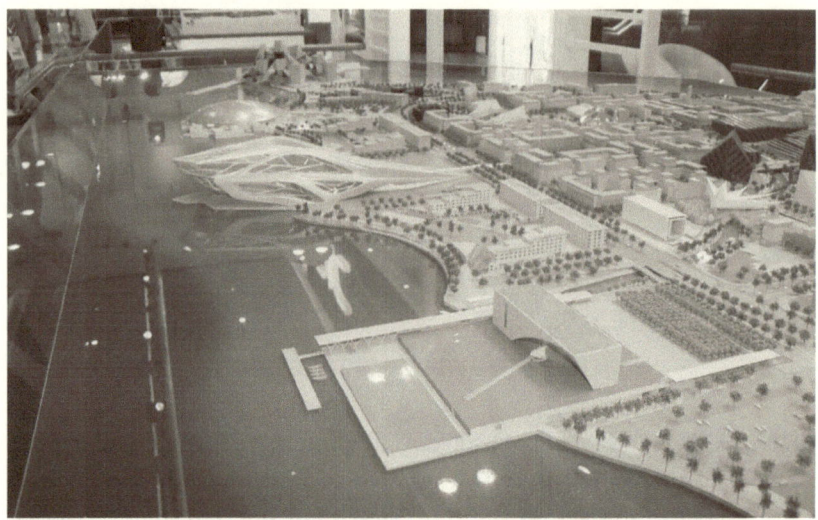

widespread push to diversify and decolonize the canon, alongside museums'
staff, holdings, exhibitions, and the art world more generally.[2] This push for
inclusivity is partly to rectify significant injustices in prior museum collection
and representation practices stemming from racist colonial and nationalist regimes, and partly to accommodate multicultural twenty-first century publics.[3]

These two phenomena—capitalization and the imperative to perform tolerance and inclusivity—in intersection fundamentally rewrite museum and
arts practice. They do so because they disrupt established patterns of who has
historically deployed museums to their advantage, and who was represented in
them and how. In the nineteenth and twentieth centuries, imperial and state
actors used museums as tools to create and promote the state, be it an empire
or a nation (Anderson 2006; Bennett 1995; Duncan 1995; McAleer and Longair
2014). In this well-documented state-culture paradigm, states have used museums and culture to inculcate citizens into the nation's heritage, deploy citizens'
cultural contributions to define a state aesthetic and cultural identity, and forge
an imagined community (Anderson 2006; Barringer and Flynn 1998; Bennett
1995; Coffey 2012; Duncan 1995; Foster 2002; Karp et al. 2006; Levitt 2015; Lloyd
and Thomas 1998; Macdonald 2006; Myers 2002; Pieprzak 2010; Prior 2002;

Sachedina 2021; Shaw 2003; Watenpaugh 2004; Winegar 2006). While such moves defined the nation and who was part of it, they also defined who was excluded and reinforced racial and social hierarchies. Tony Bennett coined the term "exhibitionary complex" to refer to exhibition-related infrastructures that represented the state and persuaded the public to identify with it, including adopting those racial and social hierarchies. In the twenty-first century, however, the social forces dominating museums have shifted, and as a result, historic patterns of representation—the ways artifacts from and artworks by marginalized and/or colonized communities are shown—have shifted too.

Marking a historical rupture, this book uses the Emirati art world to define a twenty-first century museum paradigm, in which a transnational neoliberal capitalist market has eclipsed the state as the primary nexus of power in the museum, and the imperative to diversify has reshaped art and museum practice. As capital and market logics have grown more influential, museum organizers have expanded their vision of who the museum's audience includes. This shift in the locus of power has therefore encouraged dramatic shifts in how artifacts, artworks, and communities are represented in the museum.[4] Museums and galleries can no longer use the aesthetic work of diverse communities to support their subjugation and exclusion from the body politic if museums and galleries expect that community to become patrons and support the institution, financially or otherwise. These two linked phenomena, then, are ultimately about power and inclusion in museums—and not just in the UAE, but worldwide. The UAE case illustrates how the state-culture paradigm of power in museums that dominated for a century and a half has now given way to what I term a market-culture paradigm, in which museum demographics and representational practice necessarily shift in alignment with the new power structure. In essence, the museum as an organ of the state presumed an audience of citizens; the museum as an organ of the market presumes a wider, capitalist audience.

The intersection of these phenomena—moves toward capitalization and inclusivity—create a push and pull effect: Museums grapple with how to be both specific and universal. That is, they seek to appeal to as many publics (i.e., consumers) as possible and achieve maximum capitalist reach while representing diverse constituencies with accuracy and nuance. In this way, appearing to be tolerant or multicultural can effect inclusion for the market's sake, parallel to observations about the ways that commodification can counterintuitively appear to—and even create openings to—further inclusive politics

(Hale 2005; Melamed 2006; Shankar 2015). Yet the more specific or catered the display, the less representative the museum becomes. This dialectic, balancing a universalist, maximum capitalist reach versus honoring and celebrating particularity, reorganizes fundamental elements of museum practice in ways that are distinctive to twenty-first century museums and diverge from the prevailing models of nineteenth- and twentieth-century museum practice. Using the UAE as a case study, I draw out how these epistemic shifts manifest in the daily lives and practices of artists, curators, gallerists, and organizers—showing whose cultural contributions are valued and why; how the possibilities for arts organizations foreclose certain kinds of art-making; how artists experience limits on self-presentation and expression; and the everyday inclusions and exclusions in the cultural realm.

The United Arab Emirates and a Global Contemporary Art Scene

The UAE features the two phenomena in question, and is host to a massive transformation in art and museum practice. The UAE has been studied for both its extensive capitalization (Cooke 2014; Davidson 2008; Hanieh 2011; Kanna 2011) and its diverse population (Keshavarzian 2024; Le Renard 2021; Lori 2019; Vora 2013, 2018; Vora and Koch 2015; Wright 2021). The country's capital surge after the mid-century discovery of oil spurred large-scale labor migration and has resulted in an incredibly diverse demographic of residents. From roughly 1820 through 1968, the British Empire dominated the territory of what is now the United Arab Emirates (then the Trucial States). The Crown sought to protect its maritime trade routes from India, signing trucial agreements with local shaykhs to ensure safe maritime passage through the Strait of Hormuz and the Gulf. While Britain did not directly colonize the Trucial States, they controlled foreign policy and in- and out-migration for non-locals. When Prime Minister Harold Wilson announced in 1968 that Britain would withdraw from all territories "east of Aden" by 1971, shaykhs in the Gulf region debated the names, borders, and political structures of the states that emerged. In what is now the UAE, ruling shaykhs created a federation government consisting of seven emirates, each ruled by a different tribal community (Map 0.1). The fledgling state worked to transition infrastructures from British to local control, formulating banks, post offices, libraries, and other administrative systems (Heard-Bey 1982). British architects played a key role in defining the landscape, physically and infrastructurally (Reisz 2021).

As the British had often employed the practice of secondment, or hiring out their officers to local rulers, the transition from semicolonial dominance to commercial dominance did not mark a substantial change in operating procedures. Gulf rulers also left intact British policies for managing the seasonal or contract migration of workers based on a sponsorship model, now known as the *kafāla* sponsorship system (Alshehabi 2019).

The discovery and exploitation of oil in the region, which also transpired in the mid-twentieth century, made many of the newly independent Gulf (*khalīj* or, as it is commonly transliterated, *khaleej*) states extremely wealthy, and as rulers directed that wealth toward infrastructural expansion projects, foreign workers also arrived. The city-emirate of Dubai's growth into an economic powerhouse dovetailed with significant capitalist expansion globally: The 1990s witnessed the acceleration and intensification of trade flows, rising technologization, and the rapid expansion of a global market, particularly due to the neoliberalization and deregulation of markets to promote free trade across the globe (Appadurai 1990; di Leonardo 2008; Inda and Rosaldo 2008). In the Gulf, oil wealth ushered in an era of multinational corporations and transnational capital. The Gulf states formed the Gulf Cooperation Council

MAP 0.1. The United Arab Emirates in regional perspective.

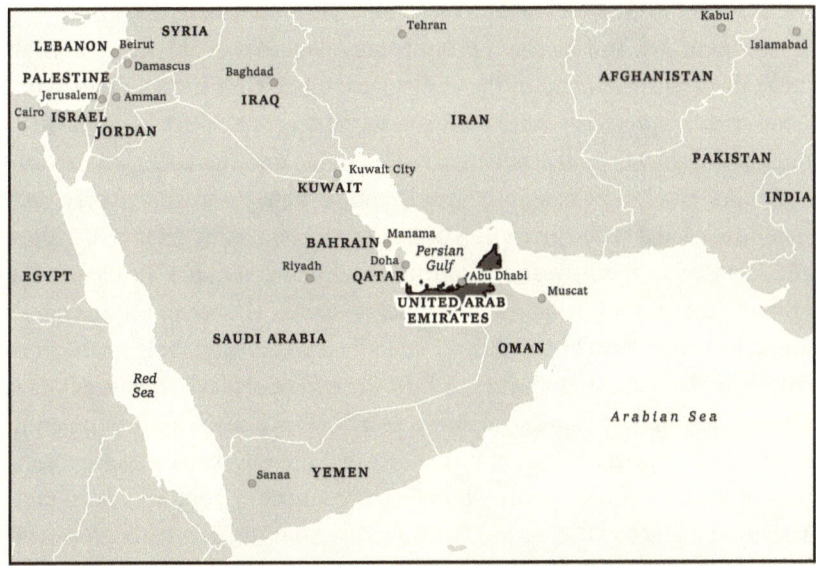

Source: Map made by Anya Shaw, University of Wisconsin Cartography Lab.

(GCC) in 1980 to encourage cooperation between member states (Bahrain, Kuwait, Oman, Qatar, Saudi Arabia, and the UAE). UAE leaders attempted to grow their economies quickly; Shaykh Rashid bin Saeed al-Maktoum of Dubai had ambitious plans for Dubai's growth, including dredging Dubai Creek to improve its harbor, opening Jebel Ali port in 1979, and installing airports (Davidson 2008; Kanna 2011; Reisz 2021). Shaykh Rashid's sons have continued his infrastructure modernization and real estate expansion vision. Between 1988 and 1998, Dubai International Airport (DXB) passenger throughput rose to 9.7 million, fixing DXB as a central node of international transit (Dubai Airports 2024). Not to be outdone by their neighbors, the rulers of Abu Dhabi and Sharjah also initiated far-reaching infrastructural projects (Bani Hashim 2019 and Al Qassemi and Reisz 2021, respectively).

Examining the significant financialization and growth of the GCC states, particularly the "internationalization of Gulf capitalism," political scientist Adam Hanieh casts capitalization and the changing social norms it entails as a process of class formation, "*Khaleeji* capital" (2011, 2).[5] Hanieh argues that *Khaleeji* (Gulf) capital does not represent a loss of individual GCC states' identities, "but rather an orientation and perspective toward accumulation at the pan-GCC scale," and in particular, on a UAE-Saudi axis (2011, 2). This ostensible recession of the individual nation to foreground capital interests, which we see in Gulf museum projects, thus has precedent in the region.

Heritage, art, and museum projects are a key part of this growth: After unification and statehood in the early 1970s, many Gulf states initiated museum-making projects, either with the support of UNESCO (Kuwait, Bahrain, and Qatar) or independently (Saudi Arabia and the UAE). These early museums were prime examples of the culture-state paradigm, as they were state-funded and state-run entities dedicated to formulating a national history and identity. In recent years, the focus on capitalization has also led to the promotion of a "knowledge economy" across the GCC, such as Saudi Arabia's museum and archive boom (Bsheer 2020; Foley 2019) and Gulf states' franchising higher education (Vora 2018). By the early decades of the twenty-first century, however, various state and private actors undertook new museum and heritage projects. Miriam Cooke notes that these "urban heritage projects have become a national priority for all Gulf countries" (2014, 101). Such projects are integral to GCC states' "authentification of modernizing processes" (Cooke 2014, 171). Knowledge economy and heritage projects "aim to restore the kind of vibrant indigenous past that promises a cosmopolitan future"

(Cooke 2014, 103)—one that somehow limns being cosmopolitan and tolerant as well as ethnonationalist.

Infrastructural and urban development projects across the Gulf region, including in the UAE, have required a vast labor force to realize them, causing significant population shifts in the country, both in overall number as well as in ratios of citizens to foreign workers. Populations in the territory that is now the UAE had historically often been nomadic and engaged in seasonal migration (Heard-Bey 1982), be it from the interior to the coast to engage in pearl diving (Hightower 2012, 2013), or between the northern rim of the Peninsula and what is now Iran, Pakistan, or the broader Indian Ocean (Bishara 2017; Moghadam 2021). In 1975, the total population of the Emirates was nearly 558,000 people, of which 63 percent were "nonnationals," per the UAE's Federal Statistics and Competitiveness Authority. The population doubled to nearly 1.4 million in 1985, rising to 2.4 million in 1995, 4.1 million in 2005, and then 9.1 million in 2016. The last year the Ministry of the Economy released the population breakdown by citizenship status was 2005. That year, 79.8 percent of the UAE's population were nonnationals. This skyrocketing population has necessitated even more expansion in transit and residential infrastructures, schools, health-care facilities, utility infrastructures, etc. Since 2006, museum and arts professionals have also been part of this migrant workforce. All these workers who came to build the UAE labor under the *kafāla* sponsorship system.

Instigated by the British, who formerly controlled in- and out-migration of British personnel and non-locals (Alshehabi 2019), the *kafāla* sponsorship system requires noncitizens to have an individual or corporate sponsor, largely predicated on employment, to remain in the country legally. Many scholars and media pundits have analyzed the Gulf states' handling of large-scale temporary populations through the *kafāla* system (Beaugé 1986; Diop et al. 2015; Fechter and Walsh 2010; Kanna 2011; Kanna et al. 2020; Khalaf et al. 2015; Le Renard 2021; Longva 1997; Lori 2019; Schielke 2020; Unnikrishnan 2017; Vora 2013; Walsh 2007, 2012), particularly the treatment of manual laborers from South Asia (Gardner 2010; Karinkurayil 2024; Ross 2015; Wright 2021). These factors have led to a stereotype of the "triptych" of residency, built on the stereotyped divisions between different groups: Gulf residents are "either (exploited) 'migrant laborers,' (consuming) expatriates or (unproductive) locals" (Vora 2015, 175). Cooke glossed these populations and the GCC states' plans for them with the term *barzakh*, an Arabic "term denoting undiluted

convergence" (2014, 10). Such an explanation for the often stark social strat-
ification in the UAE is very palatable to an ethnocentric state, whose leaders
fiercely protect citizenship transmission via bureaucratic delay and who incen-
tivize endogamy through land grants and other rewards. This very question,
of how to govern and manage a diverse population, is central to the intersection of capitalization and inclusivity in art and museums that I examine here.

The Emirati state has, in more recent years, focused more on promoting
itself as "tolerant" and "multicultural," yet in ways that maintain strict divisions between citizens and noncitizens. In fact, Gulf art scenes and museum
projects have often been accused of artwashing, or, put in Aruna D'Souza's
terms, whitewalling. Whitewalling refers to "the white walls of the gallery . . .
the notion of 'white washing,' or covering over that which we would prefer
to ignore or suppress" (D'Souza 2018, 9). In this instance, critics believe the
UAE's museum plans and tolerance discourses are an attempt to whitewall
concerns about human rights abuses and the treatment of migrant workers.
The UAE case therefore offers an excellent opportunity to examine assumptions about what art and museums do, and how they engage and represent
wide swathes of the population.

Most major studies of museum practice have focused on British, American, and European institutions as significant founders of museum practice
(Bennett 1995; Bunzl 2014; Duncan 1995; Hicks 2020; McClellan 1994, 2008;
Price 1989, 2007). Subsequently, much of the scholarly work on decolonizing and diversifying the art world has focused on attempts within a Euro-
American context, and there has been little attention to how museums in other
contexts contribute to decolonizing practice. In cases like Russia (Rogers 2015)
and Nigeria (Apter 2005), which parallel the UAE in oil wealth, state actors
have diverted petrodollars to cultural development in complex assemblages
of state and private interests and with varying degrees of success. Plans for a
museum of modern art in Kolkata have received attention (Mathur and Singh
2015) as have Qatar's museum aspirations (Erskine-Loftus et al. 2016; Murray
2017; Levitt 2015). But Qatar's museums are all individual museums, not franchises of major French or U.S. museums. Aside from an overview volume on
museum practice (Erskine-Loftus 2014), early work on the Gulf's museum
boom has focused on heritage (Exell and Rico 2014; Wakefield 2021), modernity (Exell 2016), and collecting (Erskine-Loftus 2014). Yet the UAE's plans are
exceptionally large-scale, located in a state often synonymous with obscene
wealth, and extensive media attention has sensationalized the franchising of

the Louvre and Guggenheim. The questions of how to manage multicultural audiences and how capitalization and the push to diversify representation intersect are central in the UAE. All of these factors—the Emirates' hyper-capitalization, its highly diverse population, and its ambitious contemporary art and museum aspirations—make it an ideal site to study the tensions that arise at the nexus of these forces, and to examine questions of power in the museum (via states and capital), diversifying the museum, and the operationalization of inclusion through tolerance.

Capitalizing on Diversity: The Market-Culture Paradigm

The ascent of capital and its influence on museums is controversial because of core ideas about the role of the museum in society. Integral to the exhibitionary complex were the ideas that museums were state-supported public institutions that were educational and fostered democracy, and therefore were public goods; and secondly, that true or legitimate art was not made for profit. Both of these ideas derive from Enlightenment frameworks that link art and aesthetics to lofty civilizational achievements. As Jessica Winegar argues:

> The "art as evidence of humanity" theory in Western thought is of course traceable to Kant, who argued that the aesthetic experience of beauty takes us beyond "the purposive striving of nature" and is part of "the cultivation of our higher destiny" and the "development of our humanity." (Winegar 2008, 657; citing Kant [1790] 1951, 283)

Winegar traces this idea through the work of E. B. Tylor, Lewis Henry Morgan, and Franz Boas. She defines this dialectic as the humanity game, wherein art "constitutes the supreme evidence of a people's humanity" and is a "uniquely valuable and uncompromised agent of cross-cultural understanding" (Winegar 2008, 652). Due to this pervasive belief, art and museums are often seen to be incubators of tolerance and civility, as museum visits become "civilizing rituals" that cultivate good citizens (Duncan 1995). In addition to these associations, the Louvre in Paris, which is often considered the first public art museum, was a fundamental organ of the newly democratic state after the removal of France's monarchic system (McClellan 1994), further aligning the construct of the museum with democracy, public education, and civilizational accomplishment. The universal survey museum, as a form, derives from the Louvre (France), Ashmolean (UK), and British Museum (UK), which deployed collections from non-European groups to define Europe as the apex of progress, bolstering scientific racism.

The industrial revolution of the late nineteenth century wrought changes to all aspects of society, including to art museums' form and mission, and marked the beginning of a new relationship of the art museum to capital. By the 1920s, observers such as the Frankfurt School theorists were wary of mass production in art, mostly voicing doubts about its implications for constructs of authenticity (Benjamin 1969; Horkheimer and Adorno [1944] 2002). Walter Benjamin famously argued that art loses its aura—that ineffable, transcendent quality—when it is mass produced, thereby becoming inauthentic (Benjamin 1969). These scholars were concerned about consumerism in the art world, insisting on a separation between mass markets and art to preserve the integrity and authenticity of art. In the eyes of Frankfurt School scholars, consumerism and capital interests polluted and corrupted art, rendering it illegitimate. These views resulted in a privileging of handmade art as "real" or authentic art, disqualifying photography and film.[6]

The idea that capital polluted art remained pervasive in the mid-twentieth century; then, a new phase of capital influence on the art world began in the 1980s. Until then, many states had been primary supporters of museums and many museums had continued to operate in the culture-state paradigm. Britain's Margaret Thatcher and the United States' Ronald Reagan heavily promoted neoliberal policies in the 1980s, including severe cuts to grants and aid to art museums (Wu 2002, 99; see also Alexander 1996; Krauss 1990; Rectanus 2002). Between 1980 and 2000, rising neoliberal capitalism—the "tentacles of enterprise culture"—grasped the art and museum world (Wu 2002, 303). In 1982, Reagan proposed 50 percent cuts to the National Endowment for the Arts (NEA) and the National Endowment for the Humanities (NEH) (Hall 1981).[7] Such draconian cuts, or the threat of them, forced many U.S. and European museums to seek alternative funding sources, relying more heavily on "foundations, individual donors and corporate sponsors" as well as seeking to build their membership bases (Rectanus 2002, 22; see also Wu 2002). U.S. museums "transformed themselves into semicommercial entities," one consequence of which was the adoption of corporate models of management being integrated into museum practice (Rectanus 2002, 22–23). In 1990, the art historian and influential critic Rosalind Krauss warned that museums would come to look more like institutions of leisure or entertainment (1990). These transformations were widespread: Lorna Abungu (2005) discusses

African museums meeting the challenge of dwindling state funding, and Esra Özyürek (2006) includes an example of a bank organizing a key national exhibition in Turkey. In Spain, the La Caixa banking foundation opened the first CaixaForum museum and cultural center in Barcelona in 2002.[8] Globally, many museums faced declining state funding and pursued corporate funding sources to survive.

This shift to corporate funding has reoriented twenty-first century art and museum practice. Rosalind Krauss termed the resulting institutional type the late capitalist museum. Reflecting on the cultural logic of these museums, Krauss argued that the "activity of markets restructur[ed] the aesthetic original . . . to change it into an 'asset'" (1990, 6). Akin to the Frankfurt School scholars, Krauss's concern was the conversion of artworks from art-as-pure-art into commodities, perhaps motivating her use of quotation marks around the term "asset" to emphasize the seepage of financialized terminology into the everyday vocabulary of the art world. The idea of commerce or a focus on capital remained an anathema to high-brow art communities: In his fieldwork between 1998 and 2001, Olav Velthuis noted commercial art dealers' refusal to "demean themselves to what is called commerce," revealing a strident divide between art and capital and an ongoing sense that finance pollutes art (2005, 1). Despite the rising influence of corporate models, there remains a strong belief—or perhaps the performance of one—that financial aspects pollute the arts and its institutions.

Franchised institutions like the Louvre and Guggenheim Abu Dhabi invoke these complicated histories as well as debates about the role of museums in society and how financial interests affect art and museums. They are also at the forefront of a paradigm shift, from the state-culture paradigm to the market-culture paradigm. Conceived in the early twenty-first century, their forms are deeply marked by the prevailing logics of that period. While I note a new relationship between capital and museums in the twenty-first century, I do not posit that what we are witnessing is a full retreat of the state or the nation; this work itself shows the deep imbrication of state actors with capitalizing projects. These different art and museum paradigms are intimately connected, and even dialectical: Both are formulations of how the powers that be utilize culture and art museums to various ends. In the past, empires and later nations dominated these politics, while today it is the market: The tentacles of capital link between and through the terrestrial boundaries of nation-states.

I use the term "capital" to refer to financial capital, and as shorthand for the economic "project" of neoliberal capitalism, after Hannah Appel (2019,

2), to emphasize its dynamic, processual nature. Capital as a project consists of "'privatizing' state-owned enterprises; reducing the size and cost of government through massive public sector layoffs . . . and reducing barriers to trade" (Ellwood 2007, 53). Neoliberal agents believe these practices promote "abstract equality, market individualism, and inclusive civic nationalism" (Melamed 2006, 2)—financial practices that, through the invisible hand of the market, will ultimately lead to optimal social ends (di Leonardo 2008). Capital is therefore both a financial and a social project.

State actors clearly still draw on museums in nation-building, particularly state-branding, projects. However, drawing on scholarship demonstrating how museums and the art sector have moved away from the state as a primary source of funding (Alexander 1996; Rectanus 2002; Stallabrass 2004; Wu 2002), I argue that market concerns, rather than state concerns, now dominate. Furthermore, the market is more visible as a driving force, and state concerns are often cloaked or less foregrounded. The title of this book refers, then, not only to the foregrounded nature of the capitalist market, but also to the ways that cultural capital—particularly in the art world—operates, and the ways entities and actors attempted to translate these developments into capital, both financial and cultural, to establish the Emirates' capital city, Abu Dhabi. In each chapter of the book, I closely examine one of the transformations wrought by the intersection of pushes toward capital and inclusion: in the forms of arts organizations, patterns of representation, the very definition of contemporary art, and everyday practices of artists, collectors, curators, and other arts workers.

As the forms of arts organizations evolve, so too must their typologies. New hybrid arts organizations, which are difficult to neatly categorize as commercial or noncommercial, state or nonstate, collecting or non-collecting, emerge in this new paradigm. Their forms confound simple organizational typologies like public versus private, museum, and nonprofit. Larissa Buchholz insists on the importance of scholarly attention to this "institutional diversity of globalizing cultural realms" (2022, 5). Hybrid organizations such as those in the UAE emerge through graduation of sovereignty, a process by which the state delegates others to carry out its sovereign responsibilities and therein extends sovereignty to them (after Ong 1999). Aihwa Ong describes the origination of this strategy in Asia, as the state "calibrat[es] its control over sovereignty to the challenges of global capital," showing how the practice of graduated sovereignty is deeply imbricated in and derived from capital (1999,

216). As capital moves to shrink the state, the state must abdicate functions—and sovereignty—outside. Whereas prior iterations of museums exemplified the exhibitionary complex—the representation of the empire or nation-state through display—the Emirati state now delegates much of the responsibility for its museums and arts organizations to nonstate entities, or at least operates in partnership with them. I trace these changes in Chapter 1. For example, the Louvre (Paris) is run by the French government, which signed an accord with the Emirati government to build the Louvre Abu Dhabi. Per Hassan Fattah (2007), Abu Dhabi paid France one billion U.S. dollars to lease the Louvre name, loan a percentage of its collection to the new museum annually, and benefit from the expertise of its staff. To facilitate the deal, the French government created Agence France Musées, an "international museum consultancy," to build out the Louvre Abu Dhabi, thus constituting a blend of bilateral government agreements translated into a commercial consultancy. On the other hand, the Guggenheim Foundation, a private entity, also signed a contract with the Emirati government, forming a transnational public-private partnership. These organizational constellations rewire authority in the museum—how state actors are involved, and in what capacities, for example—and at times adopt corporate logics.

Just as private and public were blurred in the UAE's arts organizations, so too were lines between commercial arts ventures and noncommercial ones. Overlaps between market-centered organizations and the noncommercial are commonplace in the twenty-first century, such as M+ in Hong Kong whose name reflects a mission to be more than a museum (Ho 2014); the Kunsthalle model in Europe that focuses on exhibitions rather than maintaining collections (Zarobell 2017); or Moroccan "marketplace museums" (Pieprzak 2010, 37). Rather than seeing commercial and noncommercial entities as distinct realms, "public institutions like museums do not reflect the [art] market but actively balance it" (Bull 2011, 187). Parallel with the rise of biennials, there has also been a boom of art fairs (Baia Curioni 2012), including a surge in corporatization and franchising of fairs to create a global art fair circuit (Buchholz 2022, 77–78). Art fairs are themselves "new organizational spaces" (Baia Curioni 2012, 130), revealing also how organizations shape-shift and take on new roles. Per Larissa Buchholz, understanding the proliferation of biennials, the rise of global art criticism discourses, and the creation of new "global institutions for artistic evaluation and consecration" is necessary to analyze recent global transformations in the art worlds, underscoring the importance of a broad swathe of organizations and networks (Buchholz 2022, 27). Indeed, this co-constitutive nature extends to the individual level as well, as scholars have noted correlations between high-profile noncommercial exhibitions and artists' commercial success (Buchholz 2022; Bull 2011; Johanson et al. 2022; Velthuis 2011).

Crossover between commercial and noncommercial arts organizations was particularly visible in staffing, especially for gig work at Art Dubai or other temporary shows. My interlocutors' backgrounds highlight this flexibility. One curator at Qatar's Museum of Islamic Art later worked as a commercial gallerist in Dubai; another gallerist left that role to become a curator at a state-sponsored royal foundation; and one organizer worked for Abu Dhabi's cultural authority before working for a commercial organizer in Dubai. Organizations such as the Sharjah Art Foundation, Barjeel Art Foundation, and Jean-Paul Najar Foundation took on educational ventures that blurred lines of easy categorization. Auction houses also sometimes hosted lectures; commercial art fairs held talks on modernism and commissioned local artists to make work. Thus my account integrates actors and organizations across the Emirati art world, borrowing Howard Becker's influential definition of an art world as "all the people whose activities are necessary to the production of the characteristic works which that world, and perhaps others as well, define as art," regardless of whether they were profit-oriented or not (1982, 34). All these organizations significantly influence artists' work, the practice of exhibition-making, and display more generally.

As these organizational forms shift, so too do the ways various actors deploy art and artists to represent communities, which I discuss in Chapter 2. Diversifying the collections, how communities were represented, and museum staff were imperative for museums to reach broad audiences, stay financially viable, and retain their position of authority in society. Museum organizers have attempted these moves in various ways. First, the integration of the economy and "pluralized contact" (Yúdice 2003, 11) between communities have shaped representational politics, particularly in the attempts to diversify the art world post-1989, when a truly global art market emerged and curators and gallerists voraciously searched for undiscovered talent to include in exhibitions and markets (Belting et al. 2013; Stallabrass 2004; see also Velthuis and Baia Curioni 2015). These competitive attempts, however, often wound up commodifying difference in tokenistic ways that consistently failed to benefit the artists themselves as much as institutions benefited from appearing "diverse" and "multicultural" (Buchholz 2022; Dávila 1999; Harris 2011; Joselit 2020; Oguibe 2004; Rey 2020; Winegar 2008) or leveraging real estate (Dávila 2012; Ho Hing-Kay 2010).[9] To promote shows and entice audiences, transnational curators and museum organizers often fixate on artists' ethnicity, citizenship, or nationality (Dávila 2020); coopt artists into "transnational cultural brokering" (Yúdice 2003, 104); or expect that artists' work will respond to politics of their homeland or heritage (Harris 2012; Welland 2018; Winegar 2006, 2008).

My artist interlocutors often spoke about the ways their citizenship status, religious beliefs, or ethnicity played into how curators and gallerists read them and their work. Olu Oguibe termed one practice that emerged in response to the diversification imperative the "culture game" (2004). In the culture game, institutions pay lip service to inclusion by adding a token artist from a marginalized community to their exhibition roster or their acquisitions schedule. Such moves, while perhaps well-intentioned, put pressure on minoritized artists to represent entire communities in ways that white artists largely do not experience, and reveal shifts in how museums and arts organizations represent diverse and multicultural communities. As Stuart Hall argues, "'multiculturalism' . . . references the strategies and policies adopted to govern or manage the problems of diversity and multiplicity which multicultural societies throw up" (2000, 209). Yet multiculturalism operating in a brokering role "contributes to the consolidation of groups that can be capitalized on by academic, art, media, and market institutions" (Yúdice 2003, 162–63; see also Dávila 2004; Hale 2005; Londoño 2020; Melamed 2006). One way that multiculturalism, and cultural brokering across categories, showed up in the UAE art scene was in how curators and organizers marshaled artists' statuses to showcase the UAE as a tolerant state.

In the UAE instance, the market imperative to diversify trumped narrow ethnonationalist patterns of state representation. Inclusion is here instrumentalized for market ends. In some cases like the Emirates, noncitizens are chosen to represent the state as proof of its tolerance and multiculturalism, showing how projects of national representation in art museums shift to appeal to a transnational audience and market, rather than to citizens, and demonstrating the value of performing tolerance. Tolerance is another mode of managing diversity, a strategy or policy to govern multicultural societies. Wendy Brown notes that the term "surged back into use in the late twentieth century as multiculturalism became the central problematic of liberal

democratic citizenship," and has often been a code word for "mannered ra-
cialism" (2006, 1–2). But it also has been an "umbrella term for designating the
virtues of openness and inclusion, and by extension . . . moral and political
goodness," such as in the Latvian context (Dzenovska 2018, 8). Tolerance, as a
metric of city or state branding, also becomes a market imperative, a prerequisite for capitalist expansion. Much of the rhetoric celebrating institutions and
exhibitions in the UAE championed ideas of universalism, multiculturalism,
and tolerance, positioning art as a natural unifier, aligning with the humanity game. Polysemous though the term is, tolerance in the Emirati art scene
seemed to mean the absence of conflict or even of disagreements. It also meant
putting up with or being nonreactive toward difference—and this in a country
with residents from many nationalities and severe income inequality.

Just as artists' identities become salient in various ways in projects to
evince tolerance, what is defined as art is itself contested. In Chapter 3, I show
how sociopolitical critique becomes a legitimating factor, and UAE-based artists must balance the tensions of market visibility, seminal to their livelihoods
and success, with the margins of freedom of expression in the UAE. What
constitutes critique—and what constitutes art itself—are contested, informed
by class (Bourdieu 2000; Lena 2019) along with race (Banks 2010; Cooks 2011;
DiMaggio and Ostrower 1990) and other social positions. Familiarity with
legitimized (or, in Pierre Bourdieu's terms, "consecrated") art, having educational degrees, and speaking in ways and terms legible to the upper class
imbued one with cultural capital, which often shored up one's financial capital. To be able to perform knowledge of a global art world's definition of "real"
art signifies having art capital.

Artists, collectors, and organizers also perform professionalism, another
key demonstration of financial capital, and an instance where market dominance is visible, as I argue in Chapter 4. An instance of what Bonnie McElhinny (2010) describes as "regimes of self" associated with the rise of neoliberal
capitalism, traits such as "being responsible, autonomous, self-sufficient and
entrepreneurial" (Shankar 2015, 17) become paramount. With the ascension of
capital interests, in the UAE case, professionalism and tolerance become ele-
vated to key codes of practice and tools for managing difference. The embodied practices and vocabulary of professionalism, however, reveal themselves
to be the expansion of Euro-American, Anglophone corporate standards and
etiquette. Chin-Tao Wu has noted that in many instances, the term "Western" has been replaced by "global"—but the underlying ontologies remain

the same (2009). In the UAE as elsewhere (Gerber 2017; Win 2014), artists and collectors alike are trained to adopt a "professional" aesthetic regime that renders them entrepreneurial in their self-presentation, ostensibly to achieve ultimate flexibility and legibility in a global contemporary art market, seamlessly switching between commercial and noncommercial modes (Chapter 4). In these instances, professionalism repackages difference for supposedly universal consumption. Yet upon closer examination, the claim of "universal" access depoliticizes what is ultimately an expansion and imposition of a Global North neoliberal multiculturalism.

Finally, museum organizers seek to minimize potential conflicts and promote easy global legibility as they devise new modes of managing and cultivating multicultural, diverse, twenty-first century publics (Chapter 5). Museums continue to be sites of civic ritual, but in producing a tolerant, multicultural *world* public rather than a national audience. Yet this "tolerance," performed to appeal to a broad audience, comes via preemptive erasure of difference, showing how difference is sanitized and edited to be palatable and commodifiable. These erasures are incentivized by the promise of easier, freer trade and exchange—the idea of compromise for the greater good, yet with only certain parties adapting for the others.

Following Wendy Brown's cue to understand tolerance not as a transcendent, universal concept but rather as a practice of governing bodies and discourses, I trace the ways that tolerance emerges as a market imperative in the art and museum community, predicated on the humanity game. The performance or projection of tolerance allows states to signal their peer status to the international community and facilitates commercial flows. Tolerance, in this way, benefits capitalist expansion while also promoting diversification—in theory, if not in practice.

In the twenty-first century, a transformed relationship to capital interests rewires museums', arts organizations', and artists' relations to power, to the state, and to a global constituency. Museums and arts organizations are now grounded in their connections to markets. Offering a microcosm of these epistemic shifts, the UAE case shows how the nexus of neoliberalism and the imperative to perform inclusivity redefine the paradigm of the art museum in the twenty-first century, resulting in the preemptive erasure of difference in the name of tolerance; a redefining of legitimacy for artworks, artists, institutions, and collectors; and hybrid organizations that blur easy categorization and accountability.

FIGURE 0.2. *The Circle Game,* 2016

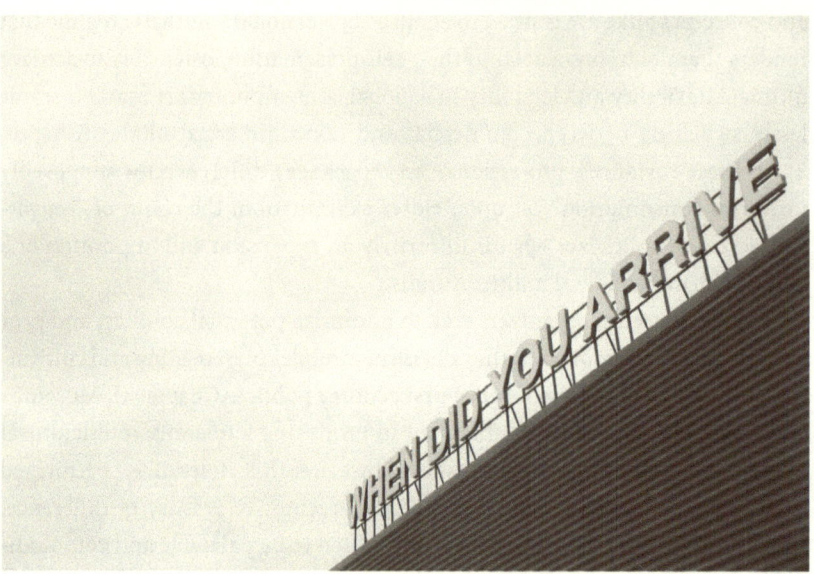

Source: Mary Ellen Carroll / MEC, studios. Installation photos by Mary Ellen Carroll / MEC, studios ©2016. Image courtesy the artist and Alserkal Avenue.

FIGURE 0.3. *The Circle Game,* 2016.

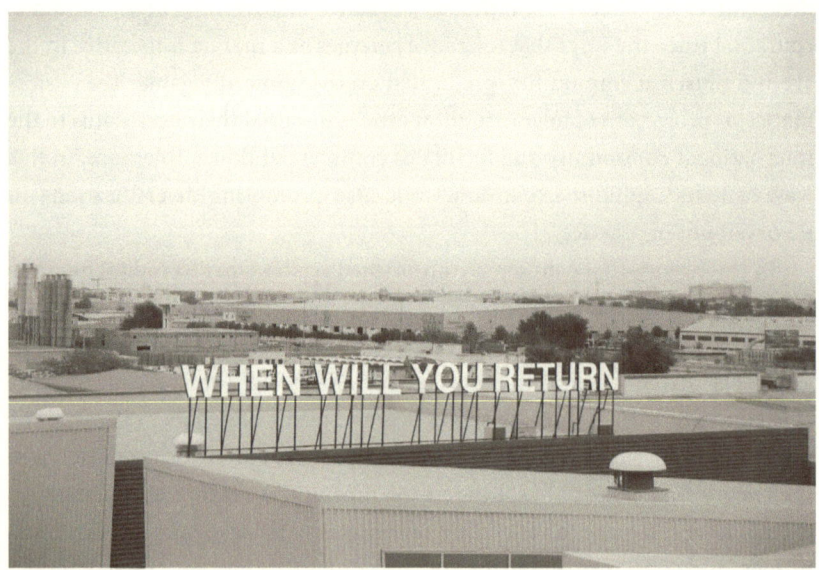

Source: Mary Ellen Carroll / MEC, studios. Installation photos by Mary Ellen Carroll / MEC, studios ©2016. Image courtesy the artist and Alserkal Avenue.

When Did You Arrive? When Will You Return?

To make these arguments, I focus primarily on the everyday interactions of individuals who worked in the Emirates' art world between 2006 and 2017. This long decade between the announcement of museum plans for Saadiyat Island and the opening of the Louvre museum was a period of vibrant growth in the UAE art scene. *Art Capital* derives from extensive on the ground observation and participation with artists and staff of arts organizations, data that often complicates or contradicts that which is issued in press releases, organizational websites, and sensationalized media reports. Museum staff, artists, curators, gallerists, auction staff, and other art professionals based in the UAE had taken seriously the Emirati government's proclamations, and they recognized that the art and museum industry was to be an area of focus and development. This community, who became my interlocutors, had dilemmas and critiques of their own, some correlated to the outside critiques of the UAE's arts ventures and others of their own making.

I arrived for primary fieldwork in October 2015, a felicitous time given that many arts organizations were preparing to celebrate their ten-year anniversaries and were reflecting on the accomplishments and progress made in the prior decade. A few factors shaped the data I could collect, the primary one being access. In 2012, I connected with a former colleague who had begun working at Abu Dhabi's cultural authority. They facilitated connections for me, and in 2013 and 2014, I was able to conduct preliminary fieldwork in Abu Dhabi's major museum initiatives. I aimed to capture art workers' spontaneous and unguarded reactions, not reproduce PR statements and official language that was already available on organizations' websites. Another researcher recounted waiting fourteen months to interview museum staff, only for their interview to be attended and policed by the organization's marketing staff, resulting in a dearth of new or unfiltered data. In contrast, longer-term immersion in these organizations allowed me access to a plurality of perspectives and experiences.

In 2015, however, Abu Dhabi's cultural authority no longer granted non-Emirati researchers access (at least, this was the cause cited for declining my request to collaborate). I began to collaborate with other institutions, undertaking a series of short-term projects with arts centers across Dubai and Sharjah, through which I recruited participants. These projects included participating in a reading group for artists, assisting with an exhibition and

editing the exhibition catalogue, organizing a series of panels, interviewing artists in residence about their experience, interviewing art teachers in
primary schools, and sitting in on a class for artists in exchange for making
photocopies and coordinating logistics with guest lecturers. These activities
helped me to meet a wide variety of people across different arts organizations,
and because many of them had worked with other organizations before in
various capacities, they spoke knowledgably about practices across the scene.
I completed primary fieldwork between September 2015 and April 2017, and
I have conducted follow-up trips in October 2018, January 2020, December
2022, and November through December 2023. This research extended the three
months of preliminary fieldwork I had conducted in the major museums to include a broader swathe of the art world, which allowed me to better understand
the wider art ecosystem and how museums like the Louvre Abu Dhabi fit into it.

Access to individuals and organizations was also a challenge due to the
UAE's highly transient population. Midway through my fieldwork, the artist
Mary Ellen Carroll created *The Circle Game* installation for Alserkal Avenue
(Figures 0.2 and 0.3). On one warehouse roof, giant letters read: "When did
you arrive?" Across the avenue, its sister sign read: "When will you return?"
These questions permeated social life in the UAE, and overshadowed—literally and figuratively—the relationships I built with my interlocutors. Approximately 20 percent of my interlocutors changed roles during my fieldwork:
leaving organizations, returning to their country of documented origin, or
relocating abroad. This transience mirrored my own.

In addition to artists, my interlocutors included institution directors, gallerists, curators, collectors, patrons, studio managers, teachers, critics, and
writers of various nationalities. While residing in Dubai from 2015 to 2017,
I crisscrossed the city in my trusty Renault rental, often debriefing to my re-
corder on my drive to the next meeting or home because driving took up so
much time and I risked forgetting details (Map 0.2).[10] I interviewed artists in
cafés in Business Bay, Al Quoz, northern Jumeirah, or at Sharjah's Qasbah or
Ratios. I visited artists in their studios in neighborhoods from Green Community Village to Nad al Sheba to Silicon Oasis to the Heart of Sharjah to Khor
Fakkan, whether those studios were dedicated facilities, rented or sponsored
spaces in art centers, or spare rooms in their homes. I traveled to Doha, Qatar,
and Kochi, India, with interlocutors to see exhibitions. I accompanied an
artist on a research trip to Mleiha, an archaeological site in Sharjah emirate,
as they prepared new works. In addition to exhibition and gallery openings

MAP 0.2. Key art locations in Abu Dhabi, Dubai, and Sharjah.

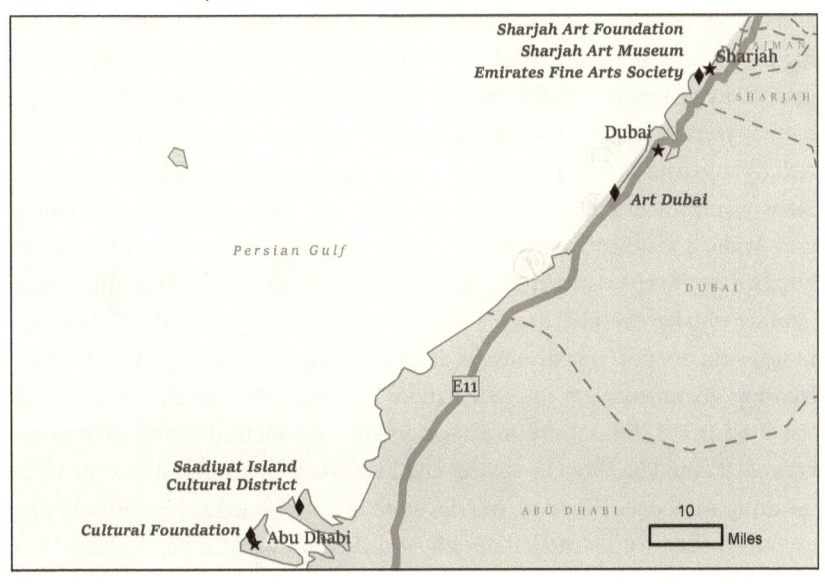

Source: Map made by Anya Shaw, University of Wisconsin Cartography Lab.

across Bastakiya, Al Quoz, DIFC (Dubai International Financial Center), Sharjah, Dasman, and Hamriya, my fieldwork took me to sleek commercial art fairs like Art Dubai and Abu Dhabi Art, as well as to popular events like Comic-Con, where I mingled with teens in cosplay and browsed comic books authored by my artist interlocutors. I visited various fringe art and film festivals at the behest of my interlocutors, because they were exhibiting or attending. By the time I left the UAE in April 2017, I had conducted over ninety interviews and collected two suitcases' worth of exhibition documentation.

My interlocutors included both male- and female-identifying members of the art world, ranging from college-age to those in their sixties. Some identified as straight and others as queer; others did not specify an identification at all. Many had been born and raised in the Emirates, and others had lived there for decades and carried formal identity papers from elsewhere: South Asia, Iran, Europe, the UK, other Arab countries, or North America. Some interlocutors had their documentary status change during my fieldwork, as government actors stripped their Emirati passports from them. The transmission of Emirati citizenship is extremely restricted and has grown more rigid, tied to patrilineal bloodlines and codified since the country's unification in 1971 (Kanna 2011;

Lori 2019). Today, one must possess both an Emirati passport and a *khulāṣat al-qaīd* family card proving one's descent to be considered a citizen.[11] Limiting the number of beneficiaries allows the Emirati state to continue to provide its citizens generous benefits, including preferential hiring through workforce nationalization (also called Emiratization), free health care and education, as well as land and housing grants upon marriage to another citizen.[12] Since the 1980s, government officials have revoked the citizenship of political dissidents, non-Arabs, and other "undesirables" to maintain power, and to further limit the number of citizens entitled to state benefits.[13] This situation means that many families who have resided in the UAE for decades—even prior to UAE statehood in 1971—do not possess citizenship, creating a large class of locals who hold citizenship documentation in other nations that they have rarely visited, much less lived in.[14] I did not ask interlocutors directly about documentary status, because it could be a touchy subject and I was wary of assuming incorrectly or insulting someone. However, interlocutors often revealed their status as they explained their work: Their status allowed them to work in particular jobs or exhibit in certain shows, or it troubled their ability to study abroad, etc.

During my fieldwork, when speaking generally about UAE society, my interlocutors generally referred to Emirati citizens as nationals, while the term "local" described both persons possessing UAE citizenship and lifelong residents who lack UAE citizenship documents. The term was therefore useful to obfuscate someone's documentary status but emphasize their belonging. "Nonnational" described anyone holding foreign passports, while "expats" (expatriates) was used interchangeably with "Westerners," referencing only privileged white, Western migrants seeking white-collar work (Le Renard 2021), aligning with other scholars' findings on the racialization of migrant labor (Fechter and Walsh 2010; Hindman 2013). The term migrant workers was reserved for those from the Global South and working in poorly paid, manual, or menial positions.[15] These labels indicated one's rank in the social and political hierarchy: Emirati and Gulf Cooperation Council (GCC) citizens held top tier, then white expatriates, followed by long-term Arab or Arabic-speaking residents, middle-class South Asian expatriates (often overlooked in studies of the Gulf; see Vora 2013; Wright 2021), and migrant blue-collar workers (Gardner 2010; Schielke 2020).[16]

While I initially aimed to study the Louvre Abu Dhabi, which had been scheduled to open in 2012, it had not yet opened when I arrived in 2015. In anticipation of the UAE's burgeoning art scene, however, many other organizations had opened up, and so I expanded my parameters to include auction houses, commercial art galleries, noncommercial art centers, biennials, and art fairs in the UAE. In this analysis, I define a museum (*mathaf*) first as a collecting institution with a space that intentionally uses displays to educate viewers, in contradistinction to displays of family heirlooms or other private collections, for example. Second, a museum must be open to the public and described or identified as such. The broad base of the public means that theoretically, the museum is open to all. In addition, the museum maintains an association with wide publics given its connotations with democracy, as noted earlier. The definition of museum I use here largely maps onto the terms *mathaf* in Arabic and *musée* in French, yet it does exclude some forms of display. Many Gulf families maintain *majlis*, or *maylis* in Emirati dialect, rooms (literally, sitting rooms; sometimes translated as council rooms) that have extensive historical displays according to "autochthonous" aesthetics rather than "Western museum models" (Exell 2016, 171; see also MacLean 2016; Wilson 2023). But these spaces are often part of residences and not necessarily accessible to everyone, nor are they cleanly categorizable as didactic. While worthy of study in their own right, majlis rooms are outside the scope of this book.

In addition to museums, I also refer to arts organizations. The term "arts organization" includes art museums as well as those organizations with studio spaces and exhibition spaces, but which were not named as museums either because they were formally incorporated as commercial galleries, because they did not have a collection, or because their primary focus was artists rather than artworks. I also include commercial galleries in the category of arts organizations because my interlocutors valued them. Galleries regularly staged exhibitions and many interlocutors toured these shows and exhibited in them. They also employed a number of people who later worked in nonprofit organizations. To encompass all these shifting modalities, in this book the term arts organizations glosses any institution dedicated to "art," its making, display, or sale. My use of arts organizations instead of museums reflects the complex hybrid nature of many twenty-first-century arts entities. The line between commercial and noncommercial was also blurry. Throughout the book I use the term noncommercial to designate organizations that are not operating as commercial businesses. Because the organizational structure of a nonprofit does not map easily onto the Emirates, using the term "nonprofit" would create false parallels.

My interlocutors came from a variety of backgrounds and generations, so I conducted interviews in Arabic, English, and French, depending on the preference of the interviewee. With Belgian and French artists, as well as the French staff who worked on projects like the Louvre Abu Dhabi, I spoke French. With interlocutors of Indian, Pakistani, Japanese, Spanish, British, and American backgrounds, I spoke English. I found a generational split in Arabic language preference: For the most part, Arab artists based in the UAE (including Emirati and non-Emirati Arabs) under the age of forty felt more comfortable discussing their work in English than Arabic, given their training in primarily English-language schools (Derderian 2021).[17] As a result, most of the "local" artists I worked with had a more precise and expansive register for discussing art in English compared to Arabic. There are also some structural reasons for English preference: There are no codified translations of some art-specific terms like "curator" and "installation" in Arabic. However, among the over-forty UAE-based artists who had trained in Arabic before English-language schooling became the norm, their overwhelming preference was to speak in Arabic. Many artists in this generation had pursued graduate training in the arts in cities like Cairo and Baghdad, which are other Arabic-speaking capitals.

My positionality as a white female ethnographer afforded me significant passport privilege (Le Renard 2021). Whiteness offers extensive privilege in UAE society. The seemingly ubiquitous security guards never questioned me about whether I belonged as they would have others: There are many news reports of malls banning single men, particularly South Asian men, under the guise of "family spaces," such as those in Qatar described by Samuli Schielke (2020). My whiteness gave me assumed, and unearned, legitimacy. It allowed me broad mobility, which facilitated my research but also renders me complicit in the Emirates' complex and problematic racial hierarchy.

Most practicing artists based in the UAE are now women, so as someone identifying as a woman, my joining social gatherings went with the grain of social norms. I have elected to focus more heavily on women and queer artists here, partly because my positionality afforded me greater access to these communities and partly as a political act, given the underrepresentation of women and queer artists in the mainstream media and scholarship more generally. Being a white woman in the UAE often garnered me respect and expedited service. I am also aware that some other female U.S. colleagues who are not white did not have these advantages, so it is not solely my gender presentation or passport privilege that gave me these advantages, but the two in intersection with my whiteness.

As is typical for anthropological research, *most* but not all of the names of individuals and organizations in the following text are pseudonyms. I have indicated where I use real names. In general, I do this during the historical overview of the UAE art scene; in the *In the Gallery* interludes between chapters where I feature artists' work, galleries, and exhibitions; and when discussing artists whom it would be fruitless to camouflage, such as the late artist Hassan Sharif (1951–2016). Using pseudonyms protects my interlocutors' identities and allowed them a measure of freedom to share things with me while shielding them from retribution, which was especially important when we discussed critique, citizenship status, and the limits of expression. Particularly in a state where criticism—or perceived criticism—of the government could result in deportation or imprisonment, my interlocutors were justifiably leery about speaking on the record at the beginning of my research. Their initial hesitation, followed by more expansive conversations we shared after I had earned their trust, also speaks to the value of deep ethnography and the kinds of knowledge it can foreground.

Throughout the book, I cleave closely to the terms used by my interlocutors. Significant literature examines heritage production and heritage museums in the region (Erskine-Loftus 2014; Erskine-Loftus et al. 2016; Exell and Rico 2014; Khalaf 2000, 2005; Sachedina 2021; Wakefield 2012, 2021) and the influence of heritage on land art (Sindelar 2017). This book offers a complementary focus on contemporary art, artists, and art museums rather than national museums or heritage spaces. More precisely, most of the book is about contemporary art, rather than modernist art, as art historians typically periodize the two.[18] My interlocutors did not often use the term "heritage" or the Arabic *turāth*. Rather, they were keen to assert a history of artistic production in the Emirates and to call attention to the historical facts of prior initiatives and organizations, such as the UAE 5 group of artists, the Emirates Fine Arts Society, and the Sharjah Biennial. These histories challenged tabula rasa narratives of the Gulf as having no art history. My interlocutors were often hostile to hints that their work dealt with heritage, perceiving it as a slight that their work was lazy or lacking sufficient critique to be good contemporary art. In an interview with an artist I call Reem, she relayed the questions media asked about her work. "I get the question, 'How do heritage and tradition influence your work?'" She rolled her eyes. "There is this assumption that I cannot think beyond these things," she said. "It's an easy way out and people use 'heritage'—certain designs, especially—but that work is"—she paused and pursed her lips—"the opposite of thoughtful." In a separate conversation, another artist remarked, "The [government organizations] try to force heritage a lot. If an artist doesn't identify that way . . . art just becomes craft." These comments capture how many interlocutors associated heritage with craft, not with contemporary art, and the pressures to present in traditional aesthetics (see also Joselit 2020; Mosquera 2003; Oguibe 2004; Winegar 2006). The construct of heritage was, for many I worked with, not a framework they saw as relevant to their art-making, although it was pushed by state actors.

As part of this practice of using the terms my interlocutors did, I also use terms common in the global art world, like "white cube," referring to the minimalist display style favored by many museums and galleries; "residency," a short-term visiting position for artists that was usually compensated and commissioned them to create new work; and "gallery." Gallery is a polysemous word that reflects crossover with market interests: It can refer to an exhibition room in a noncommercial art space, or it can refer to a commercial art organization. The *In the Gallery* interludes are so named in order to highlight this hybridity. As for residencies, my artist interlocutors regularly applied for them. They coveted these opportunities because they gave artists paid space and time to create new work, and they also increased artists' international visibility. During my primary fieldwork period, a number of my interlocutors were awarded residencies at various international arts organizations in places like Seoul, Kyoto, Baku, Kochi, New York City, and London.

While my ethnographic analysis is specific to the UAE, it is couched in an understanding of the Gulf region as a whole and derives from research conducted in the UAE; Kochi, India; Qatar; Kuwait; Bahrain; Saudi Arabia; and Oman.[19] Accessing Khalifa Al Qattan's archives and interviewing Kuwaiti art scene leaders helped me establish a more thorough understanding of the strong artist networks in the 1970s and 1980s, self-termed Gulf (*Khalīj*) or Gulf Cooperation Council (GCC; *majlis al-tʿāwun*) artists. Perhaps a vestige of these early groupings, my citizen interlocutors generally expressed a fraternity with and enjoyed reciprocal privileges in other GCC states. In keeping with my interlocutors' framings of salient geographies, I use the Gulf as a geographic unit of analysis recognizing there are limitations and politics to such geographic groupings (Carapico 2004; Green 2014; Keshavarzian 2024; Khalidi 1998; Low 2014; Onley and Nonneman 2020). Given the regional ethos I witnessed during my fieldwork, it is also perhaps fitting that the UAE's art and museum boom emerged from a regional Gulf art scene that existed in the twentieth century, which is where we begin.

IN THE GALLERY I   Exhibiting the Pioneers' Generation

WHEN I WALKED INTO *But We Cannot See Them: Tracing a UAE Art Community, 1988–2008* at New York University Abu Dhabi (NYUAD)'s Art Gallery, I stopped short in front of a massive chronological web, a set of interwoven pastel bands titled "A Timeline of Intersections" (Figure G1.1). It looked reminiscent of a subway map. Each horizontal band bore a location, and each of the delicate interlaid multicolor lines represented an artist. The timeline read from left to right, chronologically. Shows and events were marked with delicate vertical lines. The artist's individual lines zigzagged across the different locations to mark the shows and events they had participated in in those places, creating a web of connections.

Some of the different events marked were: Emirates Fine Arts Society (EFAS) exhibitions in Sharjah, Hassan founds Dubai Art Atelier (Free Art Atelier, Ministry of Education), the 3rd Cairo Biennial, the Muscat Youth Biennial, a residency at Khor Fakkan Public Library, Sand Palace Gatherings begin, 7th Havana Biennial, Sharjah Biennial 6, and the *Language of the Desert* exhibition at the Kunst Museum in Bonn, Germany. The format of the map depicted early arts organizations across the Gulf as operating in small nodes. The introductory wall text nearby read:

> This art community's work diverged dramatically from the existing art practices in the UAE at the time, but the community anchored itself in a positive attitude of aiming to grow a contemporary art audience, and supporting one another's growth in the UAE context. They worked for enhanced arts

FIGURE G1.1. Participating artists' exhibition timeline, *But We Cannot See Them: Tracing a UAE Art Community, 1988–2008*, on view at the NYU Abu Dhabi Art Gallery, March 2–August 26, 2017.

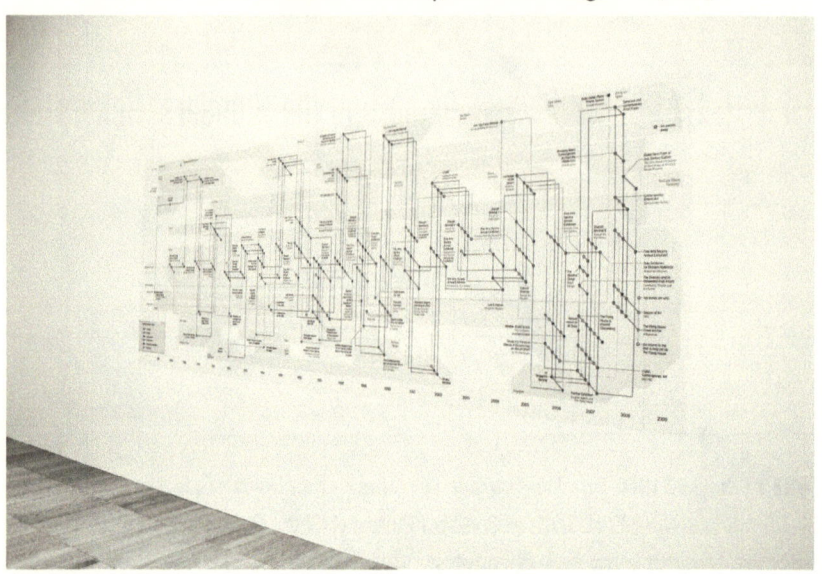

Source: Courtesy of the NYU Abu Dhabi Art Gallery.

> infrastructure and education . . . they worked enthusiastically despite their relative obscurity. In many ways, they were one another's audience, critics, and arts infrastructures.

The exhibition celebrated and showcased these connections, showing through juxtaposition the different influences this cadre of artists had on each other (Figures G1.2–G1.5).

Yet because there were no infrastructures, unearthing the archival documentation of this period was also challenging. In order to learn more about the early exhibitions in the Gulf, I traveled to Kuwait. Kuwait had experienced an early efflorescence of art in the region. The Mirror House, a private museum dedicated to the work of late Kuwaiti painter Khalifa Al Qattan (1934–2003) and his wife, fellow artist Lidia Al Qattan, also maintained Khalifa's personal archive, dating back to the 1950s.

When I pulled my white Hyundai Sonata rental car up outside the Mirror House one April afternoon, I had no doubts as to whether I had successfully found it. Located just north of the third ring road in an otherwise quiet

FIGURE G1.2. Installation view with Hassan Sharif's work in the foreground, *But We Cannot See Them: Tracing a UAE Art Community, 1988–2008*, on view at the NYU Abu Dhabi Art Gallery, March 2–August 26, 2017.

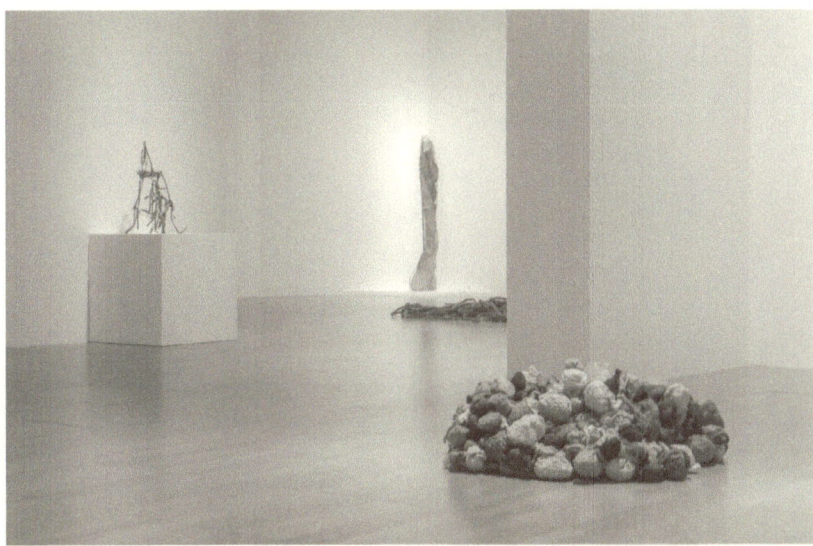

Source: Courtesy of the NYU Abu Dhabi Art Gallery.

FIGURE G1.3. Installation view with work by Mohamed Ahmed Ibrahim in the foreground, *But We Cannot See Them: Tracing a UAE Art Community, 1988–2008*, on view at the NYU Abu Dhabi Art Gallery, March 2–August 26, 2017.

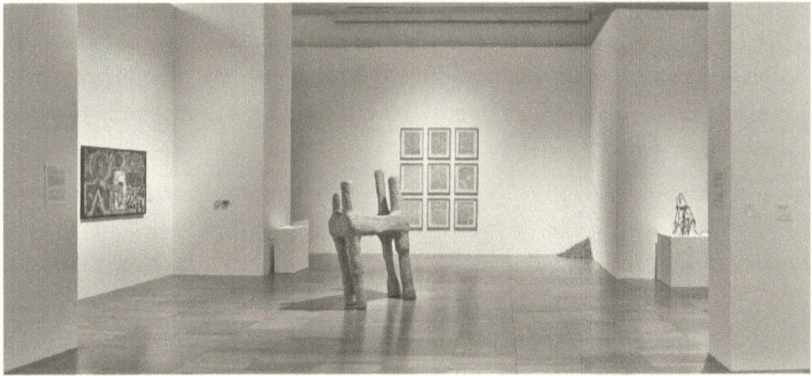

Source: Courtesy of the NYU Abu Dhabi Art Gallery.

FIGURE G1.4. Installation view, *But We Cannot See Them: Tracing a UAE Art Community, 1988–2008*, with works by Vivek Vilasini, Salwa Zeidan, and Abdullah Al Saadi on view at the NYU Abu Dhabi Art Gallery, March 2–August 26, 2017.

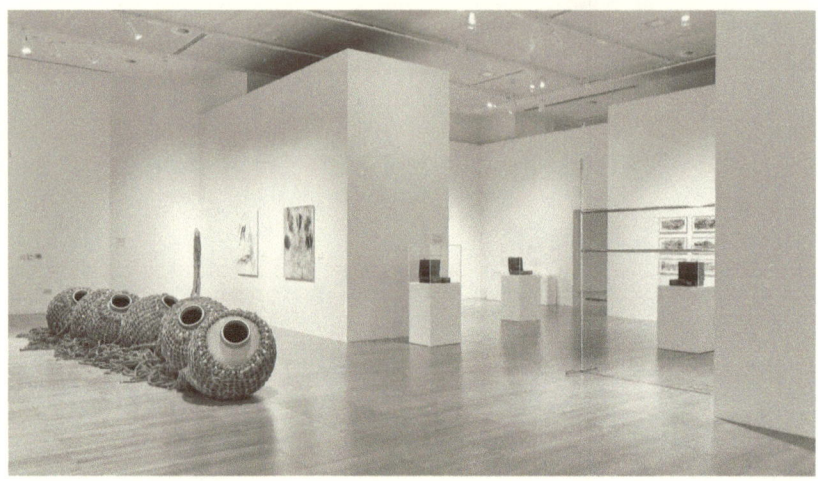

Source: Courtesy of the NYU Abu Dhabi Art Gallery.

residential neighborhood in Kuwait City, the Mirror House façade was emblazoned with butterflies, stars, and flowers made from mirror fragments assembled in mosaics on the brick of the exterior wall. The doorway was framed in a similar mosaic. Above the doors, metal text spelled out a curving, languid prayer invoking blessings, *Bism-Allah al-raḥman al-raḥīm*, decorated with more mirror fragments. Inside the house, mirror mosaics decorated walls, doorways, bookcases, ceilings, and the doors themselves. The mirror artist, Lidia Al Qattan, and her daughter Jalila graciously gave me a tour. Together they ran the Mirror House.

The Qattans possess a precious private archive documenting early arts initiatives in the Gulf. Khalifa's personal archive filled an interior room, one of a rare few without mirrors, with floor-to-ceiling shelving for his books, albums, folders, photographs, and ephemera. The room smelled vaguely of newsprint, like a library. Perhaps seeing my eyes widen at the amount of material, Jalila graciously offered me a coffee, and I accepted. I put on a pair of plastic gloves and got to work. I was looking for any documentation of exhibitions in the Emirates or including Emirati artists, particularly those in the *jīl al-ruwād*, or pioneers' generation, who had been active in the 1980s, including Hassan

FIGURE G1.5. Installation view featuring installation by Hussein Sharif, *But We Cannot See Them: Tracing a UAE Art Community, 1988–2008*, on view at the NYU Abu Dhabi Art Gallery, March 2–August 26, 2017.

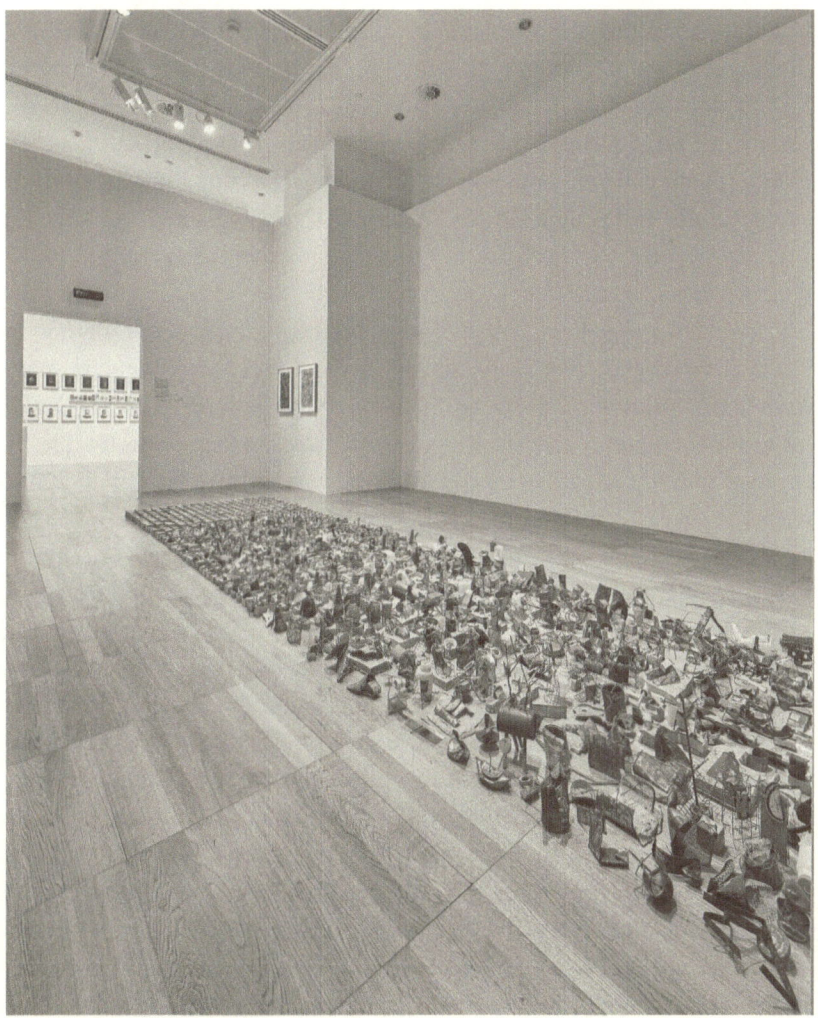

Source: Courtesy of the NYU Abu Dhabi Art Gallery.

Sharif, widely cited as the founder of contemporary art in the UAE, along with Hussein Sharif, Mohamed Yousif, Abdullah Al Saadi, Abdulrahim Salem, Mohamed Kazem, Mohamed Ahmed Ibrahim, and Najat Makki. I hoped that the archive would offer me insight into the kinds of connections and intersections documented in the wall chart at *But We Cannot See Them*. I already knew from interviews that Kuwait had been important to UAE-based artists; as one artist told me, "Kuwait was very buzzy" in the 1970s and '80s. Kuwait's government funded a number of early exhibitions, before the advent of museums and dedicated arts exhibition spaces. Among the Gulf states, Kuwait was home to a flourishing art scene (Al Qassemi 2013, 2020). In the 1950s, with early oil wealth, Kuwait's government had supported the development of a broad Pan-Arab network of scholars, sending Kuwaitis to study abroad and bringing non-Kuwaiti Arabs to Kuwait to study (Al-Rashoud 2019). It had been a time of rich intellectual foment in the country to which the arts were integral.

Qattan had organized his photos in brightly colored floral albums in rough chronological order, so I flipped through them, skipping over snaps from family vacations to focus on the images that captured his artwork and his exhibitions. Seeing that some pictures had fused to their protective plastic covers, I moved the pages gingerly. After skimming three albums, I flipped open one page and saw a familiar face. I saw Hassan.

In 1986, Qattan participated in the annual Emirates Fine Arts Society exhibition, and in 1993, Qattan participated in and won first prize at the inaugural Sharjah Biennial (Figures G1.7 and G1.8). While in the UAE, he visited the Dubai Fort with other artists. Qattan, presumably behind the lens, captured a group of artists including Hassan Sharif and Abdulraheem Salim, appearing to pause mid-installation to share a meal, clustered around plates and glasses. In another shot, Qattan posed with a group of Emirati artists including Sharif, Salim, and Mohamed Yousif (Figure G1.6) at Sharjah's Expo Center, the site of the early biennial and host to many early exhibitions: The small cubes of each carpeted stall are visible behind the artists. To one side, paintings are stacked resting against a wall. Qattan in a gray robe and loose kaffiyeh on his head looks down at Mohamed Yousif, crouched in blue track pants. In another photo, Qattan posed with Abdulqader Rais, presumably at an opening as other people nearby are contemplating a series of paintings hung behind them.

Qattan's archive provided other documentary evidence of such artistic connections and exchanges, and importantly, also documented the types of organizations, events, venues, and artists in the scene at that time. From the certificates of participation and exhibition brochures in Qattan's documents, I learned that the Kuwaiti Society for Formative Arts held its first exhibition in 1975. Qattan had also saved exhibition brochures from the

FIGURE G1.6. Khalifa Al Qattan, left, with Abdulraheem Salim
(center back), Hassan Sharif (right), and Mohamed Yousif
(center front) at the Sharjah Expo Center, 1986.

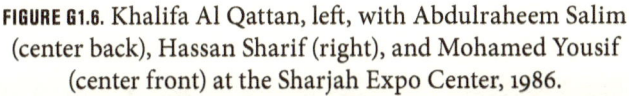

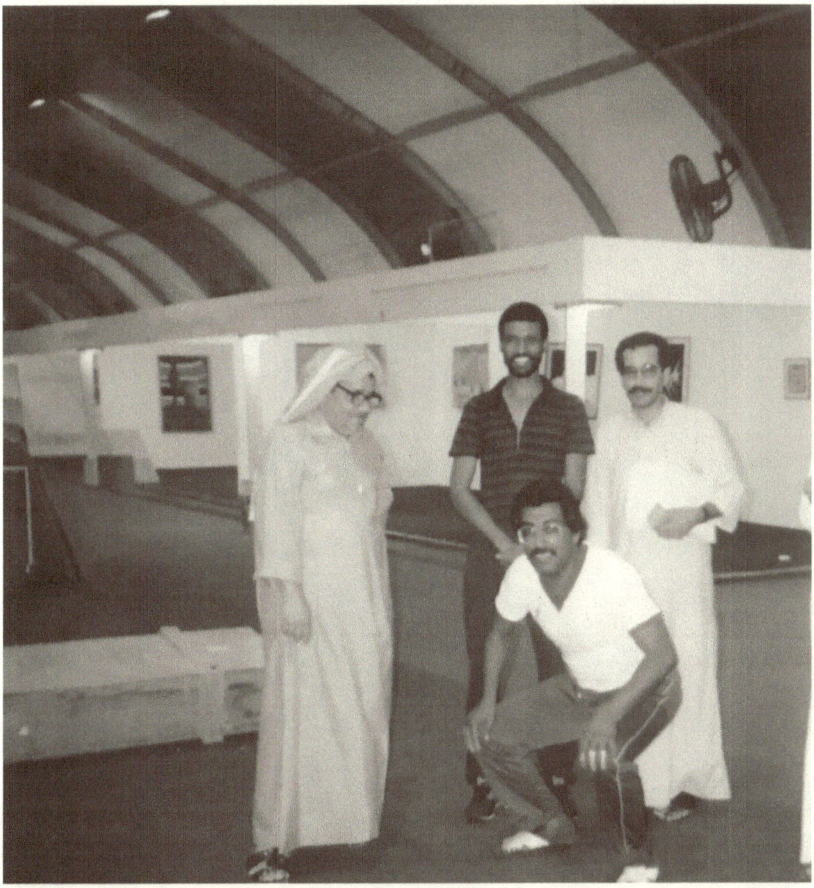

Source: Author's photo of archival material, reproduced with permission of the
Khalifa and Lidia Qattan Art Museum/Mirror House.

early years of Kuwait's *Marsam al-ḥur,* often translated as the Free Atelier.
Kuwait's Free Atelier, founded in 1960, was legendary: Founded by the government, artists were selected and given studio space and a salary. In a public
talk in February 2016, Dr. Mohamed Yousif shared that after Sharjah ruler
Shaykh Sultan Al-Qasimi was shown a flyer from Kuwait's Atelier, he was im-
pressed and decided to create a similar structure and workspaces in the UAE.
On September 15, 1980, Shaykh Sultan created EFAS (Allison et al. 2017, 205).

FIGURE G1.7. Khalifa Al Qattan received first prize in the inaugural Sharjah Biennial in 1993, as commemorated on this plaque.

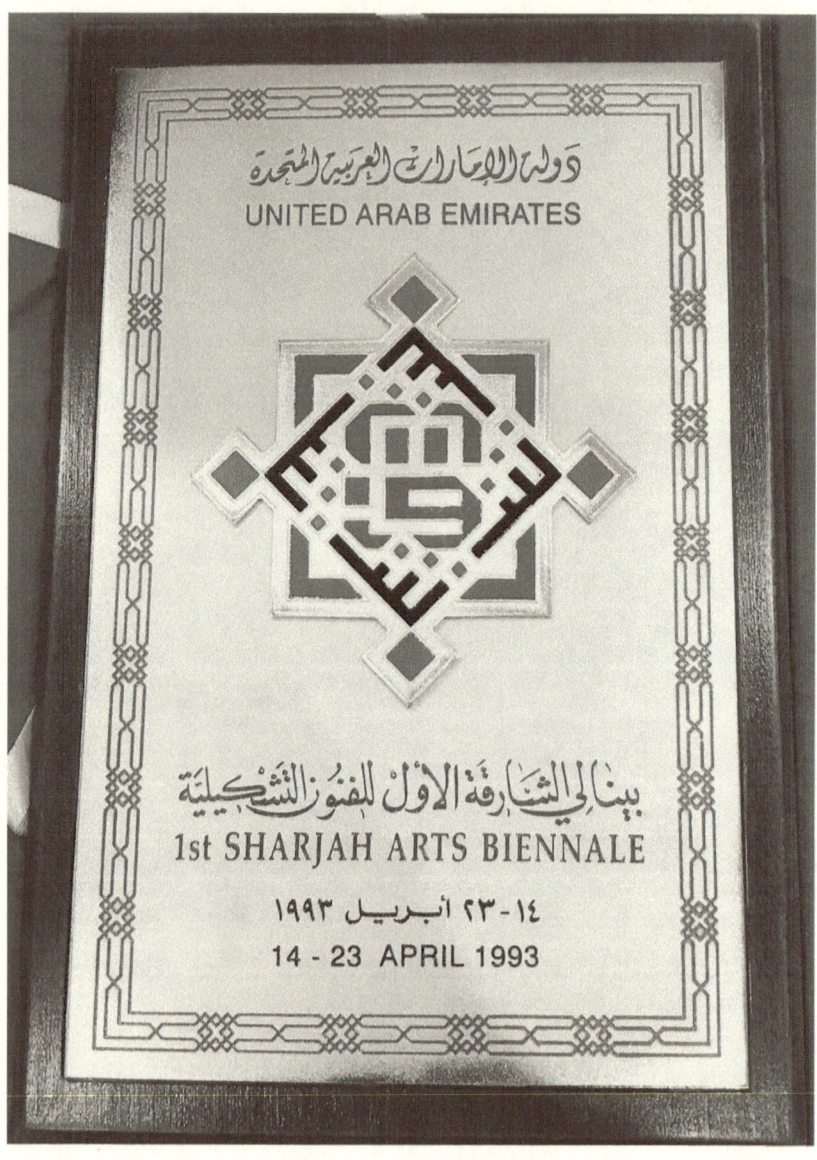

Source: Author's photo reproduced with permission of the Khalifa and Lidia Qattan Art Museum/Mirror House.

FIGURE G1.8. Khalifa Al Qattan's certificate of participation in the 1986 annual Emirates Fine Arts Society exhibition.

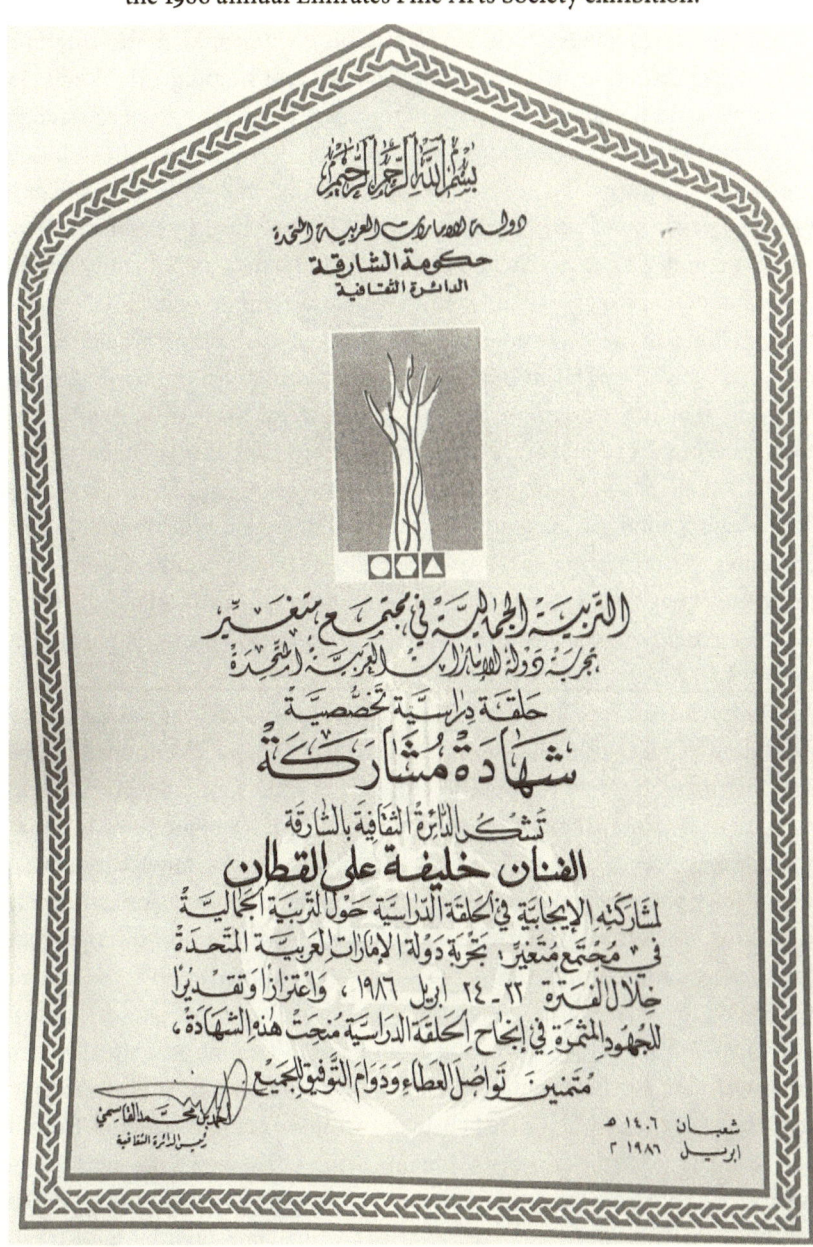

By this account, the budding arts infrastructure in Kuwait deeply informed the creation of early arts infrastructures in the UAE.

Qattan's archives also included significant documentation attesting to a vibrant regional scene, with regional biennials and rotating exhibitions. In my conversations with artists active in this generation, they often referred to exhibitions by venue rather than by titles or dates. In these various exhibition brochures, there are references to the "First Gulf Exhibition" (*ma'rḍ al-khalīj*) held in Doha, Qatar, and "Second Gulf Exhibition" held in Baghdad, Iraq, which are both unfortunately undated and do not indicate what entity hosted them, but perhaps suggest plans to have a rotating annual or biennial exhibition of Gulf artists. These shows are noted in a 1985 exhibition brochure, and therefore would have taken place prior to that year; given the chronological ordering of artists' exhibitions in their bios, it seems likely these exhibitions took place in the early 1980s. A 1994 exhibition brochure lists later exhibitions of GCC (*majlis t'āwun*) artists in Dubai (1985), Riyadh (1989), and Doha (1992).[1] The growing emphasis of the Gulf as a collective identity at this time also correlates to the creation of the GCC, a political economic alliance aimed at promoting cooperation between its members states, in 1980. Alongside these rotating exhibitions that shepherded a GCC fraternity, Kuwait, in particular, developed a robust exhibition schedule.

One of the earliest exhibitions found in the Qattan Archives was the spring exhibition of 1965, although the British Political Diaries, maintained by the senior British officer in Kuwait, note there was a show of students' work in 1960. Emirati artist Abdulqader Rais participated in the 1965 show, demonstrating early transregional connections (Rais was also the only Emirati artist whose work was on display at the Kuwait Museum of Modern Art during my April 2017 visit, although the label did not clarify when or how the work was acquired by the museum). Another recurring show is often listed as the Kuwait Exhibition for Arab Artists or sometimes as the Kuwait Biennale, which drew participants from across the region from its first iteration in 1969 (Lenssen 2018, 192) and was held regularly until at least 1989 (based on information in Qattan's archive, and a date consonant with the Iraqi invasion of Kuwait in 1990). The 1985 edition featured many of the artists now known as the *jīl al-ruwād*, or pioneers' generation, in the UAE. Kuwait also held regular shows for "full-time" (*mutafarighīn*, i.e., salaried) artists sponsored by the Kuwait Free Atelier which were clearly supported by the state financially as well as socially. A clipping of the front page of *Al-Qabas* newspaper dated March

18, 1979, shows Sadoun al-Jasim, the *wakīl* or agent of the Ministry of Information (*wizārat al-ā'lām*), gazing at one of Khalifa Al Qattan's paintings.

Kuwait also hosted exhibitions for youth (*shabāb*) artists from across
the GCC. The Second Annual GCC Youth Exhibition (*ma'rḍ al-tashkīlī al-
thāny l-shabāb dawl majlis al-t'āwun*), held in Kuwait in September 1986, was
hosted by the Kuwaiti Association of Fine Artists (*jam'at al-kuwaītīya lilfanūn
al-tashkīlī*). The cover of the catalog featured the six GCC member state flags
forming a circle around a small map with the GCC territory highlighted in
one single color, together. It included an essay on the history of the fine arts
movements in the Emirates (*tārīkh al-ḥaraka al-tashkīlīya fī dowla al-Imārāt
al-'arabīya al-mutaḥida*).

Qattan's archives reveal the nature of the early Gulf arts scene: Prior to
the arrival of the megamuseums planned for the Emirates, the scene derived
from small clusters of committed artists and curators who drove the scene
forward, and who often worked with the support of emirate-level ministries
in the absence of dedicated arts infrastructure. Exhibitions were essentially
survey shows, funded by states to represent the nation's emerging talent but
not necessarily offering viewers a single theme or aesthetic style. The arts organizations that put shows together were often loose collectives that did not
have dedicated permanent exhibition spaces and were not formal, full-time
arts organizations. The early Gulf art scene centered around events, not institutions. Qattan's archive documents the beginnings of state-sponsored arts
exhibitions and organizations in an early nationalization period. The government ministries of the time, in their nationalist and regionalist ethos, are
very different from the types of capital-centric arts organizations in operation
today. As visible in the state- and region-centric exhibitions documented in
the Mirror House archives, and in the state supports for Emirati artists in
the Timeline of Intersections, the art scene in the Gulf embodies both the
exhibitionary complex and its successor, what I term the market exhibitionary
complex.

ONE

Capital Projects: The Emergence of the Market Exhibitionary Complex

THIS CHAPTER CHARTS THE SHIFTING of organizational forms in the Gulf over the past sixty years from a series of state-based collectives operating in a regional framework to a hybrid, semicommercial model. It sets the creation of fluid, event-centric collectives in the Gulf beginning in 1957 against the backdrop of museum development elsewhere, and moves through to the present, showing how early arts organizations that were largely grassroots collectives of artists have since given way to a hybrid model of transnational institutions that are not fully state-run, nonprofit, or commercial. The first wave of arts organizations, in the period between 1957 and 1991, were often loose coalitions rather than permanent brick-and-mortar institutions with full-time staff. The development of organizations in the second phase is strongly informed by the application of commercial and corporate models to organizations across all fields, including the arts and museums. The exhibitions, artists societies, and associations of the late twentieth century paved the way for later institutions that were built in the second phase, which blends commercial and noncommercial interests.

The commercial, in the Gulf context, sometimes appeared as independent and private—that is, not state-run or the opposite of the state. Yet as one Emirati royal told me, "Almost nothing is purely private." Therefore, the term "commercial" in my analysis refers explicitly to profit-making, but should not be interpreted to mean "independent" or "private" in the sense of being fully unaffiliated with the government, as the term might be used in a U.S. context. Simultaneously, the term "noncommercial" is intentional, because the term "nonprofit" does not easily map onto the Emirates (Muslic 2017) given its lack of tax scheme, at least at the time of my fieldwork.[1] Given this complexity and to avoid invoking false parallels, "noncommercial" designates initiatives that were not primarily oriented toward profit-making. The second phase of institutionalization in the Gulf is marked by these hybrid enterprises, both commercial and not, local and not, state and not, their complex partnerships leading to difficulty in easy categorization. These changing institutional forms also inform and shape other areas of art and museum practice, as the following chapters detail.

From Collectives to Institutions

The early museums and arts organizations on the Arabian Peninsula fit into the prior exhibitionary complex model, first buttressing imperial goals and later nationalist ones.[2] In the nineteenth and twentieth centuries, imperial and state actors used museums as tools to create and promote the state, be it an empire or a nation (Anderson 2006; Bennett 1995; Duncan 1995; McAleer and Longair 2014). National museums were a "typical cultural institution in colonial states," celebrating the modern European nation-state as the apex of civilization (Joselit 2020, 30; see also Mathur and Singh 2015). Exhibitions became "the instruments of civilization . . . a concomitant to empire" (Rydell 1984, 105). In this well-documented state-culture paradigm, state actors have used museums and culture to inculcate citizens into the nation's heritage, deploy citizens' cultural contributions to define an aesthetic and cultural identity, and forge an imagined community (Anderson 2006; Barringer and Flynn 1998; Bennett 1995; Coffey 2012; Duncan 1995; Foster 2002; Karp et al. 2006; Levitt 2015; Lloyd and Thomas 1998; Macdonald 2006; Myers 2002; Pieprzak 2010; Prior 2002; Sachedina 2021; Shaw 2003; Watenpaugh 2004; Winegar 2006). Sociologist Tony Bennett coined the term "exhibitionary complex" to refer to exhibition-related infrastructures that represented the state and persuaded the public to identify with it (1995).

In Britain and France in particular, throughout the 1800s and early 1900s, the exhibitionary complex also carried imperial connotations. British imperial officials used display to illustrate the supposedly beneficial aspects of empire to domestic audiences (Barringer and Flynn 1998; McAleer and Longair 2014; McAleer and MacKenzie 2015) and abroad to instruct and "uplift" colonized groups (Longair 2015).[3] World's fairs and art museums disciplined visitors through "civic seeing," the displays inculcating civic values to viewers (Bennett 1995; Rydell 1984). Fairs in particular staged racial hierarchies to justify colonization and imperial dispossession (Auerbach and Hoffenberg 2008; Hinsley and Wilcox 2016; Rydell 1984). This practice of using fairs to inculcate civic values transpired outside European and U.S. capitals, including in the Ottoman Empire (Shaw 2003) and South Asia (Guha-Thakurta 2004; Mathur and Singh 2015).

British colonial officials opened the first museum on the Arabian Peninsula in Aden, present-day Yemen, in 1930, and a second museum (the Tawahi Museum) in 1966.[4] Small regional museums like Aden were key to projecting the Empire, and making it "manifest and tangible to those living with it as a real political, social and cultural identity" (McAleer and MacKenzie 2015, 13). British political records also note that the president of the Kuwaiti Department of Education "officially opened a temporary museum" in Kuwait City on December 31, 1957 (Jarman 1990a, 569). The British Political Agent noted that

> the aim of the museum is to preserve a record of local crafts and customs in Kuwait and to show a comparison between conditions in Kuwait before and after the many development schemes which have been started since oil was discovered. (Jarman 1990a, 569)

This kind of comparison also emphasized the conveniences afforded by British rule and their oversight of oil development, like electricity and air conditioning. The temporary museum's "prominent exhibit, and at present the only one of genuine antiquarian interest, is a stone having a Greek inscription" from recent Danish excavations at Failaka (Jarman 1990a, 569). The diary further noted that "the Department of Education has plans to build a permanent museum in due course" (Jarman 1990a, 569). The museum was but one of many to follow.

After the fall of British and French empires, and in the era of nation-states as the primary form of political organization post–World War II, art museums and world's fairs used display as a way to discipline audiences and inculcate national values (Bennett 1995; Duncan and Wallach 1980; Duncan 1995; Rydell 1984), the museum visit becoming a secular "civic ritual" (Duncan 1995). Soon art museums became "signature ornaments of any self-respecting city, vital to its civic and cultural identity" (McClellan 2012, 271). They represented cultural capital and were often located in capital cities.

Because museums were frequently elite institutions, in the mid-twentieth century various communities began to push back on the narrowness of museums' audiences and form their own museums. In the U.S., these museums were an outgrowth of the civil rights movement. U.S. examples of community museums include the Anacostia Community Museum (founded 1967), the Studio Museum in Harlem (founded 1968), and El Museo del Barrio (founded 1969). The phenomenon of community museums reflected the exclusion of communities from mainstream representation. Elsewhere, in Mexico for example, community museums were grounded in "local practices" and "relative[ly] independen[t] from the proprietary-conservationist ethos of the ideology of national patrimony," endeavoring to engage through interaction rather than through permanent displays (Yúdice 2003, 101–2). One way in which these museum organizers signaled their difference from the prior institutions was through their architecture, as many elected for non-palatial, non-sacred designs (Giebelhausen 2006).

While community museums arose elsewhere, art museums and institutions that promoted the visual arts emerged on the Peninsula in the 1960s and 1970s, coeval with independence and nationalization movements. British rule of Arabia attenuated between 1961 and 1971: Kuwait attained independence in 1961, and after several years of conflicts with various nationalist forces, the British relinquished Aden in 1967. After the British announced their 1971 withdrawal from the Trucial States, the shaykhs along the northern rim of the Peninsula whose territories had been partially administered by the British, particularly in terms of trade and migration, debated how best to incorporate, eventually settling on the national constellations present today (Heard-Bey 1982; Zahlan 1978).

In the late 1960s and early 1970s, anticipating imminent British departure, Gulf rulers engaged in more consultative and partnership projects, which continued to increase following independence. British and French consultants were deeply integrated into museum projects in the region, establishing a consultant model that drew from British imperial policies of secondment and corporate culture, a harbinger of the corporate hybridity to come. Such consultants described the mission of these new national museums variously as the "formation of a historical and cultural consciousness" (Rice 1977, 81) and "follow[ing] the country's development" (Écochard 1972, 6). These museums were largely nationalist in tone, along the lines of other postcolonial endeavors (Chambers et al. 2016; Kreps 2011; Pieprzak 2010) and the exhibitionary complex more generally.

Many focused expressly on natural history and heritage. Foreign experts were invited to build museums in Bahrain and Qatar. The Bahrain National Museum, designed by British firm Michael Rice & Co., opened after the 1969 Second Conference on Asian Archaeology; its second iteration opened in 1988 in a new space designed by Danish firm KHR Arkitekter (Exell 2016, 56). In 1977, Rice & Co. completed the original National Museum of Qatar. While Rice credited the Emir of Qatar with the decision to create a Qatari national museum, the firm also acknowledged that "the original concepts and planning, all the design phases of the principal buildings and their interiors and the direction of the research programmes were placed into the hands of Michael Rice & Company" (Rice 1977, 79). Rice & Co. formed the museum's vision and its agenda.

Following Bennett's exhibitionary complex model, Gulf museums in newly independent states were oriented toward building a national community, and focused on scientific, ecological, and ethnographic displays—with the exception of the Kuwait National Museum, which included an art section. Kuwaiti officials requested an expert from UNESCO to "study and formulate plans for the organization of a national museum" (Écochard 1964, 146). Dr. Salim Abdul Haq, the Director of Syrian Museums, was dispatched to consult on behalf of UNESCO in 1959.[5] Abdul Haq had submitted a report based on his 1959 visit with a vision for the Kuwait Museum, and in 1964, Michel Écochard won an architectural competition to design the new museum according to Abdul Haq's specifications. Écochard was no stranger to the Middle East: He had worked in Morocco, Lebanon, and Syria, arguing for cultural- and climate-specific architecture (Écochard 1954; Khodr 2017; Verdeil 2012). Écochard's planned museum for Kuwait combined antiquities and modern art:

> The museum which [Abdul Haq] recommended for Kuwait . . . its primary purpose is to offer the people an easy means of education through visual media, bringing them into contact not merely with *works of art* but also with all aspects of life throughout the Arabian Peninsula—the development of its natural resources, its history and *art* and lastly, all branches of present-day science, thus turning their gaze toward the future. (1964, 147; emphasis mine)

Much as in colonial museums, the idea was that "a visit to the museum ought to be instructive," formulating a national identity through the cultural accomplishments of citizens but also promoting education (Écochard 1964, 147). It is perhaps notable that of the many new national museum projects across the Arabian Peninsula at the time, Kuwait's is the only that appears to include art alongside more ethnological, archaeological, and general historical material—perhaps because Kuwait's art scene was already emerging at the time, as Qattan's archives at the Mirror House attest.[6]

These consultants also envisioned connections between museums and the presence of artists—largely that museums could raise the caliber of local artists, an idea that has reemerged in the contemporary period and posits the success of the Guggenheim and Louvre Abu Dhabi on a thriving UAE art scene. Écochard tied museums to living, producing artists: His planning document for the Bahrain museum noted that "the level of teaching in the visual arts is not yet high enough to have trained artists of value" (1972, 10). However, he wrote that if a "real modern museum of plastic arts, with authentic works" was not possible, he recommended acquiring a collection of high-quality reproductions "showing the various schools of painting, engraving [and] sculpture," which could "permit temporary and renewable exhibitions on selected artistic schools" (Écochard 1972, 10). Such rotating exhibitions, in Écochard's mind, could be used to train up-and-coming artists, showing he understood the emergence of these museums to be correlated to the presence of local artists. Yet despite the necessity of such artists, museum planners like Écochard and Rice make no mention of including local artists or collectives in their plans or analyses.

During the early nationalization period, groups of artists—who had been practicing prior to independence—began to form collectives and stage informal exhibitions. Even though there were no art museums yet, they began developing infrastructures to exhibit, including biennials, artists' societies with annual exhibitions, and youth exhibitions. Their work would later form the basis of a Gulf art canon and fill the first art museums in the region.

The first solo exhibition of a Kuwaiti-born artist in Kuwait was that of Khalifa Al Qattan (whose home is now the Mirror House) at the Al-Najaḥ School in 1953 (Al Qassemi 2020, 108). Qattan was the first Kuwaiti artist to exhibit abroad, in Italy in 1962 (Hussain 2012, 1). Young artist Tareq Rajab won an exhibition staged in 1953 by pioneering artist Mujib al-Dousari, who was then teaching oil painting and Islamic floral designs at the Mubarakiya School (Tareq Rajab Museum n.d.).[7] A spring exhibition of student work was begun in the late 1950s; the British political resident noted the "second spring Art Exhibition of Kuwaiti schools" in 1960, commenting primly that "a rather lurid display of pupils' work opened at the Mubarakiya School on April 23" (Jarman 1990b, 460). That same year, the Ministry of Education opened the *Marsam al-ḥur*, or the Free Atelier.

Notably, the Atelier was primarily a *marsam*, or studio: a space for making art rather than displaying it. It was located in a historic house where it remains today, after a significant expansion of the facilities in 1972.[8] In addition to giving selected artists a studio space and materials, the state paid artists a monthly salary and supported those artists' participation in state exhibitions abroad, a clear example of the exhibitionary complex at play.

Nonstate arts organizations, those with a commercial or regional focus, also began to pop up. Artists started to organize themselves into artists' associations: Sculptor and artist Sami Mohammad cofounded the Kuwaiti Society for Formative Arts (now the Kuwait Art Association) in 1967; the Bahrain Contemporary Arts Association was founded in 1970. Siblings Ghazi and Najat Sultan opened Sultan Gallery, the oldest remaining active commercial art gallery in the region, in Kuwait in 1969. In keeping with the Pan-Arabist ethos of the time, the focus of the gallery was not just Kuwaiti artists, however, but Arab artists broadly. One of its founders, Ghazi Sultan, felt that "Arab artists were 'generally overlooked by their societies,'" leading to a "weak network of artists, and artistic exchange, which [the Sultan Gallery] wanted to change" (Khouri 2014). The Sultan Gallery was certainly part of this shift and Kuwait's thriving artistic scene, which garnered international attention.

Many of the exhibitions for which Qattan has documentation in the late 1970s through the 1980s display a very regionalist focus and were coordinated by state entities.[9] The Kuwaiti state established the National Council of Arts and Letters in 1974, and in 1977, the council invited Andy Warhol to visit. While state actors pushed nationalist projects after gaining independence, they also supported a network of Pan-Arab and regional, Gulf-centric exhibitions that were developed and run by local artists. Several artists also participated in shows in other Arab cultural centers, including Cairo and Rabat, outside the Gulf; however, the bulk of the exhibitions referenced in these archives are Gulf- and GCC-oriented. This regional focus can be attributed to two larger trends: political sentiments in the region as Pan-Arabism lost much of its popular appeal, and the process of nation-state formation on the Arabian Peninsula. While Pan-Arabism was on the decline after the June 1967 war between Arab states and Israel, described as the "Waterloo of Pan-Arabism" (Ajami 1978, 757), there was a pervasive sense that a distinctly Arab art was emerging. Art historian Kristine Khouri notes, "Arab art as a category developed at this time, coming from and being defined from *within* the Arab world, by artists, cultural managers, and intellectuals, as a break from national identification" (2014;

emphasis in original). While Pan-Arabism as a political movement waned after 1967, a unifying sentiment of Arab ethnicity remained strong. By the 1970s, "regional [art] initiatives coalesced around an explicit theme of Arab unity, in part spurred by the defeat of Arab military forces in the June 1967 War with Israel, and in part enabled by the nationalization of oil in the Arabian Gulf" (Lenssen 2018, 191–92). This region-centric ethos appears in the Qattan archives as well.

The information in the exhibition brochures in Qattan's archive testifies to both a growing art scene in the region and a number of region-wide initiatives that appear to have been aimed at promoting shared regional identity. As Arang Keshavarzian notes, "regionalizations are aspirations to create homogeneous geographic units" (2024, 12), and in this instance, there is a strong discursive focus on the "Gulf" (*Khalīj*) in exhibition titles and participants' backgrounds. There were also "Gulf" exhibitions (*maʿrḍ al-khalīj*) as well as the GCC youth shows (*shabāb dawl majlis tʿāwun*), creating a regional unity especially after the 1980 formation of the GCC. These exhibitions were supported by various governments and their burgeoning cultural entities; many of these early shows were held in Kuwait. One artist, Diana, who had been based in the Gulf for nearly fifty years, told me, "Kuwait in the '80s was where everything was happening in the region." The Kuwait Exhibition for Arab Artists, sometimes listed as the Kuwait Biennial, began in 1969 (Lenssen 2018, 192) and ran until 1989. What is also noteworthy about these exhibitions is a strong focus on national representation within the overall regional framework, fitting an exhibitionary complex model and, simultaneously, an early understanding of regionality and a collectivity that has since shifted to encompass a transnational multeity over and above a regional or national one.

Across the Gulf from Kuwait in the UAE, after federalization in 1971, Emirati federal cultural policy began to take shape with the formation of a Cultural Affairs Department and the Council of Artists Decree No. 12 (1975).[10] A number of sources cite the establishment of the Cultural Foundation (*Al-Mujamʿa*), which hosted talks, in 1981 in Abu Dhabi as seminal.[11] And most important, in 1984, Hassan Sharif (1951–2016) returned from studying conceptual art in London to practice in the UAE. He then opened the Mreija (*Al-Maīja*) Atelier in Sharjah, funded by that emirate's government, and began to train art students, including Mohamed Kazem and Mohamed Ahmed Ibrahim, who have gone on to great success as contemporary artists. Sharif also translated theoretical tracts about art by prominent artists Vassily Kandinsky, Piet Mondrian, Marcel Duchamp, and Carl André into Arabic. Given what he described as "poor translations," Sharif wanted to "write for the public" to teach them about different art schools and theories. Sharif told me, "During the '80s, I was busy with writing and teaching. I was lucky." In addition to translating, he wrote cultural editorials for *Al-Khaleej* newspaper and other local papers. The group of artists that clustered around him is now referred to as the UAE 5, a loose group consisting of Mohamed Kazem, Mohamed Ahmed Ibrahim, Abdullah Al Saadi, and Hussein Sharif (Hassan's brother). The art scene was still at that time artist-centric, rather than institution-centric.

Compared to Kuwait, fewer commercial and state-supported exhibitions were held in the UAE during the 1970s and '80s, but artists grew the art scene through a variety of privately-funded (including self-funded or unfunded) and state-funded exhibitions nonetheless (Table 1.1). As in Kuwait, the UAE's scene consisted largely of events rather than brick-and-mortar institutions. A bio for Hassan Sharif notes his holding a "one-man show in Dubai in 1976." Other archives document Sharif's "One Day Exhibition" at the Mreija Studio in Sharjah in 1985 (Al Qasimi and Marta 2015, 163). Per documentation in Qattan's archives, in 1983, Sharif and three other artists held a joint exhibition in Dubai. A few artists also listed participation in exhibitions held at *Nādī Al-Muntaza*, a community center in Sharjah, in 1985 and 1986; the *Al Ahli* club also held a few shows. Private companies also sponsored exhibitions: Abdulraheem Salim's bio for the 1985 Kuwait Exhibition for Arab Artists notes his participation in an exhibition for Jasco and Adnoc (the oil company) in Abu Dhabi. A 1985 flyer lists participation in the "First Exhibition for Fine Arts and People's Crafts of the GCC" in Dubai. Sharjah also hosted an exhibition for youth artists in 1979, and per the 1985 Kuwait Exhibition for Arab Artists catalog, Hassan Sharif was involved in the Youth Care Exhibitions (1975–76, 1979, 1981, 1984; *mahrajān rʿāyat al-shabāb bi-dawla*).[12] While supporting these various exhibitions, Sharif was also working for the Ministry—in 1987, he founded the Dubai Art Atelier through the Ministry of Education. Later, Mohamed Ahmed Ibrahim founded the Art Atelier of Khor Fakkan through the Sharjah Department of Culture and Information (1997); Kazem became the supervisor of the Dubai Art Atelier in 1999 (Allison et al. 2017). These various activities show both the long-term involvement of artists in the development of Emirati state cultural infrastructures, and that the UAE state generally supported artists' endeavors prior to the advent of formal institutions. Artists spearheaded and produced these exhibitions and initiatives, in the absence of any large art institutions or museums or dedicated arts venues.

TABLE 1.1. A timeline of openings across the Arabian Peninsula.

Date	Event	Location
1930–1931	Creation of Aden Museum	Aden, Yemen
1952	Mujib al-Dousari begins teaching	Kuwait
1953	Solo show of Kuwaiti artist Khalifa Al-Qattan at the Al Najah School	Kuwait
1960	Creation of Kuwait Atelier	Kuwait
	Second Spring Art Exhibition at Mubarakiya Schools	Kuwait
1961	*Kuwait achieves independence*	
1965	Spring Exhibition held (recurring)	Kuwait
1967	Opening of Tawahi Museum	Aden
	Kuwaiti Society of Formative Arts founded (now Kuwait Art Association)	Kuwait
	Six Day War	
1967–68	*South Yemen and Yemen Arab Republic formed; British withdrawal from Aden; British announce withdrawal from all Gulf by 1972*	
1969	Bahrain National Museum opens	Manama, Bahrain
	Sultan Gallery opens	Kuwait
	Kuwait biennial of Arab art established	Kuwait
1970	*Oman becomes a nation*	
	Bahrain Contemporary Arts Association founded	Manama
1971	*UAE, Bahrain, Qatar form as nations*	
	Al Ain National Museum opens	Al Ain, UAE
1972	First exhibition featuring young Dubai artists (Al Ras Public Library, Deira)	Dubai, UAE
1974	First Biennial of Arab Art	Baghdad, Iraq
	Asian Festival Exhibition	Iran
1975	Youth Care Festival	unknown
	Cultural Affairs Dept (federal) formed; law no. 4 (1975) and Council of Artists Decree No. 12 (1975)	UAE
1976	Hassan Sharif holds one-man show	Dubai

(Continued)

TABLE 1.1. (*Cont.*)

Date	Event	Location
1977	Opening of National Museum of Qatar	Doha, Qatar
1978	Museum of Archaeology and Ethnography opens	Riyadh, Saudi Arabia
1979	6th Exhibition of Arab Artists	Kuwait
	Youth artists exhibition	Sharjah, UAE
1980	Qatar Fine Arts Society founded	Qatar
	Founding of the Emirates Fine Arts Society	Sharjah
	Tareq Rajab opens private museum	Kuwait
	Youth studio founded	Muscat, Oman
1981	*Gulf Cooperation Council formed*	
	Kuwait Exhibition for Arab Artists, 7th edition	Kuwait
	Cultural Foundation active	Abu Dhabi, UAE
1982	Exhibitions of GCC Youth	Kuwait
	Boushahri Gallery founded	Kuwait
	Kuwait Biennale for Arab Formative Artists	Kuwait
1980s	Qurian Festival	Kuwait
1983	Dar al-Athar al-Islamiyya (DAI) opened	Kuwait
	Bahrain Arts Society founded	Bahrain
1984	Formative Bazaar	Sharjah
	Hassan Sharif returns from London, begins to teach, establishes Mreija Atelier	Dubai
	Kuwait Exhibition for Formative artists, 8th ed.	Kuwait
1985	Banoosh exhibition held	UAE
	Kuwait Exhibition for Arab Artists, 9th ed.	Kuwait
	1st Fine Arts & Handicrafts Exhibition	Dubai
	Jasco & ADNOC Exhibition (Abdulraheem Salim)	UAE
1986	"Saddam biennial"	Iraq (?)
	2nd Exhibition of GCC Youth	Kuwait
	Exhibition at Nadi al Muntazah	Sharjah
1987	Ras Al Khaimah National Museum opens	Ras al Khaimah, UAE
	Hassan Sharif founds Dubai Art Atelier	Dubai
1989	Majlis Gallery opens	Dubai
1990	*Iraq invades Kuwait*	

TABLE 1.1. (*Cont.*)

Date	Event	Location
1993	Inaugural Sharjah Biennial	Sharjah
	Omani Society for Fine Arts founded	Oman
1994	Salwa Zeidan Gallery opens	Abu Dhabi
	Dar al Funoon Gallery opens	Kuwait
	3rd Fine Arts of the GCC Exhibition	Abu Dhabi (?)
1996	Abu Dhabi Music and Arts Foundation (ADMAF) opens	Abu Dhabi
1997	Sharjah Art Museum opens	Sharjah
	Mohamed Ahmed Ibrahim founds Khor Fakkan Art Center	Khor Fakkan, Sharjah
1998	Bait al Zubair museum opens	Muscat
2003	Museum of Modern Art opens	Kuwait
	Hoor al Qasimi returns to UAE, begins to work on Sharjah Biennial	Sharjah
2005	The Third Line Gallery, B52, and Ayyam are open	Dubai
2006	Sultan Gallery re-opens after Iraqi invasion hiatus	Kuwait
	Plans for Saadiyat Island cultural district announced in April, Guggenheim Abu Dhabi announced in July, Louvre Abu Dhabi deal signed in November	Abu Dhabi
	Sharjah Museums Department (now Sharjah Museums Authority) created	Sharjah
2007	Art Paris Abu Dhabi (renamed Abu Dhabi Art)	
	DIFC Gulf Art Fair (renamed Art Dubai)	
	The Flying House opens	Dubai
	Alserkal Avenue launched	Dubai
2008	Museum of Islamic Art	Doha
	Picasso exhibition held	Abu Dhabi
	Tashkeel Art Center opens	Dubai
	The Creek Art Fair (later Sikka) held	Dubai
	Dubai Culture Council reorganized into Dubai Culture and Arts Authority	Dubai
	Inaugural March Meeting held	Sharjah
2009	Sotheby's holds sale in Qatar	Doha

(*Continued*)

TABLE 1.1. (*Cont.*)

Date	Event	Location
	Sharjah Art Foundation (SAF) established	Sharjah
	Inaugural UAE Pavilion at Venice Biennale, sponsored by Abu Dhabi and Sharjah	
2010	Mathaf Museum of Arab Art opens	Doha
	Bonhams, Christie's, and Sotheby's have staff in Dubai	Dubai
	Barjeel Art Foundation launched	Sharjah
	Maraya Art Center launched	Sharjah
2013	National Museum of Oman established	Muscat
2014	NYU Abu Dhabi Art Gallery established	Abu Dhabi
	Shaikha Salama Foundation – inaugural Emerging Artist Fellowship cohort	Abu Dhabi
2015	Warehouse 421 (now 421 Arts Campus) opened	Abu Dhabi
2017	Louvre Abu Dhabi opens	Abu Dhabi
	Sotheby's holds first Dubai auction	Dubai
	Etihad Museum opened	Dubai
2018	Ithra (King Abdulaziz Center for World Culture) opens	Dhahran, Saudi Arabia
2019	Jameel Arts Centre opens	Dubai
2020	AlUla biennial (Desert X)	AlUla, KSA
2025	Zayed National Museum set to open	Abu Dhabi
2025	Guggenheim Abu Dhabi set to open	Abu Dhabi
2030	Art Mill Museum set to open	Doha

Source: created by the author.

While the 1970s and early 1980s in the UAE were marked by one-off shows, the Emirates Fine Arts Society (EFAS; *jamʿiat al-āmārāt lil-fanūn al-tash-kīlīya*) was founded in 1980 as a collective of artists and the Emirates' first artists association. Shaykh Sultan created EFAS as a rare nonprofit, an exception to the UAE's laws that nonprofits meet the definition of charity in the Qur'an, which is largely focused on helping the sick and the needy. EFAS began holding annual exhibitions in November of that same year, and established *Al-Tashkeel* magazine. Similar artists' collectives continued to spring up around the Gulf, such as the Qatar Fine Arts Society in 1980 and the Bahrain

Arts Society in 1983 (Bahrain Authority 2021; UNESCWA 2015). Oman had founded a youth studio in 1980, followed by the Omani Society for Fine Arts in 1993 (Stoby 2017b, 20). Artists across the Gulf worked within and formed emergent cultural bureaucracies. Artist-led collectives were the foundation of local art scenes, and their work organizing recurring and one-off exhibitions paved the way for later institutions. Their work "opened the pavement," as one of Sharif's group described it to me, simply by doing things in public, to empower subsequent generations of artists to come.

In this same period in the UAE, however, there were few dedicated art spaces outside of the Cultural Foundation in Abu Dhabi and EFAS. Mohamed Kazem participated in a show in Kuwait in 1986, the flyer for which attests to the *Marsam Ras al-Khaimah*, or the Ras Al-Khaimah emirate branch of EFAS established by Obaid Suroor, also among the *jīl al-ruwād*. The Sharjah Expo Center, a trade center, was the site of a 1984 exhibition, translated as the Formative Bazaar; the Expo Center would later host the early editions of the Sharjah Biennial. Art-specific venues still did not yet exist, even as burgeoning state infrastructures came on the scene. Formal arts education programs were also not available at this point.

Many members of the early generations, including Dr. Najat Makki, Dr. Mohamed Yousif, and Hassan Sharif, therefore studied art abroad on government scholarships. While the loose collectives were a source of support for artists, they hungered for more institutionalized and formal training opportunities. Artists felt this training was important: One artist from this generation told me, "If I study at university, I learn the basics [*ātʿalim ʿbasic'*]. The ABCs of art [*ālif ba fil-fan*]. But I must have teachers who have more experience than me [*lazim āḥtaj ʿalā muderis, ākbar minī ʿind al-khibra*]. They will say to me, this color here, this color here, step by step [*liānā goolee [in Fuṣḥā: qāluā], hadhā lon chi, hadhā lon chi, step by step*]." The artist noted, too, that once their studies were completed, they were free (*ānā ḥurra*) to make work the way they want (*āsawī al-fan ilī ānā*). But they felt strongly that without the foundation of a formal education, their art practice would not have improved.

While the state supported outside education, other informal networks arose to train artists. Individualized mentoring also characterized this early period—that is, artists teaching and training other artists in the absence of robust educational or other training structures. Those who could not go abroad took advantage of intergenerational mentoring. These earlier generations of artists in the Emirates were deeply involved with informal or

semi-formalized teaching and mentoring, which has since given way to institutionalized training. Sharif was active in EFAS and his work, alongside and in
the society, offered the main art training available in the country at the time.
Sharif's mentorship of a younger generation of artists in the 1980s and '90s was
instrumental to the development of the Emirati art scene. Sharif noted that
education was key because it made people curious and it grew audiences, and
mentorship was important. One such form of mentoring was the "Banoosh"
exhibitions (1983, 1984, 1985; sometimes transliterated as "Panoosh"), which
appear in artists' bios in the Qattan archives. In a February 2017 talk, artist
Shaikha Al Mazrou noted that these exhibitions were an initiative of Hassan
Sharif and Mohamed Yousif. Al Mazrou shared, "The *banoosh* is a small boat
that takes you from the shore to the big ship. And to me, I felt like Hassan
Sharif was that means of transport to the younger generation." Sharif and the
pioneers' generation created a tightly knit community of artists and writers in
the 1980s and '90s and worked in a series of state cultural infrastructures to
build out arts organizations while mentoring the up-and-coming generation.
Since then, individual mentorship and loose collectives have become more institutionalized, and informal networks have given way to commercial, hybrid
initiatives.

Rupture: The Iraqi Invasion of Kuwait

Saddam Hussein's forces rolled into Kuwait on August 2, 1990. While Kuwait
had been a vibrant host to the arts for several decades, the country had struggled financially since the 1982 crash of Souq Al-Manakh, Kuwait's informal
stock exchange. The Iraqi invasion devastated the country. The inaugural
Sharjah Biennial, held in 1993, marks the informal beginning of the UAE's
new centrality in a Gulf art ecosystem. In this new era, a thematic shift accompanied this geographic one: The arts grew increasingly linked to transnational art networks and institutions—seemingly away from imperial and
nationalist modes—and the region joined an increasingly commercialized,
global contemporary art world system that had begun emerging after the fall
of the Berlin Wall in 1989 (Belting et al. 2013; Smith 2009). As the last barriers
to a networked capitalist global market fell, and in an emergent postcolonial,
post–Cold War world, curators and gallerists began to search for untapped
art markets and undiscovered artists. The art market and the number of biennials exploded (Gardner and Green 2016; Lind and Velthuis 2012). As these

nodes grew, and curators and artists began to travel, a truly networked global art world appeared (Relyea 2013). And in the Gulf, rulers expanded neoliberal policies coeval with the art and museum scene garnering global attention. The forms of arts organizations began to shift.

The Market Exhibitionary Complex: Transnational Networks and Institutions in the Twenty-First Century

Given these tectonic geopolitical and economic shifts, the forms of arts organizations in the Gulf began to change. The noncommercial Sharjah Biennial became a major anchor of the Emirates' art scene. Saif, an artist active in the pioneers' generation, told me that the Sharjah Biennial used to be different. In the past, he said, EFAS ran the biennial and would invite artists' societies from across the Middle East to send works. EFAS had a small annual budget supplied by the state, part of its status as a nonprofit, and some of that budget was used to run the biennial. After being invited, these local societies shipped crates to Sharjah. Saif explained:

> We used to open the box and we didn't know what was inside, there was no communication about "what are you going to show," no curators following up or doing artistic direction. The [biennial] theme was there sometimes but it was mostly mixed up. Whatever comes is being shown. Shaykha Hoor took over in 2003 and this was the first biennial that was curated properly.

According to Saif, curation becomes an element of a good biennial, both personified in the form of a curator, but also in the presence of a theme—and for him, curation was lacking prior to 2003. He refers to Shaykha Hoor Al Qasimi, the daughter of Sharjah's ruler Shaykh Sultan, who assumed control of the Sharjah Biennial in 2003, when she returned to Sharjah after earning a BFA from the Slade School of Fine Art in London.[13] Al Qasimi ran the biennial before it was subsumed under the Sharjah Art Foundation in 2010; she remains the director of the Foundation, which the website describes as an independent body despite Al Qasimi's royal status. Many of my artist interlocutors described her with reverence. Under her direction, a new curator managed each iteration, created a theme, and invited individual artists based on their practice, rather than issuing open, group invitations to societies. Most of my interlocutors agreed with Saif's perspective, believing that Al Qasimi had productively reorganized the biennial. "It wasn't just nepotism anymore," Claire, an arts writer, told me. "The [former] biennial was working on a structure of, these are the artists who appear every year no matter what. Hoor just scrapped all that and started doing a proper biennial." Both Claire and Saif used the term "proper"—as I discuss in Chapter 4, ideas of what constituted proper and professional conduct were another way in which my interlocutors negotiated the integration of the commercial in everyday practices.

The Sharjah Biennial was among the first organizations in the UAE to adopt more transnational, contemporary art world practices: hiring or selecting curators with specialized training, insisting on an exhibition theme, and displaying works in a white cube style. The Sharjah Biennial began as an exhibition organized by collectives, featuring locally based artists and held every two years.[14] Since 1993, the Sharjah Biennial's form has shifted dramatically from a local art fair representing artists working in the region, without a codified display format, to one curated by nonresident art world stars and featuring international artists exhibited in a white cube display. Biennials have played a crucial role in forging a global art world, as a "single, integrated, cosmopolitan institution of art, organized transnationally" and in which members "share converging or overlapping traditions and practices at the same time that they exhibit and distribute their art in internationally coordinated venues" (Carroll 2007, 136; see also Baia Curioni 2012; Buchholz 2022; Gardner and Green 2016). Yet, as Rashid Araeen pointed out in 1978, "the current 'Internationalism' of Western art is nothing more than a function of the political and economic power of the West" (quoted in Buchholz 2022, 23). Thirty years later, in 2009, Chin-Tao Wu noted acerbically that the biennial "has, despite its decolonizing and democratic claims, proved still to embody the traditional power structures of the contemporary Western art world; the only difference being that 'Western' has quietly been replaced by a new buzzword, 'global'" (115). A uniform display style, the white cube, has been a considerable mechanism in the coordination of these various art scenes.

White cube display had emerged in the mid-twentieth century and dominates display today. The white cube aesthetic appears in commercial and noncommercial exhibitions. The mid-twentieth century saw strong movements toward professionalization (Alexander 1996; Bryan-Wilson 2009; Duncan and McClellan 2018; Rader and Cain 2014), including a move toward minimal, uncluttered displays—in particular, the adoption of the white cube display style. The white cube gallery is assembled carefully to keep the exterior world out, with windows often covered:

Walls are painted white. The ceiling becomes the source of light. The wooden floor is polished. . . . The discreet desk may be the only piece of furniture. In this context a standing ashtray becomes almost a sacred object, just as the firehose in a modern museum looks not like a firehose but an esthetic conundrum . . . unshadowed, white, clean, artificial—*the space is devoted to the technology of esthetics.* Works of art are mounted, hung, scattered for study. Their ungrubby surfaces are untouched by time and its vicissitudes. Art exists in a kind of eternity of display . . . there is no time. (O'Doherty 1986, 15; emphasis mine)

Artworks displayed in the white cube were meant to focus the viewer and to imbue the displayed objects with gravitas and authority. Between the 1960s and 1980s, the style continued to spread, despite critiques of its elitism and inaccessibility (Birkett 2012, 35; see also Cain 2017), revealing a growing tension between capital interests and inclusion. The prevalence of white cube displays in both nonprofit museums and commercial galleries also reveals the spreading crossover between commercial and noncommercial displays, and the rise of a relatively uniform display aesthetic that I examine in Chapter 4.

With the Sharjah Biennial's adoption of curators, themes, and white cube display, among other contemporary art practices drawn from a global contemporary art world, the Sharjah Biennial ceased to be a self-selecting group of regionally based artists exhibiting their recent work and became an exclusive, curated show of invited artists making conceptual work around one theme or idea—and in a display style that allowed for easy translation with a commercial art world. The regional collectives, with a strong emphasis on mentorship, gave way to a more individualistic scene. While the remade biennial reflected the standards of the contemporary art elite and garnered precious international visibility, it simultaneously became less representative of artistic practice in the region and more controlled by a single or few authorial voices.

The biennial also evinces an external focus, rather than a domestic one. It is less about cultivating citizens or UAE residents, and more about projecting tolerance and multiculturalism for external consumption. The biennial also straddles some awkward binaries: It represents the state as "cultural armature" (Levitt 2015, 3). Yet biennials are often run by individual cities, rather than nations. Sharjah's biennial has, to date, not been coopted by the UAE federal government and remains under the purview of the Sharjah emirate-level government. Furthermore, it is also oriented at a broad art world audience. It is also noncommercial in that works are not for sale, but the funding does come, at least in part, from the state. In fact, the blurred nature of the state/ nonstate, commercial/noncommercial binaries embodies the politics of this phase of institutionalization: While arts organizations and museums remain deeply connected to the state and its project of nation-building and national representation, these connections are obscured by the dominance of transnational neoliberal capitalism. The concept of the market exhibitionary complex emphasizes the prevalence of the market, which outwardly eclipses the state, although the state remains heavily involved in less visible ways.

The Sharjah Biennial's success has also been tied to commercial ventures. Across the UAE's scene, commercial and noncommercial enterprises developed symbiotically, partly due to the reality of staff working across both fields, and partly due to the legal conditions of organizational possibility. To better understand the regulations and laws that governed how arts organizations could incorporate, I interviewed two legal consultants, Siobhan and Rami. We met in their posh corporate conference room in a glass skyscraper overlooking Dubai's financial hub. The legal forms of incorporation reveal much about what can and can't be done, and also how the powers that be understand what the arts do. For example, because museums in Europe and the U.S. are often seen as public goods, rather than being subject to the standard rules of capitalism, these organizations receive preferential terms for taxes. I asked, "In terms of setting up an arts institution here, apart from doing it as a government ministry, what are options for organizations?"

Siobhan responded, trailing a spoon in her cappuccino, "If you register as a nonprofit, you get special status. You get exemptions. But," she emphasized, "there's not many options [for nonprofits]. They can be charitable, or noncharitable." She paused here. I jumped in—how was charitable defined? Charitable, for organizations in the Emirates, meant adhering to the definition of charity in the Qur'an. This definition consists mostly of helping the needy or less fortunate, such as widows, those in debt, or orphans, for example. Under this definition of charity, an art organization was unlikely to qualify as a charitable nonprofit. Administered by the emirate-level Ministry of Social Affairs, charitable nonprofits could not be located in economic free zones—sites designed to encourage trade by reducing or removing taxes—but did get exemptions on business incorporation taxes and were permitted to fundraise. Because most arts organizations did not meet the charity requirement as defined by Islamic precepts, they could not incorporate as nonprofits "onshore." Nonprofits could be registered in a free zone, legally "offshore," under the Dubai

Creative Clusters Authority. However, these nonprofits did not get the tax and fundraising exemptions, so their "ability to go out and seek funding" was effectively curtailed, Rami clarified. These organizational licensing requirements also applied commercial models, adapted from economic free zones, to theoretically noncommercial entities.

The restrictions of soliciting funding also had other ramifications for engagement with a broader art world. Siobhan said,

> We've had this question before. We've had a museum wanting to raise funds and donations in the U.S. And the problem has been, because they're not registered as a charity here, the U.S. wouldn't recognize the charitable donations [as 501(c)3s]. So they were struggling to get donations in the U.S. because people were much more willing to donate to nonprofits. The lack of being able to register as a nonprofit does hinder your opportunities for growth and accepting donations and funding.

She added that these regulations also limited organizations' ability to apply for grants or initiatives by international cultural agencies or foundations, which do not always permit for-profit entities to receive grants. Thus for arts organizations in the UAE, the particular affordances of various modes of incorporation also defined and forecast how they could—or could not—grow and develop. Thus organizations' ability to grow and acquire legitimacy was circumscribed by the compatibility of local incorporation regulations with broader transnational organizational types and established funding circuits.[15]

Siobhan summarized, "I think the problem is that it's—there's not a lot of categories available [in general], and none for culture. There's not really any categories you'd register for nonprofits, for culture, museums, arts institutions." So a lot of places, she conceded, were registered formally as commercial businesses due to lack of other incorporation options, but operating as nonprofits, putting their profits back into the organization. However, without a charity license, they could not solicit donations or receive grants for nonprofits, so they had to offer courses, studio space, membership, supplies, or other "saleables" for a fee. One gallerist, Roxy, later confirmed Siobhan's statements. Roxy reported, "We wanted to open a nonprofit space. We didn't have the intention of making it a business. But," she continued, "at the time, there was no possibility to become a nonprofit. When we went to the economic department to register, they were like, what? Okay, so we can't be a nonprofit. We had to become a business."

These conditions of legal possibility occluded most options for independent arts organizations. As a result, most arts organizations in the Emirates during my fieldwork were either government-originated or formally registered as commercial entities. Many operated and marketed themselves as not-for-profit, despite being registered as commercial entities, making categorization difficult. Even the government-originated organizations were sometimes difficult to spot, due to partnerships with international museums, foundations, or commercial galleries.

The particular structures available for incorporation as an arts organization helped spur a transition toward market-centric practices: After all, many arts organizations were by default legally commercial entities, given the few noncommercial options available. Due to this hybridity, commercial enterprises were integral in validating the noncommercial ones, and vice versa. The inaugural commercial art fair in the UAE was held March 8 through 10, 2007, less than a year after the plans for Saadiyat were announced. The fair was initially named the DIFC Gulf Art Fair and held at Dubai International Financial Centre (DIFC). In November 2007, Abu Dhabi also staged an art fair, Art Paris–Abu Dhabi, which has since become Abu Dhabi Art. Beginning in its second iteration, the DIFC Gulf Art Fair was rebranded as Art Dubai and moved from DIFC to Madinat Jumeirah, where it has been held since. The name shift reflects a more city-specific branding and can be read as a reaction to the 2008 opening of Doha's Museum of Islamic Art, as well as a desire to put Dubai on the global art world map. Such moves were part of a broader growing attention to art from the Middle East region, including an "exponential" increase in the auction market for Middle Eastern and North African artists between 2006 and 2012 (Kräussl 2015, 147). Hoor Al Qasimi of the Sharjah Biennial convened the first March Meeting, a regional forum for arts professionals to connect and encourage collaboration in 2008 as well. March Meeting also ran coeval with Art Dubai, which catalyzed both events' visibility and braided noncommercial ventures to the commercial.

In 2010, Al Qasimi also launched the Sharjah Art Foundation, which began to offer year-round exhibitions in Sharjah as well as hosting the biennial. After the 2017 edition of Art Dubai, a curator I call Abdullah told me that that year's fair "was one of the most successful fairs. All the galleries posted record sales." Abdullah named one gallery, saying, "They sold everything they brought." And another gallery did "a good job cause they sold a bunch to LACMA [the LA County Museum of Art]." Abdullah said, "Every time the

Sharjah Biennial happens, because [the biennial] pays for the curators to come here, Art Dubai does really well. The biennial brings museum acquisitions teams into the room." When artists from the region are in collections of major museums, they are more likely to be featured in major global shows, further driving up the value of their artwork. While the Sharjah Biennial and Art Dubai are vastly different entities in many respects, their futures have been entwined.

Many of my interlocutors stressed the importance of Art Dubai: One director labeled it a turning point, saying, "That's when everything became visible." Art Dubai was critical because it brought attention and visibility; another key figure in the scene noted that after 2008, "Dubai was being talked about as an Asian art capital alongside Hong Kong." A slightly cynical artist framed it differently: "Art Dubai put Dubai on the art trading map . . . on the meat market." Whatever the spin, many of my interlocutors expressed that Art Dubai raised the profile of the Emirates' art scene. It also, to the dismay of some, established an organizational model for the art field, cementing the preeminence of the commercial. One curator told me with a sigh, "Art Dubai is the model for organizations around here, and it works on [corporate] sponsorship." The private equity firm the Abraaj Group sponsored the fair during much of my fieldwork; the current sponsor as of 2025 is A.R.M. Holdings. In a context where nonprofits did not exist or were state-originated, the only option was to be, at least nominally, commercial. The sponsorship model became an alternative for nominally commercial institutions, relying on corporate sponsors to bridge financial gaps.[16] The centrality of the commercial also masked state involvement, as the focus is on the UAE's place in an international art market.[17]

Many commercial developments did also find space to develop noncommercial elements, further complicating easy categorization. Such initiatives aimed to build up a local art scene and artists for the museums to acquire from. However, these convoluted partnerships further complicated the ways that art was funded and its social role understood. Art Dubai, for example, developed Campus Art Dubai in 2012. The fair's website describes it as "a school for artists, curators, writers, architects, designers and cultural producers based in the UAE" (Art Dubai n.d.). Each year, the facilitators develop a theme around which a Saturday course is run for a selected cohort of participants who are local residents. One organizer told me that the fair's commercial success generated space for them to sneak in some educational endeavors, revealing how the commercial could create openings and hybridity for other ventures. Art

Dubai also stages the Global Art Forum, a themed symposium of talks held during the fair. The Global Art Forum is open to any fairgoer who either gets a pass or pays the admission fee. The A.i.R. residency program, with a "mandate to foster and develop Dubai's artistic community," ran for seven iterations (2010–2017). A.i.R. involved partnering with Delfina Foundation (independent British nonprofit), Dubai Culture (emirate-level government), and Tashkeel Art Center, a commercial entity operating as a noncommercial one (run by a member of Dubai's ruling family). Entities like A.i.R. might be classed as parastatal, as they enjoy some political authority although they serve the state indirectly. In that such organizations operate on behalf of the state in some ways, they are also examples of graduated sovereignty (Ong 2006).

Because of its global visibility and remit as a for-profit endeavor, the fair's relationship with the local community was sometimes sensitive. Of course, the tensions between commercial and noncommercial priorities have been cast as tensions between traditional and avant-garde art, bestsellers versus classics (Velthuis 2005, 18; see also Bourdieu 2000). In the case of Art Dubai, it was the audience that was contested. Jasim, a curator, felt that the fair staff sometimes portrayed it as a platform—here he mimed air quotes—"to ensure equal access to all organizations in the region," but that when push came to shove, they privately privileged commercial interests. Further complicating matters, given the prevalence of the gig-labor model, many fair staff had worked in other arts organizations in the UAE before taking a gig contract with the fair. They often strove to maintain collegial relationships to secure future employment, which at times affected whose work or which organizations received preferential treatment at the fair.

The experience of the fair and its content was also fraught as many interlocutors reported that they mixed genres. One artist related that her friends visited Art Dubai like it was a museum, and she had tried to explain to them the differences between a commercial art fair and a "serious" museum show. Most of all, gallerists often reported feeling that the commercial fair's straddling of the commercial and noncommercial set a difficult precedent for local galleries and their year-round audiences. Commercial galleries pay to participate in fairs, thus creating financial imperative to justify the expense; this situation has also led to a privileging of particular art forms and mediums that sell well (Buchholz 2022, 81–83). In contradistinction, museums and noncommercial galleries could showcase art that was less prone to easy commodification. One gallerist, Briony, shared with a sigh,

It really bothers me, on so many levels, that people treat these places [galleries and fairs] like museums. They do not look at [the commercial art gallery] as a commercial entity. They look at it as a small museum. I think it's fantastic that galleries can be reflective of a really interesting art scene, as a proxy, but for sure, my remit is to sell artwork. That's what I'm employed to do. We're not there to service the public. The fact that we do is value added. Our mission is not to help people here to have a better understanding of art. It's distressing that people have nowhere else to go [to do that]—I mean, maybe sometimes they go to Sharjah for that.[18]

Briony emphasized the distinction between commercial and noncommercial spaces, and visitors' inability to distinguish between them. Many gallerists, Briony included, recounted that gallery visitors often attended commercial shows with the expectation that gallerists would explain the work to them and contextualize it within a broader art historical trajectory—necessitating that gallerists serve as de facto art historians and educators. Roxy, the gallerist, noted, "The early days were hard, people were not understanding why they should buy art. There was a lot of education. We did a lot of talks, film screenings." Roxy also noted that just because the commercial gallery existed, "people aren't going to just come buy things off the wall because we put things on the wall. We did a photo show, people just could not understand how there is a value to a photograph that could be printed one hundred times." They came to her, she reported, saying, "Roxy, why would I pay for this?" In the mid-2000s, Roxy was charging $1,000 for a print and had to create this value for her clients—putting something on display does not necessarily imbue it with value. That value must be created (Buchholz 2022; Velthuis 2005). Her prospective customers at the time felt that a painting was "obviously an original. Teaching everyone from scratch, what art is, why there's value, that photography is also an art form," Roxy said, had been the tasks of her early days at the gallery.

The interpretive tools that museums afforded—workshops, talks, gallery tours—were part of a broader mission to cultivate a museum-going, art-appreciating public, which I analyze further in Chapter 5. But commercial galleries often carried part of this labor, if for no other reason than they were permanent institutions open year-round instead of a once-a-year event. The ubiquity and dominance of the commercial resulted in even ostensibly noncommercial enterprises resembling, copying, or operating on commercial models.

Art Dubai catalyzed significant growth in the commercial sector at a time when the market for art from the Middle East was also rising (Kräussl 2015). After Dubai's first gallery, Majlis Gallery, had opened in 1989, followed by Salwa Zeidan in Abu Dhabi in 1994, a growing number of contemporary art galleries began to set up shop—many in the Al-Quoz district of Dubai. Art Dubai, in its early years, did not include many UAE-based galleries: The Third Line was the single representative at the inaugural edition.[19] But with the increasing visibility of the fair, Sharjah's biennial, year-round exhibitions and programming, and the planned museums taking shape in Abu Dhabi, savvy local business people began to open ancillary businesses: Many more commercial galleries opened in the late 2000s and early 2010s, and auction houses like Bonhams, Sotheby's, and Christie's had staff on the ground by 2010. Sotheby's held its first sale in the region in Doha in 2009; the magazine *Harper's Bazaar Art Arabia* also launched. Bonhams ran a series of informal lectures to prepare collectors for auctions; an artist I call Habib created a young collectors' group, which offered visits to galleries and art institutions to nurture emerging collectors, develop their eye, and offer support as they learned gallery protocols for purchasing artwork (see Chapter 4). In 2009, the publication *Art Map*, now run by Dubai Culture, indexed forty-five arts organizations in Dubai. By 2017, it was ninety-six—the number had more than doubled.[20] As more organizations opened, the flow of staff between them also increased—workers in the art scene tacked between commercial and noncommercial entities with seeming ease.

While hybrid entities seemed to open opportunities for collaborations, there have been drawbacks, in particular the obfuscation of accountability. In 2010, Abu Dhabi cultural authorities, in coordination with a semiprivate development firm—the Tourism Development Investment Company (TDIC)—opened Manarat Al Saadiyat, a temporary exhibition space on Saadiyat Island. When outside groups like Gulf Labor began to boycott and protest the impending Saadiyat Island museums (Ross 2015), the limited accountability of such hybrid projects became apparent: An entity like the Guggenheim Abu Dhabi or NYU Abu Dhabi contracted separately with the Emirati government, an architecture firm, and various construction and labor firms.[21] Heads of the museum projects reported no ability to control the actions of their subcontractors, nor the labor laws of the Emirates (Gulf Labor Artist Coalition 2016). The hybrid nature of the project obfuscated ultimate responsibility.

Several ostensibly noncommercial organizations worked with consultants, borrowing from corporate practice and echoing the prior reliance on external consultants in the 1960s and '70s. The level of consultant involvement was also unclear, and varied. One senior manager of the Zayed National Museum (ZNM) remarked on the relationship with another consulting museum from the UK:

> What they do on our behalf is a wide variety of things. They . . . worked on the intellectual framework for the museum. They reviewed and commented on the building design in terms of being fit for the purpose of our museum. The same is true with exhibition design, and the business and operations side, you know, drawing the org chart. It's a consultant's relationship, a contract. It has its upsides and downsides.

These partnerships between private consulting firms; private foreign foundations; foreign governmental agencies; TDIC as the commercial, semiprivate developer; and the Emirati government obfuscate relationships, capital flows, and the origins of decisions. So while many of Abu Dhabi's museum projects retained these ties to the Emirati state, they were outwardly defined by transnational commercial relationships and partnerships.

These convoluted ties also meant that organizations themselves were constantly shape-shifting. For example, in 2013 a manager running the ZNM project told me, "By the end of next year, we'll be in a position where there is actually a Zayed museum, as an organization. . . . [A]t the moment, we're Tourism & Culture Authority employees who happen to be working on this project." The ZNM was, at that time, a team employed by another organization, not an organization itself. On the other side of the coin, the British Museum (a British state entity) also created teams of dedicated staff who worked on projects in the Emirates. After signing the agreement for the Louvre Abu Dhabi, the French government—who runs the Louvre museum—created Agence France Musées, a consultative agency to pool resources, human and otherwise, from twelve major French government museums to collaborate on the Emirati project. Similarly, the Guggenheim (a private foundation) spun off a small team in New York in 2008 that was dedicated to the Abu Dhabi projects. At the beginning, this team was also in a complex hybrid situation—as part of his departure as head of the Guggenheim, Thomas Krens had negotiated that he would still run the Guggenheim Abu Dhabi project (Minutillo 2008). The small and newly formed team was paid and formally employed by the Guggenheim New York, but administered by its ex-director, putting them in a strange situation vis-à-vis the Guggenheim's new boss. These ties and relationships between organizations, or the genesis of a new organization from an existing one, rendered the landscape even more complex.[22]

Alongside this growing number of organizations, initiatives to support UAE-based artists, especially Emirati citizen artists, also emerged after the inaugural Art Dubai and the remade Sharjah Biennial. As collectives were decentered and overwhelmed with the creation of so many new entities, the question of artists and support for them arose. These programs aspired to promote artists for commercial galleries as well as to represent the Emirati nation. Commercial and noncommercial growth made spaces to exhibit that had not existed previously. Maraya Art Centre, run by the Sharjah Development Authority Shurooq, opened exhibition spaces in Sharjah in 2010, with a goal of "support[ing] emerging artists and designers in a comprehensive way, providing opportunities for continual growth through research, exhibition and project development" (Maraya Art Centre 2023). Maraya held several exhibitions a year and also began running a series of residency and exchange programs for artists.

Another platform that melded commercial and noncommercial goals in programming devoted to supporting emerging artists was the Sikka Art Fair, a festival that runs concurrent with Art Dubai. Originally started by Mona Hauser of XVA Gallery in Dubai, Al Bastakiya Art Fair (2007) later became the Creek Art Fair, eventually morphed into the Sikka Art Fair, and was absorbed by Dubai Culture, the emirate's cultural authority. A 2009 Bastakiya Art Fair (BAF) brochure identified the fair's goal to "provid[e] a public space for emerging artist talent and dra[w] on the capabilities of the local artistic community: artists from the region and those who live here." BAF 2009 also inaugurated BAF Art School, a free morning art school "designed to offer an alternative art curriculum." Such programming also echoes Sharjah's March Meeting and Art Dubai's Global Art Forum, which launched around this time. Tashkeel Art Center, opened in 2008 by the niece of Dubai's ruler, also offered studio space, printing facilities, and art classes. Sustained by membership and rental fees, Tashkeel regularly held exhibitions of members' work, one of the rare spaces in Dubai where emerging artists' work was shown in the early days. Tashkeel also partnered with Art Dubai from 2015 to 2017 to run an artist residency program in tandem with the fair: A.i.R. resident artists worked with a curator for three months prior to the fair, and they exhibited their works in non-gallery spaces during the fair. Together, Sikka and A.i.R. offered UAE-based artists critical visibility during March, when well-heeled collectors and patrons would be in town for the fair and might chance upon their work displayed in a hallway or outside the café where they ate lunch. These institutional platforms replaced an informal system of mentoring with a more formal, and more commercially oriented, system.

Post-Transnationalism: What Comes Next?

In the newly postcolonial era, an overriding ethos of establishing a national and regional community suffused the Gulf scene as artists organized collectives and exhibitions. The region-centric collectives of the twentieth century have given way to more corporate, commercially oriented arts entities that privilege the market above the state. More recently, national lines are blurred with the arrival of transnational entities. Yet part of what renders the institutional landscape so complex is that organizations aiming to be noncommercial are, legally and financially, commercial. A deep hybridity marks this phase. Since the end of my primary fieldwork in 2017, the rulers have enacted new laws, creating more opportunities for freelancers and types of organizations, to which my interlocutors have been adapting.

With an eye to the past, we can also track a shift in twentieth-century museum development on the Peninsula, broadly, from using museums for colonial and early independence nationalist goals to a more expansive, complex, transnational, market-centric goal in the twenty-first century. New models of arts organizations have also arisen elsewhere, such as the "marketplace museums" Katarzyna Pieprzak analyzes in Morocco that are "attentive to the dynamics of globalization in the culture industry" (2010, 37); the *kunsthalle* phenomenon John Zarobell describes, where exhibition centers do not maintain collections (2017, 32); or experimental organizations like M+ in Hong Kong, which "seeks to establish alternative languages of cultural presentation, with an orientation toward the local, not just in terms of collection, but also in terms of curatorial perspectives" (Ho 2014, 187). The UAE arts organizational model is simultaneously profit-seeking and purportedly noncommercial and transnational, and yet it continues to bolster the reputations of affiliated states. The UAE case is perhaps a harbinger of larger shifts to come in the art world. Whether such transnational and commercial structures actually enable a more diverse, integrated art community, departing from past ethnocentric patterns of museum representation, remains to be seen. And because the paradigm of power in museums has shifted from an overt focus on nation to market, so too do the ways artists have represented the state.

IN THE GALLERY II   The Nature of Belonging

IN MARCH 2017, I made it to Warehouse 421 in Abu Dhabi to see a new show, *Bayn: The In-Between.* NYU Abu Dhabi Art Gallery's founding director, Maya Allison, had mentored the show's celebrated emerging Emirati curator, Munira al Sayegh. The opening had taken place a week prior to my visit. After I entered the warehouse through the main entry, a metal garage door, the concierge stationed behind a black metal desk at the entry to Warehouse 421 welcomed me and handed me an exhibition catalogue.

Set on a white wall immediately to the left of the entry, the title of the exhibition appeared in a smooth, bulbous teal font, styled in acrylic decals applied directly to the walls. The wall text noted to the visitor, "The role of the artist in this exhibition is to [. . .] look at the state of liminality, critically and conceptually." Later in the paragraph, the text introduced the concepts of disorientation, displacement, and the future.

Above visitors' heads, three half-spheres of dark wire mesh were suspended from the ceiling of the gallery (see Figure G2.1). White barnacles and pale green dried seaweed nearly swallowed the wire mesh of one half-sphere (Figure G2.2). Small tufts of ivory lichens had begun sprouting through the holes in the mesh, the skins frozen into delicate frills (Figure G2.3). Another half-sphere sported a lighter layer of sea materials, and the third was most visibly a fishing net, with few barnacles or lichens adhering to it. Their natural and humble appearance jarred with the industrial aesthetic of the crisp white gallery walls, polished concrete floors, and spotless glass windows that

FIGURE G2.1. *Accumulation—Deposits* by Talin Hazbar, as installed in *Bayn: The In-Between*, UAE Unlimited's third exhibition, curated by Munira al Sayegh. Held at Warehouse 421, now 421 Arts Campus, Abu Dhabi, UAE in 2017. Image courtesy Talin Hazbar and 421 Arts Campus.

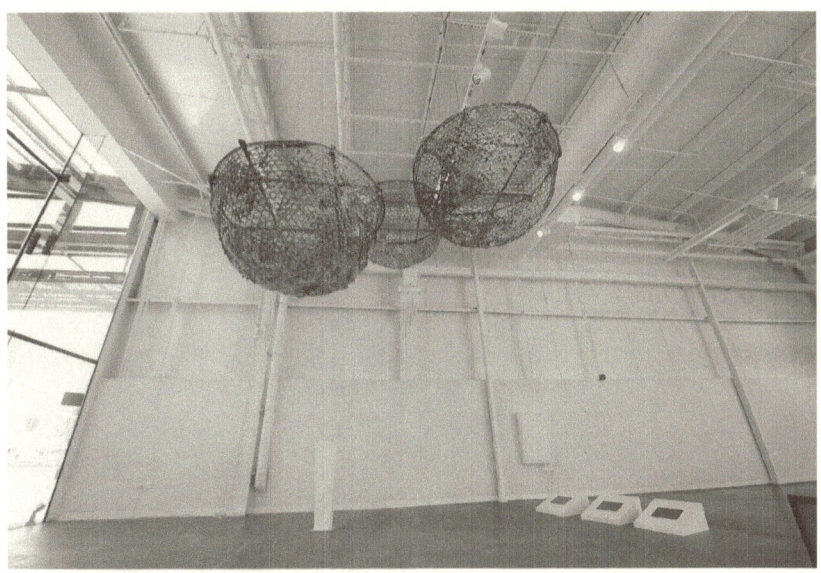

FIGURE G2.2. Detail of *Accumulation—Deposits* by Talin Hazbar. Photographer: Souad Hervé; image courtesy Talin Hazbar.

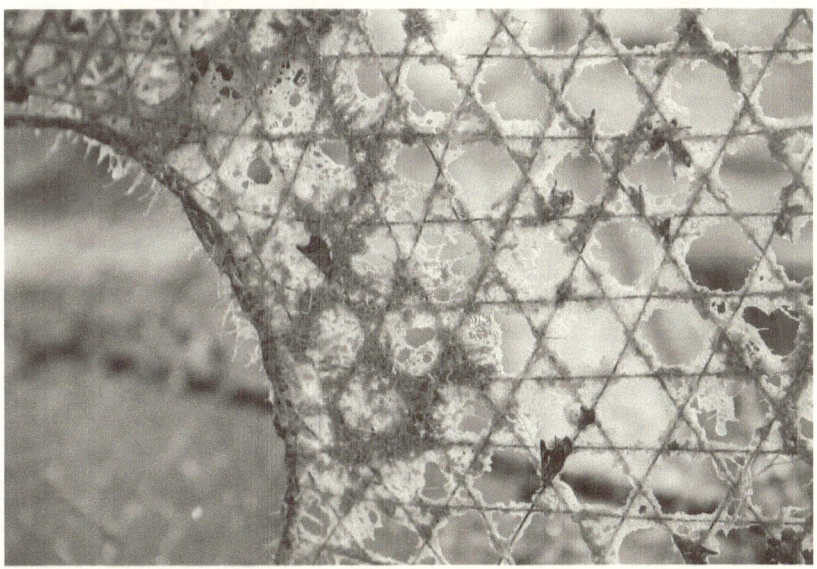

FIGURE G2.3. Detail of *Accumulation—Deposits* by Talin Hazbar.
Image courtesy Talin Hazbar.

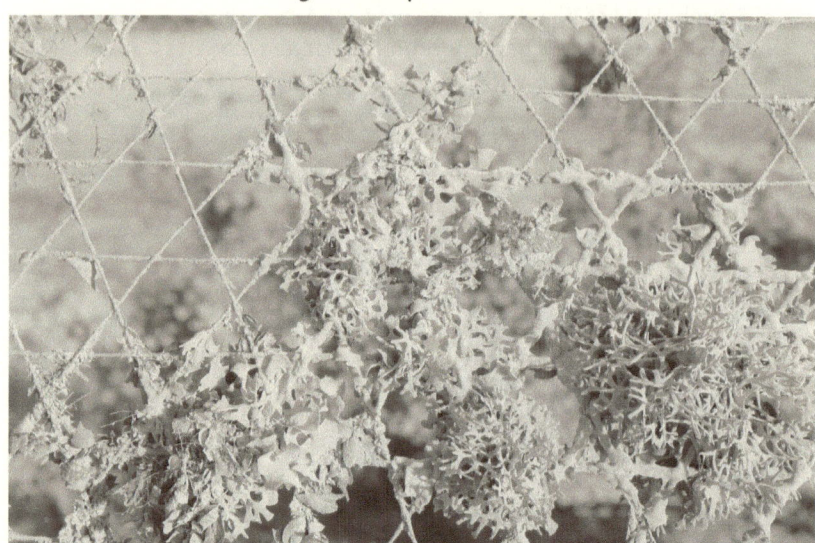

flooded the space with natural light. On the dark gray floor nearby, a series of
small digital screens in white boxes were installed in a line, each showing a
different close-up of the accumulations on the fishing nets.

Artist Talin Hazbar was born in Syria and is a longtime UAE resident.
Hazbar made the work, entitled *Accumulation*, by submerging traditional
Arabian fishing nets, called *gargour* (Emirati dialect; pl. *garageer; qarqūr* in
Modern Standard Arabic), into the Gulf waters in Sharjah for different periods of time: The longer the gargour was in the water, the more it began to resemble the underwater environment (and the less it looked like a fishing net).
On Hazbar's website, she writes that the work explores "the idea of control vs
uncontrolled processes" (Hazbar n.d.). The work, in Hazbar's description, is
"looking at their micro and macro scale where every system tries to control
its existence but a certain factor appears and things grow out of their way and
start to transform" (Hazbar n.d.). Hazbar's emphasis is on the uncontrollable
natural processes, and the work encourages us to "celebrate the transformation so we become a part of it" (Hazbar n.d.).

In this show about liminality, the work was framed with a different lens. Describing the work, curator Munira al Sayegh related, "The less time you spend

in the environment, the less of the environment you become. And that dialogue is a direct dialogue that [the artist] has with the UAE. And that sense of in-between" (Mezaina 2017). Artists who are not citizens but have spent the majority of their lives in the UAE often struggle to define themselves: They lack the documentation and status of citizens but, like the long-submerged gargour, are more attuned to and marked by the UAE environment than any other. Using a metaphor drawn from nature, and objects that are seen as traditionally Emirati, such as the gargour, allow the artist a measure of ambiguity. The work is not, as presented, about citizenship status. This work can be read as an expression of feeling more at home in the Emirates than elsewhere, yet also feeling unable to reconcile some internal element of foreignness. Note that the curator also does not render this connection entirely explicit—she does not say outright that the artist is from the UAE but holds Syrian citizenship. Curators' calculated ambiguity was also a way of protecting artists from appearing to criticize the regime, which can result in deportation and stripping of residency privileges.

The title of the work is *Accumulation*—not acculturation, not assimilation; the message of the work, as presented, is that objects remaining in a specific location for a long time grow to resemble their environment. Yet like the gargour, the accumulated layers that indicate belonging are superficial only, while the core of the object remains foreign to the environment. As framed in the gallery, the work ultimately reiterated the non-belonging of the foreign object: It looked like it belonged, but it did not. At its core, it was still a gargour. It was not native to the ocean. The work, in one reading, was essentialist—purporting that there was something essentially Emirati, or Syrian, that could not be converted or transformed. While this framing reinforced nationalist narratives about belonging, it also intimated an awareness of holding tenuous status in the UAE and the inability for noncitizens to feel truly at home.

In another show the prior year, *Portrait of a Nation*, an artist named Sarah Alagroobi exhibited a commission entitled *The Desert Rose* (2016). The work consists of conjoined discs, which at first appear to be metal but are in fact resin. The discs bisect each other at 90-degree angles to form a small sculpture, which looks like a "desert rose"—an appellation given to crystal clusters in a delicate rosette. These formations occur naturally—when salt basins evaporate, for example. I had first learned of the desert rose in 2010 when star French architect Jean Nouvel released his design for Qatar's new national museum: Nouvel's museum was inspired by this formation, a nod to a vernacular ecology.

Alagroobi covered the desert rose sculpture with dashes of sand, so the work bears streaks of coral, charcoal, and buff-colored sand across its discs and around its base. Nearby, small vials of sand, each labeled and a distinctly different color, bore the names of the seven emirates of the UAE: Ras Al-Khaimah's sand was red, Abu Dhabi's rosy, Sharjah's a beigey gray, Umm Al Quwain's redder again. The wall text for the work begins, "Sarah Alagroobi's commission offers a natural portrait of a nation. The crystalline sculpture *The Desert Rose* is formed from sand sourced on visits to all seven Emirates." In this framing, the work is clearly nationalist. Here again, elements understood as "natural" and native to the Emirates—much like the gargour—carry symbolic weight; the legibility of the work depends on their being read as native elements. The text continues, "This piece engages with the subtle material modulations in tone and texture—a celebration of diversity—while interlocking disks symbolize the strength of unity." In this instance, in contradistinction to Hazbar's *Accumulation*, however, the diversity is not a foreign versus native binary, but instead focuses on integrating the diversity within the Emirates, naturalizing diversity and emphasizing national unity. *The Desert Rose*, not only in its framing in the gallery as well as the nationalist exhibition in which it was exhibited, focuses only on Emiratis, ignoring the majority of the country's residents. Whereas *Accumulation* focused on reconciling and acknowledging natural processes of movement as well as the tensions of liminality, *The Desert Rose* bluntly naturalizes Emiratiness.

These installations raise the questions: Since typically museums have used the work of citizens to celebrate the state, how do artists represent the state in a new paradigm of market dominance? How do artists, citizen or not, belong to and represent the state? In an era of increasingly transnational migration, enmeshed global capitalism, and the waning reality of ethnostates, who represents the state—and how—have dramatically shifted away from prior citizen-centric modes of representation.

TWO

Contingent Citizens: Representing and Refusing a "Tolerant" State

THE RISE OF THE MARKET exhibitionary complex has changed the role of the state in projects of museum representation—and by extension, the roles of artists in representational projects. In this instance, state actors increasingly deploy noncitizens to represent the state, because they can showcase the state's tolerance and multiculturalism for external audiences. In this way, artists' positionalities are commodified to promote a multicultural image. I term these artists "contingent citizens" and analyze this emergent practice as a distinct departure from the existing culture-state paradigm of representation. The market imperative for tolerance and multiculturalism trumps narrow ethnonationalist patterns of state representation.

The phenomenon of contingent citizens arises from the centering of market needs, particularly the desire to appeal to a broad transnational audience rather than an internal one. The assumption of such projects is that the presence of many cultures evinces tolerance, casting diversity as a salve for social ills. Tolerance and multiculturalism, or at least the appearance of these, emerge as market imperatives in the twenty-first century. Despite the increasing emphasis on markets in art and museum practice, where we might expect citizenship status to become less important, it became more significant.

Curators and organizers considered artists' citizenship status when selecting which artists to include in their exhibitions. One evening, an artist named

Tariq and I sat at my kitchen table, eating Indian takeout from a place Tariq described as "quintessential Dubai." Between bites, Tariq recounted a recent decline of his artwork: "[The organizers] told me they already had two Jordanian artists in the exhibition so they could not accept me. I'm Jordanian now? I was born and raised here. I have spent a month of my life in Jordan, total. How am I Jordanian?" Tariq's work was informed by his life experiences—the vast majority of which had transpired out of Jordan. Because the UAE does not have birthright citizenship, Tariq described himself as "a Jordanian on paper, and a local off paper."

Citizenship status and national affiliation were major issues for my interlocutors for a number of reasons. First, they often chafed at being identified with a state to which they felt they did not belong. And many felt it limited their relevance or tokenized their identities. Many artists problematized the relationship between identification with a place and having identity documents from that place, as Tariq had.[1] Artists often disdained having a national affiliation affixed to their name. In speaking about his relationship to place, Hassan Sharif told me, "An 'Emirati artist'—this is limiting. I am an artist. A visual artist, practicing contemporary art. No ḥudūd (borders). I float from this side to this side. I don't want to be called the 'Emirati artist.'" Despite Sharif's adamant self-identification as an artist without national qualifiers, he is often credited as a pioneering or the first major Emirati artist. These artists' perspectives echoed those of their peers: In her work on Latinx artists, Arlene Dávila found that artists "do not want to be reduced to a single aesthetic or a stereotype; they seek to explore and work freely and widely" (2020, 165).

Contrary to many artists' preferences and their ways of self-identifying, organizers continued to valorize citizenship status and nationality as they configured their exhibitions. These moments of productive friction show microprocesses of globalization (Tsing 2005), revealing the "grip of encounter." Organizers often crafted multinational rosters for shows to intentionally frame and highlight the Emirates as a multicultural, tolerant state; they did so by requiring artists to submit photocopies of identity documentation when applying for open calls or exhibitions. This trend of using artists as emblems of tolerance has emerged in other contexts as well, as organizers strategically used the art and culture of Muslim-majority communities for such nation-branding efforts since the September 11th attacks (Farhat 2009; Winegar 2008). Similarly, Latinx artists experienced "national privilege" (or the lack thereof): "the benefits based on different degrees of connection to Latin

American cultures and art worlds" (Dávila 2020, 9). Conscripting citizens to perform the nation is not a new strategy, but conscripting *noncitizens* is, a practice born of accelerating transnational migration for work and the strategic uses of art and museums in globalization, what George Yúdice (2003) terms the "expediency of culture." This contingency might also be described as a specific mode of artwashing, using art as "'whitewashing,' or covering over that which we prefer to ignore or suppress" (D'Souza 2018, 9). Art is "increasingly used to smooth and gloss over social cleansing and gentrification, functioning as a 'social license,' a public relations tool, and a means of pacifying local communities" (Pritchard 2020, 179). The focus on state branding indicates the continued power and presence of the state—but there is an external, market focus that requires inclusion, not an internal cohesion effort as in the prior paradigm. This shift is one example of how the intersection of capitalization and diversification reorganizes representational politics.

The UAE example reveals how extensive transnational migration and sustained expatriate residency can fundamentally reorganize the established paradigm of state-culture engagement. As migration increases and populations become majority-transnational or majority-foreign and diverse, multicultural populations become the norm, state actors must consider how to draw on and draw in long-term foreign residents in their nation-making project, especially as museums have become "signature ornaments of any self-respecting city" (McClellan 2012, 271). In general, the recent rise of populist fascism and anti-immigrant rhetoric worldwide reveals how many states are struggling with the disruption of the ethnicity-state homology (however imagined or constructed it might have been in the first place). While globalization is not a new phenomenon and populations have moved and intermingled throughout history (Wolf 1982), many nation-states maintain the fiction of ethnic homogeneity, especially in their representational projects. In transnational states like those in the Gulf with majority-foreign populations and others facing rapidly diversifying resident populations, it is not financially sustainable to target only citizen audiences for domestic museums and cultural projects, nor to exclude noncitizen cultural contributors in the population. Transnational market pressure to be a "good" place to live, to be welcoming and not xenophobic, infused much of the Emirates' branding efforts.

The UAE case extends frameworks of citizenship that capture the ambiguous and messy realities of legal and extralegal migration and naturalization (Coutin 2007; Gomberg-Muñoz 2016). A constituent part of the nation that can never be acknowledged as such, these individuals are not necessarily ethnic minority citizens who come to represent the nation, as in the case of Aboriginal artists in Australia (Myers 2002) or Asian, African American, Latinx, or Native American artists in North American contexts (Davalos 2004; Dávila 1999; Davis Ruffins 1992; Fuller 1992; Lavine 1991; Marzio 1991; Tchen 1992). Nor are these communities a postcolonial, external other against which the nation defines itself, a phenomenon several studies have analyzed (Lionnet 2004; McLeod 2004; Pieprzak 2010; Salamandra 2004). In this research, I use the term "citizen" to refer to a legal status rather than to designate belonging.

This strategy of using artists to prove the state's tolerance is predicated on two core notions: First, it relies on the humanity game (Winegar 2008). The idea that art "constitutes the supreme evidence of a people's humanity" and the perception that it is "a uniquely valuable and uncompromised agent of cross-cultural understanding" lead to the deployment of art as a critical demonstration of a people's humanity and civilized nature—in this case, the UAE state's (Winegar 2008, 652). If art were not correlated to these constructs of humanity, civilization, and tolerance, it would not be an effective bridge.

Second, the use of contingent citizens is predicated on their permanent exclusion. For the UAE to appear tolerant, these noncitizens must remain within the nation and yet never be a part of it. Were they to become citizens, there would be no one for the UAE to tolerate. That is, to perform receiving the state's generosity, noncitizens must be outside the nation. Paradoxically, these noncitizens are chosen to represent the state precisely because they can never be a part of it. These inclusions were also a temporary phenomenon, mirroring the fleeting belonging through labor afforded by the *kafāla* system (Gardner 2010; Unnikrishnan 2017; Vora 2013) and paralleling a rise in gig labor in the art sector generally (Relyea 2013). Their temporary inclusion is a branding tool, demonstrating the "imperative of marketability" (Wu 2002, 214), of showcasing a thriving, multicultural population.

Often engaging in strategic acts of refusal and ambiguity, many artists and cultural producers largely dismissed the idea that citizenship status qualified one for an exhibition, pushing back on various actors' attempts to discipline the representation of the state. Regardless of citizenship status, they judged "good" art worthy of exhibition by aesthetic and conceptual rubrics rather than by the nationality of the work's maker. Artists navigated their own responses to these opportunities and state actors' attempts to conscript them into projects of national representation, often pushing back to assert a definition of good or worthwhile art untethered to citizenship in a state, themselves espousing a "global art world" standard and discourse. Depending on the stage of their career and the potential exposure certain projects could offer, artists at times refused to participate, accepted, or obfuscated their citizenship status altogether.

Exhibiting Bureaucracy

Farah and I sat at her kitchen table, her artwork stacked all around us. Her laptop flickered to life at her touch, and she showed me the open call application she was working on. On the organizer's online form, she needed to upload a pdf of her passport as well as "Select artist's citizenship" from a drop-down menu. Farah had Palestinian and Canadian identity documents, and she chose which to submit depending on the opportunity. For example, for a residency in the U.S., she submitted her Canadian passport. For an exhibition at a West Bank art center, she submitted her Palestinian papers to credential herself as a member of the diaspora.

Exhibition organizers in the UAE often requested proof of citizenship status as part of open call or exhibition applications, a primary and material instance where citizenship status came to the fore in the art community. In these instances, paperwork can enact violence or exclusion (Gupta 2012), making order and disorder (Hull 2012). One curator, Vic, who worked at a UAE arts center, noted that her organization was under "massive pressure to hire Emiratis" as well as to "include" Emirati artists in shows. She related that her boss told her, "We have to make a balance between Emiratis and non-Emiratis." The unspoken goal among the arts organizations I visited appeared to be to have a substantive number of citizen artists in the show, and then as many other diverse nationalities amongst the remaining half of the participating artists. This tenet of the selection criteria was not made public or explicit, but I found myself conducting tallies, as every show listed each artist's national affiliation, and this breakdown appeared repeatedly. Citizenship status mattered in national representation, as state actors drew on the contributions of citizen artists to establish a cultural lineage for the nation, and noncitizen artists to evidence the state's benevolence, tolerance, and multiculturalism for an external audience. To these ends, artists' citizenship status often appeared in exhibition collateral, seemingly oriented toward an international art audience rather than an internal, national one.

In the UAE, the humanity game had two parallel tracks: The cultural contributions of citizen artists reveal the country's humanity and civilized nature, whereas the contributions of noncitizen artists demonstrate the country's tolerance. This twofold strategy attempted to counter negative tropes of the region, particularly in the news media and popular culture (Said 1978; Shaheen 2001), and paralleled the efforts of neighboring Gulf states to rebrand the nation in the eyes of the international community (Cooke 2014; Gardner 2010). Art has also often been used as "a smokescreen for displacement" and other class-based erasures (Pritchard 2020, 179). While in the past art and museums justified colonialism, now they smooth the unevenness of globalizing neoliberalism (see also Melamed 2006)—especially in a place of chasmic inequality like the UAE.

Key cultural figures in the UAE reiterated and validated the humanity game narrative, further heightening the importance of citizenship status.[2] Comments from high-level cultural bureaucrats in the press and exhibition catalogs praised the UAE as "a dynamic vibrant and multicultural society, where people live in harmony and tolerance" (Louvre Press 2017), in a region where "global concerns of multicultural co-existence . . . have been a reality" (Stoby 2017a, 40). Yet others described the forthcoming Louvre Abu Dhabi as a place to "define our humanity" through "the universal languages of the arts" (Al Muhairi 2013, 15). This kind of lofty language aspires to gloss over differences and frictions, which theorist Kwame Anthony Appiah (1994) has pointed out is typical of multiculturalism discourses. These state discourses are in and of themselves a technique of governance: "'Multiculturalism' . . . references the strategies and policies adopted to govern or manage the problems of diversity and multiplicity which multicultural societies throw up" (Hall 2000, 209). Museums are part of cities' "cultural armature" that include "a diversity-management regime—how diversity is regulated and distributed" (Levitt 2015, 3). To manage the UAE's diversity and minimize any perceived frictions between the country's various constituencies, organizers promoted an image of tolerant multiculturalism to defray criticisms of the UAE as incompatible with a thriving art scene.

Alongside claims to multiculturalism, tolerance discourse in the UAE was ubiquitous. The state launched a major tolerance initiative: "With more than 200 nationalities living peacefully and successfully in the UAE, the UAE society has been [sic] an undisputed example of being a tolerant and inclusive country" (UAE Government 2016). UAE rulers appointed a minister of state

for tolerance, passed several anti-discrimination or anti-extremism laws, created two Twitter accounts devoted to promoting tolerance (@VOTolerance, or
ṣawt al-tasāmaḥ, and @uaetolerance), and launched the National Tolerance
Programme, which includes archaeology and history, as well as humanity,
among its seven key pillars.[3]

Yet tolerance, like multiculturalism, is not a neutral concept, as Wendy
Brown has argued. According to a liberal, Euro-Atlantic definition of tolerance predicated on multiculturalism and democracy where the meritorious
(supposedly) prosper, the UAE is routinely portrayed in international media
as intolerant because of its illiberal, authoritarian government; its ethnonationalist (as opposed to multicultural) citizenship regime; and its well-documented abuses of human rights standards in the treatment of migrant workers.
Brown writes that as postcolonial states would not draw on the same logics as
Western states, "an Islamic state seeking to develop codes of tolerance inflects
the term differently than does a Euro-Atlantic political imaginary within
which the nation-states of the West are presumed always already tolerant"
(2006, 3). Indeed, the UAE has developed such a code in a different lexicon.

Organizers constantly highlighted the duality of residents' citizenship
status to emphasize the state's generosity and that communities of different
backgrounds reside harmoniously in the country. This narrative "twinning"
strategy emerged as a discursive technique of governance and managing
difference. One organizer claimed to "giv[e] opportunities to all emerging
artists, curators and writers be it our own Emiratis, but also foreigners, to
develop their skills, crafts and careers while at the same time advancing our
own cultural landscape" (bin Sultan 2016, 11). Another proclaimed that the
organization "has supported emerging Emirati artists and UAE-based artists"
(Warehouse 421 2017, 23). In another instance, a curator wrote, "Our residency
programme is important for the UAE as it offers artists based here, be they
Emiratis or other nationals, to develop their practices in new environments
and take time to focus on artistic research" (MacGilp 2016, 10). While this pervasive twin narrative tactic was perhaps intended to show inclusivity, it simultaneously othered and reinforced categorical distinctions between the artists.

This consistent marking of co-residents' otherness also emerged in talks
and public events: When describing the constituency of the Salama Foundation
at the Sharjah March Meeting in 2016, the manager of the foundation's arts
program said, "We are investing in the future of the United Arab Emirates by
investing in its people. Our definition of the people is both UAE nationals, and

the long-term residents of the United Arab Emirates. The people living here." By repeatedly underscoring the presence of nonnational artists living and working peaceably alongside citizen artists, organizers portrayed the state as generous, welcoming, and tolerant. Throughout their contingent and temporary inclusion, however, they simultaneously and consistently reaffirmed nonnationals as outsiders. Organizers' multiculturalism discourses in effect served to emphasize differences amongst the UAE population in order to allow the state to appear tolerant to an external market. Yet artists pushed back on the use of citizenship status as relevant to their art-making, responding in a variety of ways.

Navigating Contingency: Representation, Ambiguity, and Refusal

Noncitizen artists and arts workers often felt a deep sense of belonging to the UAE due to their lived experiences there, yet they felt the impossibility of citizenship keenly and chafed at the state's occasional acceptance of them as "Emirati enough" to represent the state but not to be granted citizenship. Long-term resident artists strategically disclosed or refused to clarify their citizenship status, aware organizers drew on it selectively. Artists and art workers chose carefully when and how to define themselves. Individuals struggled to balance gaining exposure and exploitation by the state, and in essence navigate their contingency. These choices were calculated according to a complex rubric and not always consistent: They at times resisted, submitted, and acted in ways that can be categorized as neither/both.

For example, Eman was an arts organizer and writer in her late twenties. She traveled to the Venice Biennale one year as part of a delegation representing the UAE. The Venice Biennale, founded in 1895, is one of the most—if not the most—elite contemporary art events in the world, and the display is organized by national pavilions. Describing her work with the UAE pavilion at the Biennale, Eman shared, "We stood out a lot in Europe. It was me and three other Emirati girls." Eman remarked, "We were all staying in one house, we were doing everything together. The locals would ask us where we were from. They'd say, we're Emirati. I'd never get a chance to say where I'm from. I'm Palestinian." Eman continued, pushing her curly hair back behind her ears:

> So I started asserting. My close friend at that time was like, "Why do you feel the need to continue to assert that you're Palestinian? I see you doing this." I'm not Emirati. Why should my identity be sort of sweeped [sic] under the

carpet when it's convenient because you wanna represent the UAE? She said, "You don't identify with the UAE?" Yes I do, but I'm not a citizen. It's hard for me to wholeheartedly just say, I'm from Dubai, I'm from the UAE, when I don't have any rights in that place. That was the first time it actually dawned on me that I'm not Emirati.

Eman's wording reflects her ambiguous situation as someone born and raised in the UAE, but who carries foreign citizenship documentation. She notes "three other Emirati girls," implying they are like her, even as she marks her difference by emphasizing her Palestinian identity. Such remarks were often how my interlocutors revealed their citizenship status to me: Even though I did not ask about it outright, their status affected the kinds of jobs they could have, how they were able to stay in the UAE, their ability to go abroad for education, their marriage prospects, and even whether they felt it responsible to have children. For example, one interlocutor I call Talal had been born and raised in the UAE; his family were Palestinians forced off of their lands in 1948, and they made their way to Kuwait, living there until the 1990 Iraqi invasion, after which they were expelled. They later qualified for asylum in Canada, and after obtaining Canadian citizenship, relocated to the Emirates. Talal was able to live in the UAE under his father's residency visa until he turned twenty-one; at that point, he had to find a job. Because his ability to stay in the UAE was dependent on having a job, he felt unable to move positions until he had another job lined up. He also considered himself lucky, because even though he did not think of himself as Canadian, if he were to lose his UAE residency, he could relocate to Canada. Other interlocutors had no such safety net: One curator migrated from Syria with his young family when the recent civil war began. Return was not on the horizon. Another interlocutor born in the UAE, Layla, held Iraqi papers; even to visit her family in Iraq at the time of my fieldwork, the government required her to have a special escort to ensure her safety as a nonresident.

One evening, I invited several artists I knew to an open conversation about the local art scene. We gathered at a Dubai art center where several of the participants—three European-born artists and four UAE-born Arab artists—had studios. The artists joined me for a lively conversation that eventually turned to the arts scene in the UAE and state cultural policies. During the conversation, one of the European artists, Renata, asked if the "local" artists wanted to work for the government to change cultural policies and pedagogy in the UAE, revealing assumptions that citizens

felt ownership over their government and also that citizens' input was welcomed by that government. These assumptions were perhaps true in the socialist democratic context from which Renata came, but not necessarily applicable
in the Emirates. Activism and civic participation—or even agency—do not
necessarily occur in the same forms everywhere (Atshan 2020; Mahmood
2005; Yúdice 2003). The local artists diplomatically changed the subject.

Having noticed this, I discussed the conversation a few days later with
one of the Arab artists, Asma. Asma noted that while Renata assumed all
four Arab artists were Emirati citizens, only two of the four present possessed both the passport and family card at that moment. She then shared she
had held an Emirati passport but not a *khulāṣat al-qaīd* family card, and that
a year prior, the UAE government had rescinded her UAE passport, claiming
their family was "clearly Iranian and not Emirati," and therefore not entitled to passports from the UAE.[4] The UAE is not a democracy, birthright
citizenship and naturalization do not exist, citizens and residents are not
guaranteed due process, and there was no legal process to complain or peti-
tion. Asma's family was rendered stateless overnight. As she shared her situation with me, I wondered why she had not corrected Renata when Renata
assumed she was a national; when I later witnessed Asma deftly sidestep
questions about citizenship status, I realized her disclosures were strategic,
not just an issue of shame or emotional difficulty. Revealing one's status at an
inopportune moment, or to the wrong person, could damage one's standing
in the community. Asma—among others who had spent the majority of their
lives in the UAE but did not carry unambiguous rights to UAE citizenship—
carefully weighed when to disclose their status out of self-protection.

Opting to not disclose or clarify one's citizenship status, as Asma had, is
one response to organizers' push for information, yet this choice can mean
being excluded from exhibitions. A few years back, when Asma still had an
Emirati passport, she was invited to exhibit in a prominent all-Emirati show.
She reflected:

> I was upset, I knew they had picked me and they had accepted me as Emi-
> rati, but many other times I wasn't because I didn't have *khulāṣat al-qaīd*. I
> wanted to be Emirati, but a lot of times I got rejected because I wasn't, really.
> After the show I was in this pool [of Emirati artists], and people would ask,
> "What's it like to be an Emirati artist?" And I'd say, "As opposed to what?"
> When it works for them, you are considered Emirati.

In Asma's careful responses to questions about being Emirati, even as she spoke to someone who knew her situation, she neither confirmed nor denied her citizenship status. Her reply ("As opposed to what?") rather overtly poked at the utility of citizenship status to one's art-making: In fact, why would Emirati citizenship make one a different, or better, artist?

At the time, Asma believed the organizers were under pressure to produce a certain number of promising emerging artists who worked in a particular medium; the exhibition included a residency with a well-known artist and was part of a larger state-sponsored initiative to support and develop citizen artists. The market imperative to present a number of recognized, emerging local artists in this instance mitigated Asma's liminal status and prior patterns of state representation. As Asma put it, it worked for them. In this case, she was "Emirati enough." In another instance of exception, a UAE-born artist with Palestinian papers was invited to join a cohort of all-citizen artists; the excellent caliber of his work and the potential of that work representing the country overshadowed the material fact of his nationality. At certain moments, when an artist's contribution has the potential to improve the state's brand, their official status can be obscured or papered over to temporarily include them. Market viability, via the appearance of tolerance and peaceful multiculturalism, supersedes ethnonationalism.

Asma had elected to participate in the all-citizen show, recognizing that the organizers' acceptance of her status as an Emirati citizen was not permanent, and that she was being deployed selectively. Given the stage of her career at the time of the exhibition, she felt the exposure was important, yet she was aware that "no institution is neutral" and she had to accept serving as a representative of the Emirati state in order to get the exposure the show provided—a rather painful experience given that she had, in many other instances, not been "Emirati enough" to represent in this capacity. Furthermore, participating in the show also put her in a difficult position going forward: As it was well-publicized that the exhibition showcased "Emirati artists," other arts organizers assumed she was an Emirati citizen.

In the next couple of years after the exhibition, Asma received an onslaught of emails inviting her to participate in exhibitions as an Emirati artist. Yet most of these shows required a photocopy of the artist's passport to participate. No longer having this passport, she largely ignored them, opting not to clarify her citizenship status. If the curator followed up, she would politely defer and explain she was busy. Many older news articles about her and her work cited her as an Emirati citizen, so many people assumed her citizenship status remained the same. Because many curators in the UAE are relatively short-term foreigners, partly due to the gig nature of labor in the art world (Menger 1999; Relyea 2013), they were not necessarily aware that citizenship status in the UAE was a shifting category and that revocation of an Emirati passport was a possibility. While Asma shared her status with me privately, she did so after several months of us spending time together. She therefore knew me well, and her disclosure was also likely related to the fact that I was an academic, not a curator who might approach her for shows. She declined to identify herself as either a citizen or a noncitizen publicly or in large group conversations. She strategically employed ambiguity, partially because she considered her status in flux and hoped for it to be restored, but also because her affective sense of belonging to the UAE and her lifetime of living in the UAE were at odds with her identity papers. Refusing to disclose her status to organizers allowed her some measure of control over which exhibitions she participated in and under what terms; aware that organizers hoped to deploy her work and presence as an artist to paint a particular narrative, Asma simply declined to allow her status to be known. While not disclosing her status prevented some damage to her social standing, she did forfeit some exhibition opportunities because she did not submit identity documentation for verification. Her choice empowered her in some ways and disadvantaged her in others.⁵

Noncitizen artists frequently expressed frustration and confusion about how to describe and situate themselves. For example, Layla described to me the first time she realized she was Iraqi, not Emirati, tacking between English and Arabic as she spoke:

> [It] was in 1990 during the Gulf war, because these kids from Kuwait started coming throwing pebbles on me. I said why are they doing this? My dad said, "You're Iraqi." *Shū* "Iraqi" [what is "Iraqi"]? I'm from Sharjah. . . . Kids would say, *ānti bint 'saīf al-'arab,' ānti bint Ṣaddām* [you're the daughter of the "sword of the Arabs" (Saddam Hussein's nickname), you're the daughter of Saddam].

Layla struggled with how to identify herself, as her formal citizenship status chafed with her experience. She smiled ruefully and said, "I was born an immigrant. Millions of Arabs, South Asians, whites [grow up here], but come age eighteen, they have to go back. Go 'back' where? You don't know." Layla's comment, that she was born an immigrant, highlights that for many in the UAE, the state categorized them as migrants—as outsiders—from the moment of their birth. The concept of return, or going back, was also laden: In effect, it often meant going to a place they had never been, much less lived.[6] In these communities, they do not always belong, either: Their dialect, their habitus in Pierre Bourdieu's (2000) terms, and their pop culture references were often at odds with the place of their documented "belonging" and the place they have lived. To date, Layla remains in the UAE, aware that her residency is not guaranteed, but rather is "ambiguous, tenuous . . . I tell myself, 'Don't get too comfortable, this is not your place.' In my head, my bags are packed. There are no treaties that can protect me. I have no place to go."

Likewise, Amira was born in Syria and raised in the UAE. She described her ambivalence toward the UAE as simultaneously her home and not her home: "At a certain point, should I submit and do things the way they're done, or should I just leave? . . . A lot of my work deals with home and nostalgia and connections to places that are not home, but could be home, but could not really be home even though you're surrounded by people and places and memories."

Other artists also shared that they had channeled their complicated emotions about their status and belonging into their work. Ghada, an artist of Palestinian descent, told me, "I was born here. I don't have a passport from here. But amongst the current generation, you find people who say, you're Emirati just like us. You know the country, the land, the culture. And then I go back and say"—she paused and clicked her tongue—"but not really." This sense of always being an outsider, and the tenuousness that comes with her lack of rights and citizenship status in the country, pervades her artistic practice as it does Amira's. Many artists felt state-centric definitions of artists to be an archaic mode, a strategy out of step with the convoluted transnational realities of life in the UAE and the diversifying of populations that came with that reality.

Aside from strategic disclosures and ambiguity, some refused in other ways, channeling their responses into their artwork, emphasizing their affective belonging and identification with other places, or, in some instances, leaving the UAE altogether. Eman, who worked on the Venice Biennale as described earlier, was born and raised in the UAE. She grew increasingly uncomfortable representing the UAE, despite considering it home. She expressed frustration that she was Emirati enough to represent the country abroad while working on exhibitions, but this representation did not afford her rights or status at home in the UAE. She shared her dilemma about where to live and how to engage, pausing throughout:

> I'm thinking about my future. The Gulf is a big part of my sensibility, especially as a Palestinian.[7] I feel like I can't do meaningful work that doesn't include that, in some ways. But it is a place of conflict for me. Whatever work I do is going to reveal that conflict. I still have family that lives there. Am I willing to compromise on their safety?
>
> The thing about the Gulf, and the UAE, it's an arbitrary place. You literally don't know what you might say or do that might push someone's buttons and okay, you're out. It's not structured in a way that you know clearly what goes and doesn't go.
>
> There's a sacrifice, either in the work I do, or my family's safety.
>
> If I wanna be honest, I do, I wanna talk about what it means to live in a place for decades and go back as a tourist. What does that mean on a psychological level?

Eman alluded to the fact that because she no longer works in the country, she must apply for a tourist visa in order to visit her place of birth where her family still lives.[8] While Asma utilized ambiguity to make her citizenship status opaque, Eman referenced the parallel uses of strategic ambiguity employed by the state. Because the laws are vague and policies can change overnight with no process of public input, many UAE residents preferred to stay on the safe side, reining in their behavior to avoid any gray areas that might shift and result in loss of residency privileges.[9] The state's calculated reliance on ambiguity frequently resulted in the population self-censoring. The end result was that the society was more conservative than its laws would indicate.

Eman also referred to the contingency of workers, whom the state accepts so long as they are useful—much like the artists I worked with. Eman was frustrated that those who had lived in the UAE for decades were forced to leave upon retirement or when they turn eighteen, given that the residency visa system was predicated upon employment or being a dependent child of an employed person.[10] Without a job or a family member who can sponsor dependents, a residency visa was not possible. Eman grew animated: "Our parents, that generation of men and women who are rendered invisible and irrelevant when they are no longer working and have no visa or jobs to sponsor them. It makes me angry and I want to do something about it. But what?" When a noncitizen no longer benefited the labor market or the state's marketing projects, their contingent inclusion evaporated too. Eman struggled against her experience of contingency and disenfranchisement as someone who was raised in the UAE but who had no rights there, and who would never be able to fully claim citizenship and belonging there.

Some outside groups have critiqued arts organizations in the Gulf, particularly the franchises of the Louvre and the Guggenheim. For Eman, some of these attempts that addressed circumstances in the UAE appropriated the terms of the discourse, and patronized Gulf-based workers by speaking for them, instead of with them, resulting in a double alienation. She spoke of the organization Gulf Labor, which has circulated boycott petitions and staged protests in New York, particularly targeting the Guggenheim, in an attempt to raise awareness about the working conditions of migrant laborers at Saadiyat Island's various sites including the Louvre Abu Dhabi, Guggenheim Abu Dhabi, and New York University Abu Dhabi. Members of the group are extremely (and justifiably) critical of the human rights violations in the Emirates, but many in the group have limited experience with the region and have not resided there. Eman said:

I have some grievances with Gulf Labor, those people who are not people who live there or have deep connections to that place, and jeopardize the people that *do* live there.

They come from the luxury of being in New York and criticizing systems and structures they want to change without understanding how it actually affects people living on the ground.

I share the sentiment of this conflict, I wanna be a part of the conversation, but if it's not a conversation that speaks to my experience, I don't know if I can be a part of it.

In these discussion groups, Eman felt there was no space in the conversation for those who were not Emirati or poorly paid migrant workers. Those who could not claim legal citizenship in the UAE but felt it was home did not fit into the neat binary portrayed by activists and the media: savior activists or downtrodden exploited laborers.[11] Looking beyond a highly curated public image reveals the ways organizers curated a tolerant, multicultural image to brand the UAE, showing the capitalization of diversity and the dominance of capital interests over ethnonationalism. Artists also, albeit rarely, challenged these discourses publicly.

Expressing the Emirates

In the UAE art world, a shift to market dominance also meant changes to the role of the state, often putting state actors in the backseat. State actors were certainly still influential, although often acting under the guise of transnational art market networks. As the established pattern of representation shifted away from an openly ethnonationalist mode, museum actors endeavored to showcase diversity and multiculturalism to connect with a broader transnational art world. Tolerance for multiculturalism and diversity were market imperatives, necessary for an art world to flourish. One of the most significant ways the market exhibitionary complex reveals itself is in how the state uses artists in projects of representation, with the shifting importance of citizen and noncitizen artists. These practices parallel the ways corporations have used art and cultural initiatives to improve their reputations (D'Souza 2018; Rectanus 2002; Wu 2002; Yúdice 2003) and the branding of diversity more generally (Melamed 2006; Shankar 2015).

On a bright November day, I arrived at Manarat Al Saadiyat to attend talks during Abu Dhabi Art. The first talk featured artists involved in the *Emirati Expressions* show that was staged in an exhibition hall adjacent to the fair itself; the artists were all Emirati citizens in their mid- to late twenties. Afterward, I took a quick tour of that exhibition while waiting for the second talk to start, which was to focus on the Zayed National Museum and its growing collections. Both talks and *Emirati Expressions* centered on supporting and promoting Emirati artists.

The talk featured a curator from the British Museum alongside four UAE-based artists. Dim salmon light bathed the seating area, while the stage and its rows of black leather chairs and white side tables were illuminated in an orb of bright white. This talk boasted the most diverse audience I had seen so far at Abu Dhabi Art: Half the attendees were wearing Emirati national dress such as the *khandūra* for men and the *abaya* for women, and half sported so-termed "Western" attire. The speakers mirrored this breakdown: All but one artist and the white British Museum curator wore Emirati national dress in some variation.

The moderator, a woman I call Hind from the Zayed National Museum (ZNM), started the talk promptly. Hind opened the talk by saying in Arabic that if audience members had questions in Arabic, they should feel free to ask, although the talk would be in English. She then transitioned to English, saying:

> Shaykh Zayed would always use words such as *insh'Allah* in his quotes and his speeches. And he always depends on his faith and his values and his beliefs. And he also tends to use words like, especially when he addresses Emiratis, he would not say the UAE, he will tell them your land, *bladkum, 'ardkum*. So really, the content of the museum, the narrative, the build-up of the museum is all inspired by those words, by his values, by his beliefs, and his wisdom, his compassion, his vision, it's really the guide throughout the development of the narrative. And we really want each and every Emirati to feel the belonging to this museum, to feel the pride and to be part of this development.
>
> We also want the visitors to be able to understand our loyalty and love to the country and our leaders. And we want the residents of the UAE to be part of this history, to be part of this build-up of the history. And of course, Shaykh Zayed himself was behind the build-up of the first national museum in the United Arab Emirates in Al Ain in the '70s. And the Zayed National Museum will be a legacy of Shaykh Zayed's beliefs and values, and have his rather compelling passion to protect, preserve, and share with the Emiratis, and the world, the history and culture of the United Arab Emirates.
>
> We are all indeed writing a new chapter of the history of the UAE, which will continue for more generations to come. And then an essential component of the museum's collection, of course, part of this collection will be having contemporary exhibitions. And our talk today, which is a continuation of Multaqa–Zayed National Museum, will focus on the evolving nature of museum collections.

Hind felt no need to translate *insh'Allah* for this audience; it means "God [Allah] willing." Her inducement to Arabic speakers to ask questions also asserted an Emirati-first outlook in line with her position at a national museum. Yet the use of English privileged international visibility. Her integration of contemporary art in the collection of a national museum, albeit quick, was noteworthy. Her comments did not clarify *whose* art would be featured in the national museum. Perhaps because the talk was part of programming attached to the commercial fair Abu Dhabi Art, Hind strove to highlight the relevance of a national museum, more often associated with heritage or older art historical periods, to the contemporary art market and the commercial art fair in which the talk was held. These talks also revealed the hybridity of commercial and noncommercial arts enterprises, and were also one method of cultivating audiences, which I discuss further in Chapter 5.

In some ways, plans for the new ZNM revealed threads of continuity with prior practice of drawing on citizens' artwork. Hind continued, "So these are some samples of the collection of the Zayed National Museum and for you to understand what will be in the collection as part of the contemporary collection of the ZNM. We just started the build-up of it. And of course, it will be a continuation of the development of this collection." Her slides featured works by mostly Emirati citizen artists. Hind also made it a point to highlight the UAE's first museum, the Al Ain National Museum, establishing a cultural lineage for the projects of today. The history of museums, and contemporary art production, in the region were often contested (see also Derderian 2020), and a number of talks and exhibitions made sure to focus on early initiatives.[12]

At the conclusion of the British Museum curator's overview, Hind was quick to draw out that collections included "everything that is related to what's happening around the world right now. The same thing is happening with our development of the collection of the Zayed National Museum as well. It's not only historic objects or manuscripts," she offered, again underscoring that the national museum would hold a collection of fine art in addition to these other types of collections. Hind's invocations clearly defined a scope for the national museum—perhaps even the answer to the questions: What is a national art museum in the twenty-first century? Whose artwork and what objects should be displayed in a national museum? Whose art defines the nation?

After all the speakers gave their spiel, Hind opened the floor for questions from the audience, which was when the complexity of citizenship and changing national representation in the Emirates began to filter through. In response to an audience member asking an artist I call Khaled to talk about one of his pictures, which she had heard was about his experience as a Palestinian, he shifted in his chair. Khaled responded, "I'm Palestinian Kuwaiti and I've been here twenty years, which is longer than I've been anywhere. And this country has taken me in," he said, emphasizing a sense of commitment and belonging to the UAE. "But," he continued,

I don't like to be called a Palestinian artist, Kuwaiti artist, or Emirati artist. I think any artist that I know would rather be called an artist, or a photographer, rather than by nationality. I think it's been a blessing and a curse. I think it's really great that Middle Eastern art has gotten a lot of attention. But on the other hand, I think many artists are getting locked into certain labels.

These labels can benefit artists, certainly; there is what Arlene Dávila terms a "currency of categories," and distinctions between categories such as Latinx versus Latin American can entail market success or market failure (2020, 79–103). Such examples emerged in the UAE as well. Khaled concluded with the example of Mona Hatoum: We don't call her an Arab artist, he said—she's an artist, full stop. Khaled referred to the phenomenon of "crossover" artists—"when they 'graduate' from [regional] art sales into contemporary art sales" (Dávila 2020, 89). He continued:

I think it's a problem, if nationality is the endpoint. If it's the beginning of the discussion, I don't have an issue with that. But I think many people stop at that. And then they start to project so much of their understanding of the history of the country onto the image, which maybe has nothing to do with the image.

A look of confusion briefly crossed some faces, as the audience processed Khaled's comments that problematized the connection between artists, representation, and the nation—and that troubled the neat lines Hind had laid out for them. Khaled offered in its place another discourse, one that detached artists from a nation, placing them in a broader global sphere. While some state organizers engaged in performatively inclusive talk, presenting noncitizen artists as evidence of the state's tolerance to brand it on the market, artists themselves chafed at such moves, denying the relevance of one's citizenship status to the caliber of their art. State actors wanted to use artists' status to project a tolerant image to a world market, while artists themselves often aspired to be detached from such moorings to legitimize their own work in precisely that market.

Beyond Citizenship: The Transnational Paradigm

Since 2007, with the announcement of the Louvre Abu Dhabi, the beginning of commercial art fairs in the UAE, national pavilions at the Venice Biennale, and all-Emirati shows, many UAE-based organizers continued to mark citizenship as a relevant category in the cultural nation-making project. They used museums and exhibitions, long recognized as tools of state-building, to exploit the precarious status of noncitizens and showcase the Emirati state's tolerance and cosmopolitanism, privileging transnational market pressures toward inclusivity over an ethnically limited framework of citizenship.[13]

While forces of capital and calls for inclusivity transform museum politics, artists continue to navigate their contingency through strategic ambiguity and refusal. Their creative and agentive responses show how projects of national representation shift in a market-dominant paradigm. These artists prove that hegemony is fragile because, as Raymond Williams points out, "it has to continually be renewed, recreated, defended, and modified" (1977, 112). Hegemony must continually be made and remade. These artists disrupted the hegemonic ethnonationalist discourses that previously defined art and museum representation, demonstrating the malleability of aesthetic forms and the power of refusal in the ways their citizenship status was used—and also in the ways they strategically offered their critiques.

IN THE GALLERY III   *Melting the Sky*

ON A WARM OCTOBER EVENING, I attended the opening of Cristiana de Marchi and Monira Al Qadiri's joint exhibition *Melting the Sky*, held at the commercial art gallery 1x1 Gallery in Dubai's Alserkal Avenue. De Marchi, who was born in Italy, had lived in the UAE for several years at that point. A poet and multimedia conceptual artist, she worked across words, video, fiber, wood, and installation. Al Qadiri is a Kuwaiti artist, born in Senegal and educated in Japan. Her work is also multimedia and focuses on "cultural histories of the Gulf region," particularly "petro-culture" (Al Qadiri 2025). *The National*, the state-run media outlet, posted a brief note about the exhibition's opening: The artists "address the idea of a nation state in a new exhibition . . . [which] looks at blurred lines of territory in our modern world and man-made borders that shift every day" (Seaman 2016). Standing outside the gallery's windowed entryway, I could see the title of the exhibition in plain black typeface and a strip of white wall through the windows.

In the first room, directly opposite the visitors' entry, the gallery had installed Monira Al Qadiri's *Father of Pearl* (2016). A grid of white silkscreen prints, six tall and seven across, was installed on a large mat board propped against the wall. The white prints looked nearly featureless at first, the black pushpins holding them in place being the only visible markers. But as I walked closer, the pages shimmered, and I could see the prints actually had opalescent portraits of an older *Khalījī* man, wearing distinctively Arab head coverings. Al Qadiri made the prints from the sole surviving photograph of her grandfather. Her late grandfather had traveled around the Gulf, India, Iran, and Africa, working as a singer on a pearling boat. Japanese businessman Kokichi Mikimoto successfully cultured pearls in 1893, and the expansion of the cultured pearl industry rendered pearl diving, previously an economic mainstay of the Gulf, obsolete over the next fifty years; in its place, Gulf rulers built oil economies. Pre-oil lifeways, which often entailed the dangerous work of pearl diving and sometimes involved seasonal migrations, seem rather distant from the experiences of Gulf residents today. The label noted, "This work describes the artist's feeling towards this disappearing history, and her absolute inability to grasp or understand it." I also saw the disappearance of shaykhly figures, a potentially sensitive topic. Political scientist Christopher Davidson had angered the Gulf rulers after the publication of his 2012 book titled *After the Sheikhs: The Coming Collapse of the Gulf Monarchies*, so I was surprised to see work that depicted Gulf elders disappearing.

Another of Al Qadiri's works, *Prehistoria* (2016), consisted of several one-by-one-meter wafer-thin metal panels hung from the ceiling. The panels, cut to resemble the "technical drawings of patented oil drills" per the wall labels, cast shadows against the white walls of the gallery, creating lacy images dancing along the walls. The exhibition fact sheet noted that the forms might "resemble marine creatures, decorative patterns, or science-fictional tools." Finally, the sheet concluded, "The artist imagines that in the future the oil industry and its inner workings will appear as a cryptic ancient reality, an illusion of past dreams, where shiny aspirations and mirroring fantasies cast their shadows on entire landscapes and peoples." While the work undermines outsider critiques and stereotypes of the Gulf states as shiny urban fantasies with little substance, it also pokes at the two-dimensional nature of oil state aspirations and the real effects brought onto the populations living under them.

In the middle room, de Marchi's *Possible Worlds* (2014) series was displayed (Figure G3.1). These monochrome weavings—red, beige, green, white, blue, and black—depicted continental and national outlines. The shapes of the continents or nations were the same color thread, but stitched differently than the surrounding oceans and nations so the sheen of the embroidery floss created a barely perceptible difference. De Marchi interrogates the constructed and arbitrary nature of boundaries through her work. I remembered visiting de Marchi in her studio, when she had described the *Possible Worlds* series to our group of visitors: "This one is one of the maps where I'm working on the ideas of borders, so it's the first piece I made working with the MENASA

FIGURE G3.1. *Possible Worlds* (2014) by Cristiana de Marchi, installed in *Melting the Sky*, Dubai, 2016. Courtesy the artist and 1x1 Gallery, Dubai.

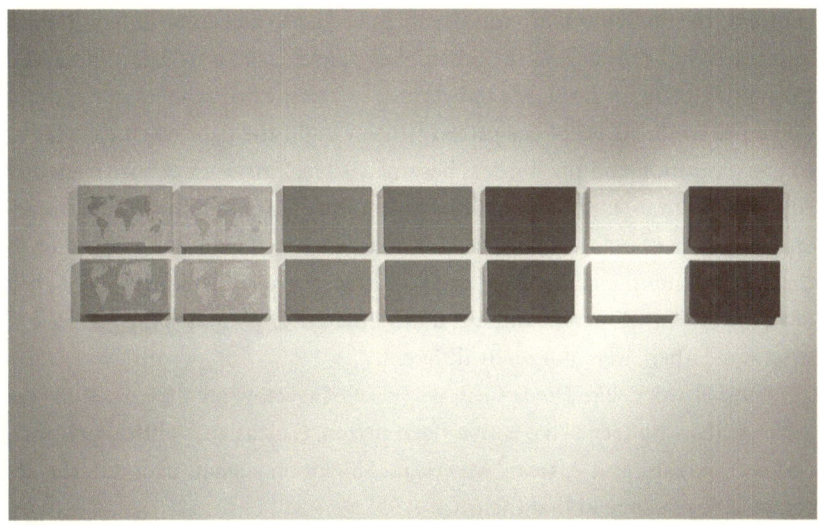

FIGURE G3.2. *Sustainability* (2015) by Cristiana de Marchi, installed in *Melting the Sky*, Dubai, 2016. Courtesy the artist and 1x1 Gallery, Dubai.

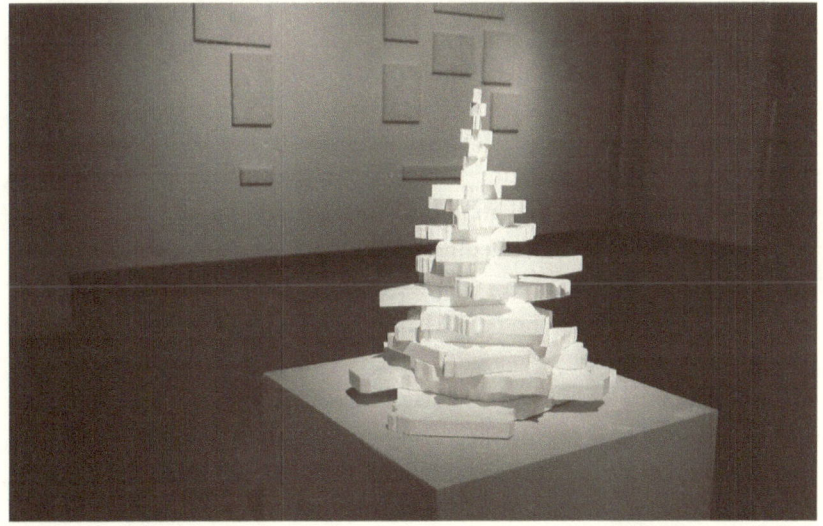

(Middle East North Africa South Asia) region. So you can't actually see much, but if you have light, you can see it. I'm using monochrome and using different kinds of stitches to maintain the shapes." The lack of color differentiation mimicked the arbitrariness of borders. Self-conscious in the posh commercial gallery, I bobbed my head side to side to see what she had pointed out, a slight difference in the luster of the thread which caught the light when the viewer changed position and the borders became visible. This work echoed Benedict Anderson's (2006) idea of "imagined community," highlighting for me the arbitrary nature of political borders and their fabricated nature: As she stitched the borders into the cloth, de Marchi could have made the borders an eighth of an inch in any direction without much difference. What was the nation and what was "other" were not really different.

Another work, *The Die is Cast*, was a set of seven white dice. Each di was laser-etched with terms like native-born citizen, Caucasian, political prisoner, widower, female, and African American. Shown on a small pedestal, the accompanying label read that the work

> reflects on issues of identity from a perspective of potentiality and actualization. By blindly engraving on seven white dices [*sic*] the 42 elements that characterize identity according to international standards and including gender, age, social and political status, religion and geographic origin, [de Marchi] address[es] the component of irrationality in defining one's identity, knowing that identity is a highly abused concept in the context of political and cultural inclusion, and exclusion.

That these factors are on di evokes a gamelike quality: one's future determined by chance, but with devastatingly important consequences. For example, in the UAE, one's national affiliation determines if and for how long one can receive a tourist visa, the difficulty one will face obtaining work and what privileges will be attendant (e.g., sponsoring one's family, driving, purchasing alcohol, paid return trips home), the relative rank of one's salary, and one's general social mobility. As we saw in the last chapter, citizenship status remained influential, even if only for marketing purposes. One's social position also determined how openly they could critique and the kinds of critiques they could issue: Among my interlocutors, they were wary of criticizing the state, including the royal families, and Islam, in particular.

In the back of the gallery, de Marchi's work *Stand Up* (2016) was installed. *Stand Up* consisted of a series of wooden cutouts of the GCC states, almost like thick puzzle pieces, stacked into a tower formation on top of a circular mirror (Figure G3.2). The tower becomes a kind of monument, representing the ways in which territory comes to stand in for the monument of the state. To see the territorial outlines—the nation-state's territorial outline becomes a logo of the state, as Anderson (2006) reminds us—almost as game pieces seemed, to me, to poke at the legitimacy of such fabrications by calling them out as such. The precarity of the stack of pieces also hinted at the temporary nature of states and empires. The work was part of a larger series called *Sustainability*, raising the question of the sustainability and future possibility of nation-states, especially given the historic precedent of changing borders and formations of polities.

As I quickly learned, stereotyped assumptions that censorship was rampant in the Gulf states often led many to dismiss the possibility of making critical artwork there. However, claims of censorship could often create spaces to play, pushing artists to find productive edges of tension. And indeed, the contemporary limits on freedom of expression were different from those navigated by the artists of a generation prior. One evening, after attending a class on critical practice for artists and arts organizers, I spoke with the instructor, Sofia. European-born and an artist herself, Sofia had passed around a book to illustrate her lecture. "I was surprised," I told her, and pointed at one of the caricatures in the book, an image of an old man cupping a hand around his ear to hear. The administrator at the passport department says to him, "Get three witnesses over the age of 80 and get your father to come see me." The caricaturist was Hassan Sharif, a pioneering contemporary artist in the United Arab Emirates. In this piece from 1974, he lampooned what he viewed as the state's problematic and often impossible requirements to obtain citizenship in a newly unified Emirates. Sofia laughed knowingly and responded, "Yes, I know. In the 1970s and '80s, Hassan was making critiques that would not be possible now."

The politics of expression in the UAE have shifted over time; the sharpening of restrictions around particular kinds of expression occurred coeval with the rising importance of performing a political and social critique in contemporary art, which has emerged since the 1980s (Drucker 2005; Fraser and Rothman 2017; Joselit 2017). Critiques such as those published by Sharif in the 1970s, which Sofia had shared with our class, would not be published in the Emirates today, and the country's reputation for censorship often makes headlines even for seemingly unrelated developments (Voon 2017). Some of

the critiques Sharif published in the past might perhaps seem tame by contemporary American standards: He satirized the state's deployment of petrodollars, the UAE's then-growing citizenship bureaucracy, and the nepotistic
privileging of relationships and social capital (called *wāsṭa* in Arabic). In one
caricature, a line of people stands outside, queued to enter a building. Above
them, a giant figure is poised to step over them to reach the head of the line,
holding in his hands a paper reading *wāsṭa*, or influence. In another, a scantily
clad, busty woman creeps past an old man asleep in a chair, scissors by his
side; the caption, *al-nawm Sulṭān*, is glossed as "censor fell asleep" in English.
In another example, Sharif depicts a pipeline with people wearing Emirati
national dress emerging from it with the caption: "Emirates University—Developing people [*bina' al-ānsān*]." Other caricatures focus on the media's con-
tentious relationship with the public (Figure G3.3) and administrative snafus
that prevent medical patients from receiving expedient care (Figure G3.4).

FIGURE G3.3. "Cease fire" caricature by Hassan Sharif, dated 1975. The
newspaper reads, "Cease fire." One journalist says to the other, "Where will
we get our news from now?" Image courtesy the estate of Hassan Sharif.

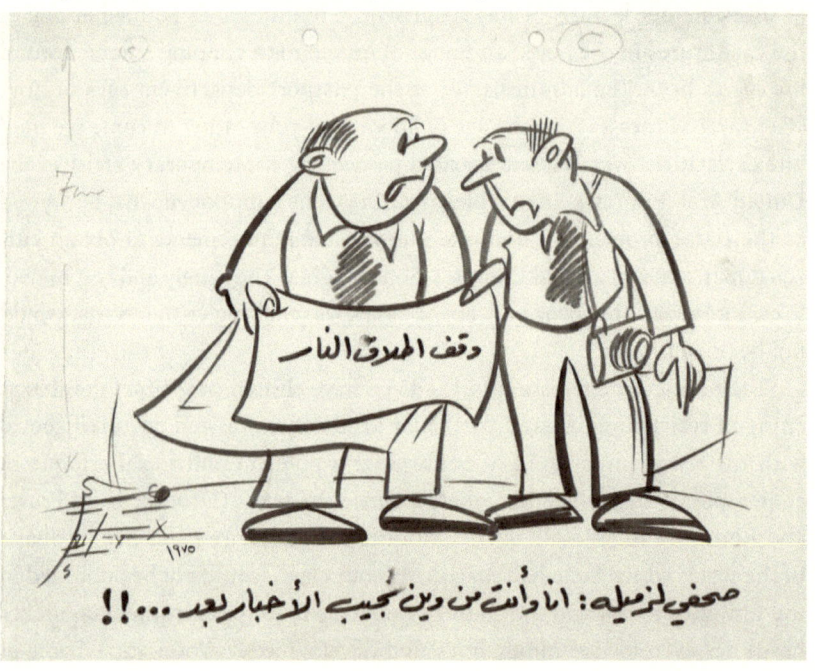

FIGURE G3.4. In this caricature by Hassan Sharif dated 1976, the doctor
says to the patient, "You need an operation ... and the operation
needs a room ... and the room needs a budget ... and there is no
budget yet." Image courtesy the estate of Hassan Sharif.

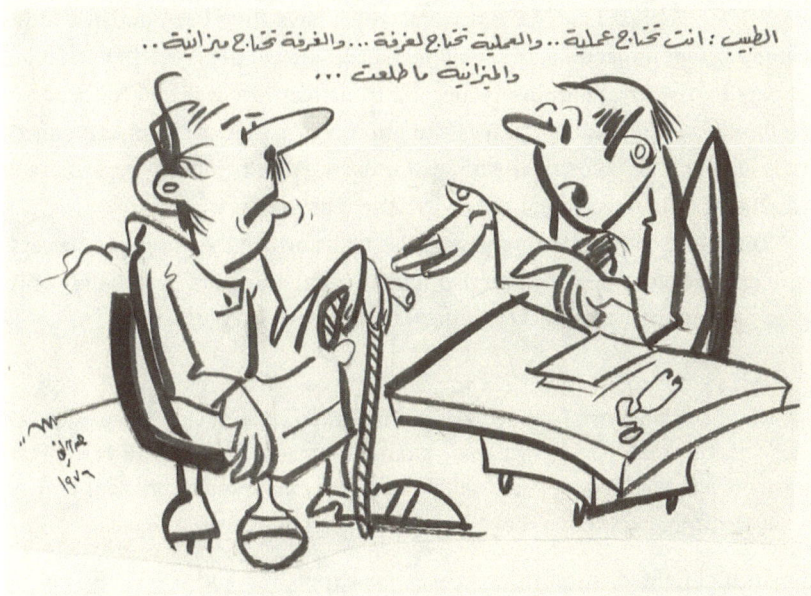

Abdullah, a curator, described the early years after the dissolution of the
Trucial States Protectorate and the 1971 national unification of the Emirates
as a time in which artists enjoyed a great deal of leeway in their expression.
Abdullah commented,

> At that time, the nation was busy with lots of other things. Electricity,
> roads—art was kind of a luxury. [The early artists] were not neglected—they
> were just doing something that people didn't understand. No one banned
> you. They were exhibiting in every public space in the UAE in the '80s and
> '90s. [Hassan Sharif] started in caricature. He was criticizing a lot of stuff
> but he was publishing in public. The real question is . . . about the margin of
> freedom that was present, and how it's now changed, and it's a dictatorship
> and you can't say things.

Sharif himself had noted to me, "Before, we had a little bit more space to talk."
He felt that "the space became less" over time, and expressed these shifts

deepened his commitment to teaching and mentoring. While the period after unification was more relaxed, around the mid-1980s, the population of the UAE began to accelerate dramatically. Concerned about retaining control over the growing and diverse population, the country instituted anti-slander laws (UAE Federal Law No. 3 of 1987), which have since been updated to include strident protections in social media and virtual domains. In particular, criticizing the royal families is illegal and slander is a criminal (rather than civil) offense. In addition, judges can and do aver that criticism can constitute slander if it "affects the honor of a defamed individual"—regardless of whether the claim is factual or not (Abdel-Nabi and Lester 2019).

The so-called Arab Spring of 2011 also transformed the margins of acceptable expression in the UAE, further narrowing the scope of permissible criticisms. Eman, who had worked at the Venice Biennale, commented:

> There was a time in the UAE where it was possible to protest, to be vocal about how angry you are because [your homeland] was being bombarded. With the Arab Spring that space shrank dramatically. The UAE became more paranoid about dissent and protest. Everyone became conscious of it and there were real stories of people being deported. I internalized it.

Eman highlighted the shifting spaces for expression and the changing parameters for acceptable speech. Her comment also reveals the politicization of particular topics and the depoliticization of others. Desirous of retaining power, Gulf governments reacted strongly when the Arab Spring occurred in Egypt and Tunisia, with violent crackdowns on budding protests in Saudi Arabia, Oman, and Bahrain (Fibiger 2017; Lulu 2011, 2012; Matthiesen 2013; Wilson 2023). The acceptable range of topics dissipated further with the Saudi-Emirati blockade of Qatar (June 5, 2017) and the normalization of Emirati diplomatic relations with Israel in 2020.[1] Within a few days of these announcements, the Emirati government had implemented laws prohibiting residents from posting criticism of the state's actions on social media platforms.

Given the (outwardly) mercurial nature of these policy shifts, many residents rarely offered direct, negative commentary about situations for fear of instigating trouble with the authorities or losing these residency privileges, resulting in what Nancy Demerdash has termed "an aesthetics of (self-) censorship and circumvention" (2017). The widespread publicization of instances of defamation and its extreme consequences, combined with the government's monitoring of social media, quite effectively engendered self-policing amongst residents at precisely the moment when a global contemporary art regime valued critical expression. Yet artists in the UAE were not—nor were they ever—silenced; their positions and critiques required more contextual knowledge and commitment to place to understand. Simultaneously, as the UAE inched toward inclusion in a global art world, artists based in the UAE were keenly aware of market metrics of success, which reconfigured different elements of their practice. One such metric was critique—in particular, critique of the state.

THREE

Con/Forming Critiques

THROUGHOUT MY FIELDWORK, I heard the term "critique" often from my interlocutors, who were artists, curators, gallerists, and arts organizers involved in the UAE's art scene. Critique encompasses a variety of meanings, but I use the term following my interlocutors' usage, to mean adopting a dissenting position on states, governments, religions, or the status quo. Scholars have analyzed the death of critique or a perceived attack upon it, both in the art world (Birnbaum and Graw 2008; Elkins and Newman 2008; Fraser and Rothman 2017) and in social theory more broadly (Boltanski and Chiapello 2005; Fassin 2017; Koch 2002; Latour 2004). The performance of critique is also subject to norms that privilege particular politics, as Sa'ed Atshan (2020) has shown. As my interlocutors used the term, however, critique denoted art criticism as well as political dissent, subversion, resistance, or opposition. They referenced the lack of critique both structurally (e.g., the absence of art critics) and socially, in the dominant language ideology, which eschewed dissent, criticism, critique, and negative speech. My interlocutors perceived critique to be explicitly political and subversive, often targeting the state. They also referred to critique to signal their knowledge of and adherence to a professional register and code of practice.

Interlocutors telegraphed these beliefs in everyday conversations. One evening, I attended a reading group at a local arts center. Alana, a visiting British artist, asked me for a ride home from the lecture. As we sped along on a huge highway back to our neighborhood after the lecture, I asked her about the commission she was working on, which would be exhibited at a commercial art fair and which had brought her to Dubai in the first place. She said, "I want this work to reflect on the politics here. So many people said to me, how can you go *there* to make art?" Alana noted she felt pressure to produce a suitably critical piece for the sake of her career broadly. She explained her idea for her work, which included a critique of Emirati government surveillance and the monitoring of speech and expression. Coming from another context, Alana chafed against the particular constrictions on expression in the UAE, which differed from the constrictions on expression she was used to at home. I could relate: When I first arrived in the country, I self-censored because I was not sure what I could say. I too had heard comments decrying the possibility of doing serious academic scholarship in the Gulf. For Alana, and for me, putting forth some kind of critique in our work seemed necessary to prove our politics and be taken seriously in our respective fields.

Artists' and curators' use of the term and its accompanying valences signified their participation in a transnational contemporary art market, wherein critique is highly valorized. In the mid-1980s, criticality emerged as a central hallmark of the prevailing art world definition of "real" (i.e., legitimate or authentic) contemporary art. Art historian David Joselit notes, "In the 1980s a new critical desideratum arose: to subvert . . . the locus of aesthetic value shifted from quality to criticality—from the 'good' to the 'subversive'" (Joselit 2017, 13).[1] Prominent international curators and gallerists privilege art that overtly challenges the status quo and offers a political, social critique. The oppositional or avant-gardist model is, most simply, a paradigm of the subversive or radical artist as critic, using their position to critique power, most often in the form of the state, capital, or religious authority. Especially for critics, curators, and funders within the Middle East region, the term "contemporary" in contemporary art "became synonymous with . . . politically subversive qualities" (Toukan 2021, 69). This definition of critique is deeply imbricated with the definition of what constitutes contemporary art. In essence, sociopolitical critiques have become a seminal component in contemporary art, a phenomenon derived from a liberal democratic social fabric that comes to stand in tension with the multeity of political forms in a globalized world. This tenet of contemporary art practice renders challenges for artists living in authoritarian regimes to gain legitimacy and remain safe from potential retribution.

Regardless of age or national affiliation, nearly all my interlocutors expressed that critique was an integral, and legitimating, feature of contemporary art. For their artwork to be recognized as good contemporary art, it needed to be conceptual and critical. They were also aware that certain forms of critique were prohibited by UAE law, which could therefore get one kicked out of the country.

The stakes for artists were high: Performing critique in the condoned way—that is, overtly and directly—legitimized artists in a global art scene and propelled their careers forward. My interlocutors believed that links to elite institutions can propel an artist's reputation forward and can spur success in the contemporary art world (Fraiberger et al. 2018). They also believed that the validation of inclusion at elite events, like the Venice Biennale, could catapult an artist's career, "speed[ing] up sales, get[ting] artistic careers going, crank[ing] up price levels and help[ing] artists land a dealer ranked higher in the market's hierarchy" in what is labeled "the Venice effect" (Velthuis 2011, 22).[2] One curator said to me, "We all know that once your work is in Venice [i.e., the Biennale], your price changes." My artist interlocutors balanced the stakes of global visibility alongside their own positionality, especially as citizens or noncitizens, or as ethnic, religious, or queer minorities in UAE society. In my interviews and observations with my artist interlocutors, they talked about how they navigated curatorial selection to gain recognition and advance their careers. For example, in the UAE, artists invited the curators who select the artists-in-residence for Art Dubai or the Sharjah Biennial—venues with much broader global visibility—to their shows at local art centers or for studio visits. Notably, Art Dubai and the Sharjah Biennial were commercial and noncommercial, respectively, but both were seen to have similar legitimizing potential. As Arlene Dávila has observed in her study of Latinx artists, "more and more POC artists must depend on galleries and markets to also validate their work, rather than the nonprofit institutions and museums that have historically opened the door" (2020, 116). I found similar beliefs among UAE-based artists of Middle Eastern, Iranian, or South Asian descent. Be it Art Dubai or the Sharjah Biennial, those opportunities in turn can put artists on the radar of influential international curators, or help them score a solo show or representation with one of the UAE's well-regarded galleries.

Curators have grown increasingly important; "the dominant role of the [art] critic . . . has been replaced by the curator who either works for a museum or is independently in charge of highly regarded exhibitions" (Velthuis 2005, 12).[3] In addition, "private collectors have allegedly come to influence the rise and fall of artistic careers" (Velthuis 2005, 12). Artists whose work does not meet the parameters of what these influential curators and collectors define as "real" art tend to disappear from public view—they are selected less frequently in open calls and are awarded fewer exhibitions or residencies. Gallery representation could be difficult to secure if gallerists did not deem artists' work attractive to collectors and key curators. Artists working elsewhere in the Arabic-speaking world also aspired to the recognition bestowed at these art events: Hanan Toukan quotes a Jordanian gallery director who noted that "every young artist from [the Arab region] feels the need to be acknowledged by the Emirates art market . . . to be invited to Sharjah [Biennial]" (2021, 101). These events, both commercial and noncommercial, afforded serious recognition and visibility for artists' careers.

Yet overt and political critique as a legitimating factor can pose barriers for artists living under regimes that punish criticism of the state, a phenomenon documented elsewhere as well. Ai Weiwei is perhaps the most well-known example of an overtly critical artist in exile. Chinese artists like him who demonstrated "bad boy political dissent" were often celebrated (Welland 2018, 7; see also Ho 2014, 195 on Hong Kong).[4] Furthermore, in international exhibitions, "expectations of explicitly dissident art had led to a neglect of Chinese conceptual art" (Wang 2014, 3). In the case of the Emirates, international art professionals expected artists to adopt an explicitly critical stance of the state's policies, in essence a kind of litmus test of an artist's politics and general support for human rights norms. After widely publicized incidents of censorship, such as the firing of Sharjah Biennial director Jack Persekian in 2011 and the 2015 denial of visas to scholar Andrew Ross and artist Ashok Sukumaran, international curators and organizers tended to ascribe legitimacy based on such performances of suitably liberal politics.[5] Among other topics, criticizing the Emirati royal families, certain governments including the UAE's, or Islam is forbidden by law in the UAE. Punishments for criticism and slander can include seven years of jail time, deportation and revocation of residency visas, or substantial fines.[6]

As discussed in the last chapter, gaining and maintaining residency privileges are perhaps more fraught in the UAE than many other places: An estimated 85 percent of the UAE's population is made up of noncitizens who depend on residency visas to live there. My interlocutors regularly shared instances of unanticipated deportations and visa refusals: One person was on vacation and only learned of his deportation when returning "home" and being denied entry at the airport; another interlocutor described pressure to prove he was a Sunni Muslim (rather than Shiʻi) to successfully renew his work visa. Performing critique, then, can have serious consequences. It can offer desirable visibility—and also undesirable exposure. To that end, all artists in this chapter, save Hassan Sharif (1951–2016), have been anonymized, given the topic. While I want to fully acknowledge the creative intellectual labor they undertake, I also take seriously the first tenent of the American Anthropological Association's Code of Ethics, "do no harm." Due to the anonymity, unfortunately I cannot share images of these works.

Artists based in the UAE were caught in a seeming double bind: If they did not make artwork that is legible as political critique to gain global market visibility, their residency privileges remained safe, yet their work was unlikely to be popular in a global art market. On the other hand, if they produced work that critiqued the state, they would likely garner the support and validation of an international art community, yet they might lose their ability to reside in the UAE. This chapter examines the ways that artists limned the double bind and managed these competing politics of aesthetic expression through a tactic I term "conspicuous omission." That is, they would create strategically legible gaps—they would leave something obvious out, communicating their message through absence rather than presence. Faced with market pressures and state constrictions, they remade critique to be more social, more contextual, and less absolute, even as they reproduced a framework of criticality as integral to contemporary art and seemed to favor market interests. Their iteration of critique offered a more expansive framework that accommodated a plethora of social contexts and politics, and shows how the imperative of market viability reshapes expression toward a more nuanced, perspective-based definition of critique.

In writing about the ambiguous forms critique takes, my goal is not to reproduce the dominant terms of a contemporary art world and assert critique as a necessary component of contemporary art, or to romanticize and retrieve some unknown underground resistance movement (Abu-Lughod 1990) by offering examples of these artists' work. Rather, I aim to examine the forms and forums in which critique was legible, and how artists navigated market visibility through forms of critique that are differentially recognized. Artists from the Global South transformed paradigms of what constituted good or real art—revealing how emergent scenes in illiberal contexts like those of the Emirates rewire norms in art worlds and the way tenets of legitimacy are kaleidoscopic, multiple, and perspective-based, rather than universal. The practice of conspicuous omission reveals the ways artists are rewriting what constitutes "good" art in a globalized form, and how critique can appear in ways legible to a global market while also remaining palatable in illiberal political contexts.

Optical Allusions: Visual Modes of Conspicuous Omission

Conspicuous is a key piece of this strategy. Conspicuous omission as a mode of critique relies on a shared understanding of what is conspicuous, or obvious—it therefore relies on a community of people and an understanding of shared knowledge. Conspicuous omission refers to the intentional creation of a structured absence, or lacuna; these artists critique through glaring omission rather than overt criticism or direct reference. Thus to understand the intended critiques, viewers must look at the gaps as well as what is formally presented. This tactic is deeply social because it relies on a shared knowledge community, which is inconstant, ever expanding and contracting, rather than explicit verbalized criteria. Conspicuous omission has parallels to other modes of deploying silences and gaps.

Others have noted the use of "strategic silence" to expedite cumbersome state bureaucratic processes (Lori 2019, 45); popular media has also tracked how Iraqi artists deployed silence as dissent (Abramian 2019). Alice Wilson described Omanis' use of euphemisms or "suggestive avoidance," such as non-participation in state celebrations, as modes of marking "silent disagreement" (Wilson 2023, 225–26). One of my interlocutors, Mai, explained that I should look for the absences or silences to find a critique. For example, Mai said, glancing quickly at what I was wearing, "I'd compliment your blouse and your shoes, but say nothing about your pants." Because the pants were the only item of clothing I was wearing that she had not referenced in her compliments, Mai singled them out. Conspicuous omission was a way that my interlocutors communicated critiques, but it did not conform to a mode of critique as direct and explicit.

I first noted—or, failed to note—conspicuous omission at a busy exhibition opening in Sharjah, held in a cavernous warehouse space. Against the back wall hung a series of six large prints. Each print had a series of colored, pixelated boxes on it, so they resembled a kind of palette—like the cubes of color on paint samples at the hardware store, or like the small color boxes adjacent to an item in advertising to denote different colors available. The pixelated blocks of color ranged from ceruleans and jades to chalky ochres. The work's title referenced the color of happiness, but the wall text did little to clarify. It read simply, "What happens when happiness gets color coded and commodified?" As I strolled past it, I did not understand what made the work worthy of inclusion. I had been in the UAE for six months at that point.

Four months after the opening, a number of interlocutors had recommended that I meet with Alaa, the artist behind the color block prints. Alaa was an Emirati citizen in her late thirties. During our first meeting at the art center where she had her studio, she mentioned the government preoccupation with becoming the happiest nation on earth. Several months prior, the UAE government announced an intention to become the happiest nation on earth (UAE Government 2016). Ohood Al Roumi was appointed Minister of Happiness, and the ministry undertook a number of initiatives with Orwellian names: Happiness and Positivity Councils, Customer Happiness Centers, and the Customer Happiness Formula. References to happiness had started appearing everywhere, especially affiliated with government ministries and agencies. For example, a mini survey popped up as one logged in to pay their electric bill: "How do you feel about today's process? Click the corresponding smiley face." Alaa sighed: "You have things like this happiness report [the government had released] . . . Am I happy because I got out of the [government office] in five minutes instead of two hours?" She expressed frustration with the definition of happiness as commodified and weaponized by the state, as well as attempts to brand Dubai with happiness. Alaa remarked, "I did a piece—looking at pictures, what does happy look like?" She then shared her process. Alaa had collected marketing materials for a series of government advertising campaigns around happiness and distilled the colors into palettes—one per advertising campaign.

The resulting work deployed a kind of visual conspicuous omission. Alaa used the marketing or consumer imagery of the color palette, which many would recognize from online shopping, and presented only blocks of color. She steered clear of using smiley faces or other iconic visual signs of happiness. She avoided using any visual, or textual, references to Dubai lest they be interpreted as critical speech. The piece thus visually referenced marketing and commodification, in its design, but avoided any iconic references to Dubai or to happiness. For the artist, the language of the work and the title would give it away—especially given the widespread campaigns for happiness all around us. The key part of conspicuous omission can best be framed as a question: conspicuous to whom?

In the UAE context, absence and ambiguity are generative—they can house critiques.[7] UAE-based artists intentionally craft lacunae—they conspicuously omit—and these conspicuous omissions should be understood as a technique of knowledge production and a mode of critique. Much like the discursive conspicuous omission I describe next, visually conspicuous omissions such as this work relied on social contextual knowledge to work. Those not steeped in the community and current events would not get the allusion and the critique. Similar to Oscar Ho's observations in Hong Kong, "artistic qualities are linked to socio-historical concerns that are generated by a specific time and context meaningful to their particular local community" (2014, 188). Paradoxically then, the performance of critique in the UAE art scene was contextual rather than universal, showing how the market consumed and produced diversity. My artist interlocutors maintained the importance of critique as a tenet of le-gitimate contemporary art, but they redefined how critique could appear and the politics it accommodated.

Mind the Gaps: Conspicuous Omission

Another instance showcases the collision of different modes of critique and reveals the tussles over performing—and recognizing—critique in different modes, and the social and textual forms of knowledge needed to make such distinctions. One afternoon, I began assisting Abdullah on materials for a show he was curating. Abdullah had generously allowed me to observe the show's process for my research in exchange for assistance producing the show's written materials. He had commissioned several local artists to pro-duce works, and I worked with the artists to produce the texts that would accompany their artworks. While offering English writing and editing skills was one way I could contribute something back to my interlocutors, I was also wary of my role in co-creating the text and the ethics of analyzing such a product. In this particular instance, I was more participant than observer.

One artist I was to work with was Mayyid, an artist in his early twenties who held Emirati citizenship. Mayyid shared a draft description of the art-work, with a note at the top: "Not sure if the description is any good." He had also annotated, "Maybe it should be more minimal." The description read:

> Have you ever wondered if your identity is influenced more by your genetics or your surroundings? [The artist] explores the difference between the two aspects of human development by using the different—sometimes false—interpretations of Islam through a daily performance where he reads and writes the Qur'an.

Reading this description, I had trouble imagining how we could make it any more sparse. I set up a meeting with Mayyid to discuss.

At a coffee shop near the gallery one afternoon, Mayyid described the performance piece he had planned: Each day, he would enter the gallery and transcribe a page of the Qur'an with his left hand. Mayyid had been punished for writing with it in school; his teachers believed that left-handedness was a sign of Satan, evil, and to be avoided. Yet for Mayyid, it seemed incongruous that Allah would make him left-handed, and then punish left-handedness; in a similar vein, the artist argued, any such instincts or predilections one was born with—including homosexuality—could not be evil because they were Allah's creation. Mayyid shared with me that he read his work as a critique of a certain reading of Islam, which was directly drawn from his identification as a gay man. It was not, he emphasized, anti-Islamic—rather, it was critical of selective *interpretations* of Islamic tenets. His work was about the ways in which different groups construed religious texts to condemn natural, inborn human behaviors.

As I worked with Abdullah and Mayyid to draft the text for the exhibition catalogue, we all agreed we needed to frame the work in such a way that Mayyid could not get in trouble for criticizing Islam, which is against UAE law, but where art audiences could still gather the critique. It was also necessary to avoid outing Mayyid, especially in a documentable way. While some things might be understood, Mayyid demurred, they were accepted socially only inasmuch as they were not spoken directly. My mind flashed to another conversation I had had with a gallerist who was upset that a journalist had specifically noted the gallery's lack of women artists on the roster. The information was public, the gallerist admitted, but calling attention to it as the journalist had done was a political—and critical—act. We did not have to deny Mayyid's sexuality, we just needed to avoid clarifying it in any particular direction.

After much deliberation back and forth on Google Docs, we crafted a careful summary of the project. We shifted from "development" to "personal identity" because the latter lacked the valences of teleology or evaluative judgment. Instead of using the second person "you," we opted for the impersonal "one." We preserved "explore" and "investigate" because they were ambiguous and noncommittal, rather than offering a definitive answer or argument. Rather than discuss sexuality outright, and potentially subject Mayyid to legal or social fallout, the text carried no mention of it. The text we collectively produced read:

> [The artist] draws inspiration for this work from his curiosity about the ways personal identity is formed. While engaging with the question of whether one's sense of self is shaped to a greater extent by genetics or experience, he explores the differences in human development arising from varying—and sometimes false—interpretations of Islam. He will carry out this investigation through a daily performance in which he reads and writes passages from the Qur'an.

The underlying themes of Mayyid's work remained in this description: identity formation, interpretations of the Qur'an, and genetics versus experience (a reframing of genetics versus surroundings, or nature versus nurture). We preserved Mayyid's original text alluding to false interpretations of Islam because it is vague—as in, it does not specify *which* interpretations might be false. Yet the relationship between left-handedness and homosexuality was not articulated or rendered explicit, in order to protect the artist. The title of the work contained the word "left" in it—for Mayyid, this was the flag, or conspicuous clue—as most of the long-term UAE resident community would understand religious proscriptions against writing left-handed, especially writing the Qur'an.

On opening night, the gallery felt spacious. The works were separated by fair amounts of open space, and they sat in the glowing orbs of their own individual spotlights. That meant the rest of the large, white-walled gallery was bathed in indirect light, which was pleasant after the bright, bleaching heat of June outside. Held during Ramadan, the opening started to get crowded about an hour after Iftar, when Muslims broke their fast.

As I was chatting with two of the artists and swirling a fruit juice in a plastic cup, a colleague came and joined our group. Sabine self-identified as an artist, but she had made some unfortunately direct comments that ruffled feathers amongst the longer-term UAE artist community and at times had expressed difficulty viewing things from a non-European perspective.

Accordingly, many of my interlocutors assiduously avoided her. She pulled me aside, her chin down and her eyes askance: "This is not art. These are just things. I don't know what they mean."

I took Sabine by the elbow and turned to the artists: "Mayyid, let's go look at your work, can you tell Sabine about it?" After we spoke with Mayyid, I guided Sabine to a few other artists and asked them to speak with her about their work. A short while later, after chatting with some other colleagues, Sabine approached me before she left the opening: "I just did not understand the concept of what they were trying to do, and the catalogue wasn't clear either. Thank you for explaining—the works make a lot more sense now."

Sabine's response reveals a few things. First, her comments reveal the rubric by which she legitimizes art as good or real art, or not-art. In this paradigm of contemporary art, it must be conceptual, critical; it needs to "say something" or to offer some social critique. While she was not an international curator coming to evaluate artists, she was active in the UAE art scene and her mindset reflected prevalent frameworks of artistic legitimacy by which visiting curators and patrons evaluated UAE-based artists. Second, in fairness to Sabine, she was not the intended audience of Mayyid's work. But her quick dismissal of what was, or was not, real art echoed the kinds of judgments often made by curators and gallerists who did not have a local frame of reference. Because Sabine could not read the critiques in these artworks, and in particular did not have the contextual knowledge to read the conspicuous omission as such, she had initially dismissed their legitimacy. Finally, Sabine did not recognize that the catalogue being "unclear" was intentional, and her comment had in fact caused the curator and me to sigh in relief, as it signaled our attempts to camouflage the critique had been successful.

Mayyid came to the free, public gallery every day throughout the run of the exhibition. Because he did not announce in advance when he would arrive to perform, some of his performances were unattended. Sometimes visitors just saw someone sitting and writing in the gallery and were likely unaware that it was a performance. Yet Mayyid performed daily, and did not hide. He attended the opening and spoke to visitors about his work. Thus in some ways, his work was very public, but the critical component of the work was communicated orally and never recorded in writing or otherwise documented. The word "left" in the title pointed to this critique, albeit obliquely. Mayyid therefore circumscribed the audience for the piece; while technically public, only people who visited the opening and spoke with him would understand the intended critical valences of his work, and he ensured that there was no text or recording that could circulate and expose his critique to authorities who might intervene. In this way, Mayyid offered a critique of some interpretations of Islam by flagging left-handedness, but drew strategically on ambiguity and indirectness in doing so in order to protect himself from potential legal action.

The modes in which Mayyid made that intent explicit were intentionally limited, undocumented, and ephemeral. This mode also offered plausible deniability, as Mayyid could deny criticizing Islam and there would be no evidence to rebut this claim. Yet while this strategy would protect artists like Mayyid at home, as a fellow artist was quick to point out, it can also render the work of these artists unintelligible abroad if international audiences do not see these works' criticality, which is seminal to their being designated and seen as contemporary art. In this way, paradoxically, protecting artists at home to support their careers can stunt those careers internationally—even as there is more focus on achieving transnational visibility and adhering to a market push for a particular version of critique.

Because art allows for flexible expression and multiple interpretations, and can avoid textual or explicit critiques, it becomes a rare space for critical expression in the UAE. When artists do share the omitted link, they can also do so in undocumented ways to protect themselves. Conspicuous omission requires contextual knowledge of the politics in a particular sphere, which circumscribes the audience and therein limits the legibility of artworks and the visibility of their makers in a global contemporary art world. As such it is a deeply social mode of critique. The practice of conspicuous omission did not deny critique as a tenet of art, but artists rewired how it appeared.

Alana, whose proposed work would have focused on Emirati government surveillance as described at the beginning of the chapter, discovered the deeply social nature of expression in the UAE, coming up against the etiquette for how to express critique. About a week after I had given her a ride home, I learned through another artist that Alana had to change her project. The next time we rode home together, I asked Alana about it. She explained how her idea for her work was not received well by the other artists and curators at the art center where she was working. In the passenger seat, Alana nervously toyed with her long wavy hair. The curator in charge told her to come up with a new one for the commission. Now, she recounted, she needed to come up with and develop another art piece quickly in order to have it finalized by the time the commission would be exhibited. Time was running out. Ultimately

Alana did produce a work for the fair, but it did not address issues of surveillance or of the government at all. She mused whether or not she would include the work in her portfolio.

The topic of Alana's first project came up in discussions with another artist, Maha, who had also been commissioned to make a work for the same fair organizer. We sat on the veranda of a shisha café, and Maha's eyes flashed with frustration immediately when we began to talk about it. "You don't think it's been done before? You don't think it's arrogant to come in and say, this is the most significant place to do it? . . . You can't say, I have the better point of view because I'm from out there," Maha stated, emphatically exhaling the smoke from her apple shisha into the warm spring air. Having long resided in the Emirates, Maha had grown tired of the media portrayal of the UAE as a place where making art was not possible because of government clampdowns on speech, and tired of outsiders with minimal knowledge of local politics asserting what it was like to live and work there as an artist.

She continued, "I was in the meeting where Alana was being told, change the wording of it so it doesn't come across as what it is." Maha noted that the framing was essential: One way of managing the politics of expression in the UAE was to avoid being explicit. It was not that you couldn't do things, she explained, it was that you had to frame it benignly to simultaneously protect yourself and for the art audience to get it. Based on my conversation with Alana, she appeared not to have understood this as an option. Maha emphasized that if Alana had omitted the explicit critique of the state in her framing of the project, she could have still performed the work as planned. At issue was more that Alana, as an outsider, did not understand why this omission was necessary, or that conspicuous omission—the practice of creating a gap that was strategically legible as such—could function as a mode of critique.

In Maha's recounting, Alana's peers first asked her to conspicuously omit elements of her project—namely removing the explicit reference to Emirati government surveillance—so it would appear benign, linguistically shielding herself and anyone else captured on the surveillance. In addition, they were frustrated that Alana, who was not a resident of the UAE and whose Western passport meant she was not subject to potential damages that those with precarious residency privileges remaining in the country might be, did not seem to be aware of the potential fallout for others. As Maha intimated, the consequences for UAE residents who would be on the recording could be serious (e.g., deportation and banishment) in ways that Alana hadn't considered, because she was unfamiliar with the country. One's social position, then, also influenced what they could express. Those more familiar with the political realities of the UAE were frustrated at Alana's seemingly careless endangerment of them and their colleagues. While they may have agreed with her opinions or even liked the proposed concept, her work was explicitly political in a way that her fellow artists deemed unacceptable. They thus blocked her project, deploying their leverage as locals to protect their community. Because Alana did not share the communal understanding of how to express critique, her project did not come to fruition as she hoped. The tensions between Alana and Maha highlight both how artists, curators, and observers who do not know the UAE's language ideology and context can fail to read critique because it doesn't appear in a particular register, and also the shared knowledge required for conspicuous omission to work.

These examples also show how curators and organizers hold artists to particular standards of what their work can speak to and about—and how the political requirements for artists that are defined by their perceived origins. For example, in her study of Latinx artists, Arlene Dávila observed that many gallerists often viewed Latinx art as "too political to be commercially viable . . . too representational and lacking intellectual rigor, or too ethnic identified" (2020, 149). These tropes that Latinx art was always already "politically radioactive" and must be commentary on U.S. racial politics influenced how these artists' works and positions were read (Dávila 2020, 149). Similarly, in the UAE, artists experienced pressure to be visibly against Gulf labor policies and thereby demonstrate suitably liberal politics.

This instance also complicates ideas of censorship that are often top-down, rather than peer-to-peer; censorship is not a hegemonic practice. Alana's fellow resident artists laid out for her the limits of expression—the requested changes were not due to direct government oversight or top-down censorship. Community members transmitted to one another the limits of what could and could not be expressed against the specter of potential state retribution. They also argued that this preference for oblique or indirect speech was not censorship, which is often a practice focused on shaping knowledge in a particular way (Boyer 2003), preventing knowledge from being transmitted (Gill 2017), or on circumventing the dangers between mass affect and collective meaning (Mazzarella 2013). Conspicuous omission, rather, was a mode of critique employed to maintain safe and polite social interactions and still communicate a negative opinion, a way to harmonize market requirements with the realities of transnational migration regimes. The strategy of conspicuous omission has emerged to accommodate the shifting parameters of politicized expression after the Emirates' 1971 unification. This practice of performing critique was part of the disciplining of artistic knowledge and practice as the Emirates moved toward its perceived entrée to the world art scene.

Critique as Visibility, Critique as Refusal

While perhaps we can read these artists' strategic choices as a validation of the dominant definition of contemporary art as that which is politically critical or offers a critique, and thus a reproduction of that paradigm of art, these choices can also be read as a refusal of another key art world tenet that is perhaps taken for granted: that widespread visibility is desirable. Such an idea is hard to square with market logics of visibility and the increasing primary status of commerce in the global contemporary art world. But in spaces where visibility means exposure, one might ask, what is the vulnerability of visibility? Refusals can be crucially informative: "Rather than stops, or impediments to knowing, those limits may be expansive in their ethnographic nonrendering *and in what they do not tell us*" (Simpson 2014, 113). Sometimes the point is not for everyone to understand it. Sometimes the opacity is the point, to borrow a concept from Edouard Glissant (1997); sometimes the goal is to elude the grasp of appropriation.

By limiting audiences, artists can avoid the push to translate their work into the registers and codified modes stipulated by transnational elite institutions and exhibitions, and they can communicate with communities they desire to interact with. In doing so, they assert the importance of context and the local. Moreover, in the UAE, they can safeguard precarious residency situations.[8] These artists' choices to circumscribe their audiences is a kind of refusal, one that ostensibly stands in tension with art market values of exposure and access to a wider global contemporary art world. UAE-based artists limit their audiences by avoiding explicit documentation or references to the critique in the texts accompanying the work, or by performing or exhibiting in venues to which they control access. They thus limit the legibility of their critique—even as they reproduce the idea that critique is a legitimizing factor for contemporary art and acknowledge that critique furthers the recognition of global elites and achieving art market success.

In addition to such molding of the content of contemporary art and supporting the rise of a decolonized, contextually informed understanding of politics, my interlocutors also had ideas about aesthetics and appearances. Specifically, they had conceptions of what art should look like, how it should be displayed, and how "professional" artists should comport themselves in order to achieve success. One definition of success included having one's work exhibited at major commercial art fairs, such as Art Dubai, another way the market exhibitionary complex reorganized art worlds.

IN THE GALLERY IV   Art Dubai

ART DUBAI WAS AN ANCHOR event in what my interlocutors termed "March Madness" (like, but distinctly different from, the NBA March Madness in the United States). Every year, March witnessed the confluence of Art Dubai's commercial art fair, Sikka Art Fair for emerging artists, the academic-style symposium of March Meeting, and the Sharjah Biennial. Every UAE-based gallery and art center had a new show bespoke for the month, to put their best foot forward. And being seen at the posh openings for these events was an important way of asserting or maintaining one's status as a key player in the UAE's art world.

A curator friend, Corinne, texted me she had a VVIP pass plus-one for Art Dubai. A VVIP pass—very very important person pass—meant we could get in before the fair opened to the public on Wednesday and tour the fair with the important collectors who got the first chance to buy. As we got closer to Madinat Jumeirah, the blue and white stripes of the famous Burj al-Arab grew bigger in the car window. We arrived at 4 p.m., pulling into the small roundabout off busy Umm Suqeim Street and showing our passes to security. Passing under the intricate arches with Islamic star motifs outlined in the molding, we noticed on our right the white wall was emblazoned with a list of all 2017 Art Dubai participants, establishing a rather blatant "who's who."

While Corinne wanted to check out all of the galleries' stalls, she was especially interested in seeing the Abraaj Art Prize show and a special pop-up called *Homage without an Homage*. Winning the Abraaj Prize was a significant achievement, crowning an artist as both a significant contemporary artist and an artist worth collecting, partly because it represented validation from the curator as well as the members of the selecting jury. The prize also promoted the fair's then-sponsor, the equity firm Abraaj Holdings. Such visual arts awards have become tools of corporate culture diplomacy. As Chin-Tao Wu has noted, art prizes "become a most valuable promotional vehicle [for multinationals in search of national and global market domination]" (2002, 161). Such prizes also whitewash artists: For example, gallerists and curators could position artists "in more 'universal' ways, avoiding any mention of their backgrounds or histories . . . highlighting anything that is 'achievement based,' such as fellowships and prizes, or else that is global, such as international residences or exhibitions" (Dávila 2020, 147).

Artnet described the Abraaj Prize as "the most significant art prize in the Middle East, North Africa, and South Asia" (Buffenstein 2016)—and not only because the winner received $100,000. Winning such a prize threw an artist into the orbit of important curators and collectors, generating significant visibility for the artist (and linking the Abraaj firm to cultural elites). Omar Berrada, director of Dar al-Ma'mun in Marrakesh and former curator of public programs at the Centre Pompidou in Paris, curated the 2017 edition of the Abraaj Prize show, which featured the winner of the prize and the runners-up. The jury included Hans Ulrich Obrist of London's Serpentine Gallery; patron Dana Farouki; Antonia Carver, former director of Art Dubai; and Defne Ayas, Director and Curator of the Witte de With Center for Contemporary Art (now Kunstinstituut Melly), among others. Of the more than three hundred proposals submitted by artists, Berrada and the jury selected Rana Begum as winner and short-listed three artists, Sarah Abu Abdullah, Doa Aly, and Raha Raissnia. Further contributing to the show's gravitas, Sternberg Press published a catalogue of the show. Begum was to debut the work commissioned for the fair later that night, so we would have to wait to see her work. After browsing the Abraaj show, *Seepage/Ritual*, Corinne and I visited the gallery stalls and *Homage without an Homage*.

The wide hall of the conference center hosted an info desk, a shop, and a number of plush beige leather benches. We went to the first hall. The room was cavernous, with a dark ceiling rising above the white cubicle stalls allotted to each gallery. In the busy halls, we did more people-watching than art evaluating, at first. There were many well-heeled visitors in sharply ironed suits and *khandūras*, and one woman wore a gold chiffon ball gown.

Corinne and I wandered around the grid of booths, and she graciously indulged my focus on UAE-based galleries. At one, she noted the artist's name and said, "That's an interesting choice. Usually galleries choose their best or most exciting artists to represent at fairs." It did not take much contextual knowledge to recognize that comment as a critique of that artist. Perusing the works in Gallery IVDE's area, I recognized the artists immediately. Vikram Divecha's series hung on the back wall, a series of abstract works that featured road textures, one a gray rectangle with a thick stripe of bubbling yellow rubber banded across it. Three works by Mohamed Kazem hung nearby, all beginning in solid black at the top of the painting and dissipating slowly into white by the bottom, the thick strands of color filtering down into tiny threads. A large rope sculpture by Hassan Sharif hung in the center of the booth: giant tassels of beige rope braided together, stretching from the ceiling to curl in piles on the floor. Another gallery showed an aerial, sepia map of a city split by a wide, curving river, the map constructed by individual photo tiles arranged on a wall. Elsewhere, five works by noted Saudi artist Ahmed Mater were on display, long rectangular strips of film with watercolor-like patterns in black and white in blonde wood frames. One booth deviated from the white cube pattern, the walls painted with leafy branches of rose bushes stretching upward, and ceramic vases interspersed onto wall mounts that blended in with the roses. Nearly all the works were "art fair art"— they were suitable for display in homes or businesses and were aesthetically pleasing or interesting, rather than engaging with troubling themes like war, poverty, or disease. They were also made at a domestic scale. There were a few pieces of institutional scale, either in size or in medium. One of the more striking pieces was a metal sculpture, several droplets of a silvery metal flying and folding as if they were water splashing, one curving upward from the floor, another scooping down suspended from the ceiling to meet it, other frozen splashes of metallic liquid hanging above from the ceiling. "Who would buy this?" I asked Corinne. "An institution," she said. This piece in particular seemed an unlikely acquisition by anyone except an institution or the ultrarich—only they would have the space and resources to install such a work with so many suspended parts.

After touring the first hall, Corinne and I wandered over to check out the *Homage* show, one of the fair's noncommercial initiatives. Sponsored by the Swiss investment firm Julius Bär, the show was curated by Dubai-based artist Cristiana de Marchi. *Homage* occupied a relatively small freestanding building in the courtyard, filled with plush seating, with the art hung on the walls or as centerpieces. The space gave off a very posh vibe. Upon entering the lounge, the visitor saw a large mirror emblazoned with acrylic labels, which read from top to bottom: Julius Bär, *Homage without an Homage*, a listing of the participating artists, and Curated by Cristiana de Marchi. Mohamed Kazem's work, a listing of coordinates, shrink-wrapped the windows. The simple white brick walls bore Salwa Zeidan's painting and art objects by Mohamed Ahmed Ibrahim, as well as a large flat-screen TV playing the video work *Foolad*, created by Hesam Rahmanian, Ramin Haerizadeh, and Rokni Haerizadeh. Metal sculptures by Layla Juma and Shaikha Al Mazrou sat installed on low plinths. The show's physical space differentiated it from a commercial gallery stall at the fair, but it was not quite so formal as a museum display. The lounge atmosphere, including waitstaff in white button-downs, black vests, and neckerchiefs, as well as plush couches, gave off a leisurely feel, an interesting mix of a curated museum gallery cut with decidedly commercial elements.

Afterward, Corinne and I retired to the Abraaj Lounge. The Lounge opened onto a private seating area, including some risers leading down toward the canal that wends through the bigger Madinat Jumeirah complex. As we chatted, dusk fell and the lounge patio became more and more crowded; soon we were moving purses from seats to make more space for neighbors. Corinne, who had been texting, looked up at me: "Can I borrow your pass?" She was going to use it to get her boss in. These small favors were the currency of the fair: Everyone in the UAE's art scene wanted to get into the Abraaj Lounge, and few locals got VVIP passes because they were typically reserved for wealthy collectors. Being seen in the Lounge indicated your status: You were important, you knew people.

Around 7 p.m., spotlights cranked on, illuminating an area next to the canal where something bulky and pointy was covered in white plastic. A man in a crisp suit with a microphone called our attention: "We are gathered here to see the unveiling of Rana Begum's work." After some theatrics, the cover was removed to much applause: A series of large transparent plastic triangles of various colors were arranged in rows, creating staggered ridges of kaleidoscopic, overlapping smaller triangles. The reveal concluded, the conversation grew louder as clumps of visitors continued their banter in the gloaming. The Lounge area was filled with stylishly dressed patrons: lots of asymmetrical, loose blouses or oversize blazers; asymmetrical haircuts; loafers; winged eyeliner; bold lipstick; and designer handbags. I was reminded of a gallerist interlocutor's comment: Clarissa had said, "A certain look is king in the contemporary art world. Contemporary art is cool, intellectual, stylish, and it's expensive." She was right—as I mentally clicked through the display spaces I had seen, the successful ones all looked similar: sparse, uncluttered displays in a white cube style. Even the displays at Dubai's affordable art fair, World Art Dubai, mimicked the same pattern (Figure G4.1).

We sat for a while—a gallerist acquaintance, Anya, joined us, and we began to discuss her career plans: She wanted to transition from gallery to noncommercial work. Many of my interlocutors moved between commercial and noncommercial arts organizations. Corinne herself had worked at two commercial galleries before shifting into a curatorial role; another interlocutor had worked at Abu Dhabi's cultural authority before moving to a commercial gallery complex. Yet another worked for a major museum before going to a commercial gallery. As described in Chapter 1, commercial and noncommercial were two sides of the same coin, in many ways, not easily parsed. Another outcome of the integration of commerce and noncommercial institutions was visible in aesthetics and displays, and in particular, the way that professionalism was constructed.

FIGURE G4.1. Photograph of World Art Dubai, the affordable art fair, in 2020. Photo by Arnold O. A. Pinto (Shutterstock).

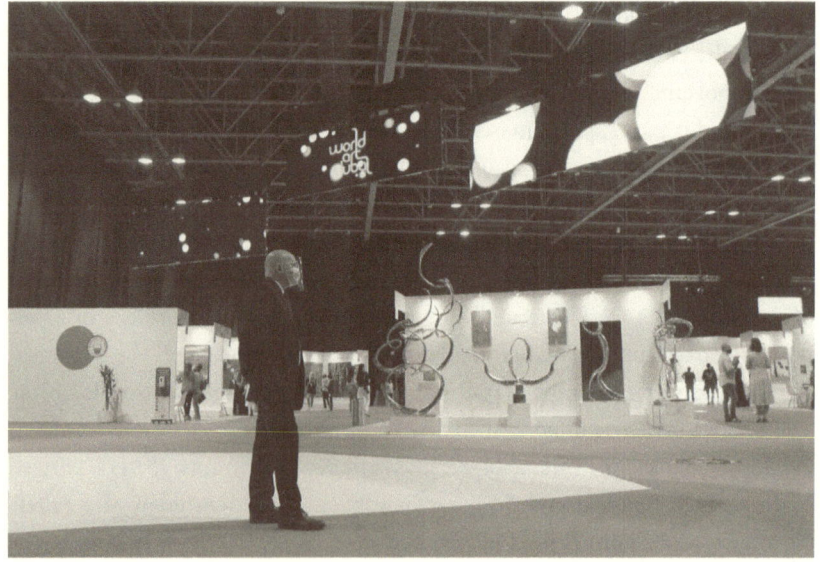

FOUR

Cultivating the Aesthetic Grammar of Professionalism

OVER THE COURSE OF MY FIELDWORK, I came to understand that my interlocutors used the adjective "professional" to index a linguistic register, a set of embodied practices, and adherence to a set of visual principles. They also rarely used "professional" as a noun (as in, "he is a professional"). Paying attention to "the qualities inhering in things gives us a way to think about how a variety of seemingly unrelated objects can be united into a coherent style—an aesthetic" (Fehérváry 2013, 8). Several of these qualities, cumulatively, forge a broader aesthetic that my interlocutors referred to as professional. One of these qualities was the white cube display style, another was the medium of the artworks on display, and yet another was the amount and type of information provided with the work.

Professional designated not just one facet or quality, but a series of them that together coalesced into an aesthetic. For example, when I ran into Carolina, a Spanish artist, at Dar al Funoon art center in Sharjah one June afternoon, she was dropping off two works that would be included in Dar al Funoon's summer exhibition. As we briefly caught up, standing in the air-conditioned corridor, Carolina leaned forward. "It's so different than the other place," she whispered, referring to her prior residency at another arts center, where we had initially met, and then paused. "It's so *professional* here. They did a condition report of my work when I dropped it off, and they asked for high-res images of them to put in the catalogue and in marketing materials. And all a month before the show, not at the last minute. It is so nice!"

In this chapter, I analyze the aesthetic grammar of professionalism—the rules for behaviors, appearances and display styles, words, and practices that instantiated professionalism—as these rules were taught through courses for artists and collectors. Texts, vocabulary, and practices, alongside material and sensory qualia, were also part of conveying the aesthetic of professionalism.[1] Clarissa's comment that "a certain look" was central in the contemporary art world, for example, included display styles—but it also included how much and what kind of information was presented with works, and what tone the words used conveyed. Visual style was decidedly central, but it was one component of a broader set of practices and qualities that contributed to the overall aesthetic. I refer to this expanded repertoire, including material and sensory qualia, texts, vocabulary, and embodied practices, as an aesthetic grammar to emphasize both the visual and linguistic components; the term "grammar" captures the concept of a system that one uses in order to make oneself legible to others but also the ways small errors in following the rules may impede total success or legibility without fully failing it. Hence while someone might adhere to the majority but not all of these principles, they would likely still come across as professional. This aesthetic grammar constituted a linguistic register and dispassionate mode of self-presentation for artists, art spaces arranged in a particular way, and knowledge of protocols and a codified set of visual practices for collectors.

These components of presentation were also interlinked; an artist's behavior and self-presentation informed how their work was perceived, just as the art's textual and verbal presentation were also integral to its reception. As Fred Myers established, "[art] criticism is not *external* to the aesthetic significance of objects" (1994, 11). The same goes for exhibition and auction catalogs: As Mukti Khaire and R. Daniel Wadhwani point out, auction catalogs "hel[p] translate aesthetic value into economic value" (2010, 1294). Isabelle Graw refers to the "market of knowledge" (2009), summarized as "the range of symbolic and prestige-giving institutions and publications that help position artists as 'priceless'" (Dávila 2020, 18). The texts that go with a work, such as with Mayyid's in Chapter 3, are seminal to its interpretation and reception. Not only were artists and collectors encouraged to become proficient in particular registers of professionalized vocabulary—that is, the content of the text—they were also taught to appreciate the visual appearance of the text. The concept of language materiality refers to how "the material aspect of language as a medium may matter to what it is, does, and means" (Cavanaugh and Shankar 2017, 4). Language materiality is critical in the visual-centric context of the contemporary art world, so I also pay attention to the aesthetic appearance of texts, including elements like font or typeface, color, and design.

Alongside adroit performance of critique, the mastery of the aesthetic grammar allowed artists to achieve status and visibility on the international art market, assimilating different backgrounds and subsuming difference for universal consumption. In essence, adherence to and performance of the aesthetic grammar sanitized difference to appeal to a broad market. The visual styles and language cultivated through these practices mimicked those used by international curators who visited the UAE during March's fair season. The aesthetic grammar defined by the art world as "professionalism" is also correlated to the changed relationship and significance of the commercial. Given that the prevailing relationship of museums and art to power is now via capital rather than the nation, capital and the commercial are also central to artists' subjectivities in new and emerging ways across contexts (Buchholz 2022; Chumley 2016; Gerber 2017; Menger 2014; Relyea 2013; Robinson and Novak-Leonard 2021; Win 2014). Adroit performance of the aesthetic grammar of professionalism also allowed fluid transitions between commercial and noncommercial spaces, which were often all white cube spaces. The "professional" aesthetic is representative of and contributes to an increased blurring of the commercial and noncommercial, facilitating the transfer between spaces and reinforcing the primacy of the commercial in the era of the market exhibitionary complex.

My interlocutors applied the term "professional" not just to galleries but also to noncommercial spaces. The widespread usage of the term highlights the creeping enmeshment of the commercial into everyday work in the field and into the habitus of artists. The term also focuses attention on artists who made a living through their art, rather than pursuing art as a hobby or side endeavor (Chumley 2016; Gerber 2017; Menger 2014; Win 2014), and on the adoption of certain codes of behavior to achieve validation within a given industry, or "professional vision" (Goodwin 1994; see also McElhinny 2010). Through conversations, interviews, and exhibition visits with my interlocutors, I learned that the designation of "professional" was an important tool for making hierarchies among exhibitions, venues, and artists, and it was a mode of establishing the UAE scene's legitimacy in a global art scene. Parallel concerted efforts to address issues of standards and quality have emerged elsewhere: in the contemporary art scenes in Egypt (Winegar 2006), China (Welland 2018), and the U.S. (Gerber 2017; Win 2014). Historically, the post–World War II art boom in the U.S. led to concerns about "a lowering of standards, a decline of expertise, and a loss of status" (Guilbault 1983, 92). In U.S. museums in the 1990s, curators "used 'professional' to refer to the careful adherence to specific art historical standards," whereas "professionalization" meant "the introduction of outsiders who specialized in fields other than art history" (Alexander 1996, 101).

In what follows, I detail how artists and collectors learned and were socialized into the aesthetic grammar of professionalism, following the artwork from the artist's studio through a display space and through the eyes of prospective collectors. Their mastery of this aesthetic regime was manifest in market success: For artists in particular, selling works meant the ability and time to produce more. The stakes were high. My interlocutors were keenly aware that they were, in many cases, building networks, and were doing so with the explicit intent of merging with an international global art world. Therefore, they needed to approach certain processes in the same way, to ease transactions with that global art world to minimize friction (Tsing 2005) and maximize flow, so often cited as a metric of neoliberal globalization (Appadurai 1990). Yet minimizing friction often entailed minimizing difference, standardizing in pursuit of enhancing flow. To achieve this flow, curators, gallerists, auction staff, and funders cultivated and reinforced this aesthetic grammar of "professionalism" in a number of ways, including through a class on professional practice for artists.

Professional(izing) Practices: Shaping Artists' Behavior and Self-Presentation

Stepping inside the tinted glass doors into Riwaq Art Center, I blinked and paused for a moment, allowing my eyes to adjust from the unrelenting sunshine outside, before passing into the spacious kitchen bursting with greenery. Riwaq was fairly well respected by artists, although better known by long-term residents than by shorter-term residents, perhaps because of its location in an Emirati residential area rather than in a trendy industrial neighborhood. In addition to studio space, Riwaq offered courses for artists and held rotating exhibitions.

Sitting down at the long wooden kitchen table, Anna, Rashid, and I began discussing a course Rashid would soon teach for the center, entitled

Professional Practice. Anna, the programs director at Riwaq, served us scalding espresso in small, traditional Arabic coffee cups, and we talked through the course syllabus and allocated roles: Riwaq had contracted Rashid, a North American curator of Arab heritage who had previously worked in one of Dubai's most prestigious contemporary art galleries, to run the course. I would sit in as Riwaq's liaison, reporting needs or concerns back to Anna in exchange for attending the class for my research.[2] The goal of the course was to train artists on how to present themselves professionally; Anna had designed the course to address areas where she felt artists needed to level up. Rashid had worked for several important galleries and art institutions, both commercial and nonprofit, across the Gulf region in the last five years and thus had a range of experience. Noting practices like the display of price tags next to artwork or a lack of artists' statements, Anna said, "Some of this stuff just has to be cleaned up if we want to be professional." Anna used "we" to mean the UAE's art scene, showing how arts staff often expressed a collective ownership—and a collective direction—for the arts scene in the UAE. Being professional, for Anna, meant attaining a certain look, but it was also behaviors and display practices. The Professional Practice class met weekly for three months, covering different aspects of professionalization for emerging artists, including writing artist statements and bios, cataloguing artwork (including condition reports and photo documentation), invoicing and managing contracts for commissions and galleries, creating certificates of authenticity, applying for residencies and other open call programs, managing one's social media presence as an artist, and understanding basic exhibition design to work effectively with curators. Riwaq billed it as a workshop series devoted to practical skills for artists. It was, then, a course on "theories, artifacts and bodies of expertise that distinguish[ed]" contemporary art "from other professions" (Goodwin 1994, 606).

Dressed in a smart button-down shirt, suit pants, and brown leather lace-up breaker boots with impeccably round Parisian glasses, Rashid looked perfectly at ease in the contemporary art space in which we were meeting. He laughed: "My pet peeve is the 'I'm so passionate about art' sentence in the artist's statement. Can we please get rid of that?" Anna chuckled in agreement. This distinction between passion and professionalism also has lengthy historical roots in the art realm. Serge Guilbault notes that in 1947, critics like the influential Clement Greenberg were stressing that "pure expressionism was to be avoided; paroxysm and romanticism were

very grave dangers that threatened the development of avant-garde painting" (Guilbault 1983, 161). The excision of emotion has long been a means of
separating "high" art from hobby, part of the work of making art a form of
"serious" labor.

Rashid did in fact do his best to eradicate passion language from the students' writing throughout the course, and indeed, linguistic self-presentation was an important component of being a professional artist. In an email
a week prior to the first session, Rashid asked participants to bring drafts of
their artist bios and statements, if they had them, to the initial class. On the
first evening, the twelve attendees trickled into the classroom, filling the seats
at the back of the long table first. After presenting the premise of the course
and inviting each student-artist to introduce themselves, Rashid told them I
was a visiting researcher and explained how I would observe the course. We
paused to answer questions and ensure their consent before continuing on.
Other than his own presence, one major way that Rashid communicated a
professional contemporary art aesthetic was through the images and words he
showed and the tone of those words that he used.

Rashid styled the appearance of his words to align with the aesthetic he
cultivated, reflecting an adherence to typeface ideology. Typeface ideology
refers to the idea that "certain *kinds* or genres of discourse and the particular
text forms that give literal shape to those discourses should semiotically align
in some recognizably suitable way" (Murphy 2017, 65). The aesthetic qualia
of typeface—size, weight (thick or thin), kerning (spacing between letters),
style, and color—"can become critical sources of meaning and sites for cultural intervention" (Murphy 2017, 69). In essence, the appearance of texts in a
display contributes to how viewers interpret them and how the exhibit's visual
aesthetic coalesces. Text displays with artworks, including the tone of the
words chosen, were a key way to create an aesthetic. One artist who was also
a graphic designer, Najla, noted to me that she read Papyrus fonts and dark
red text as distinctly Orientalist aesthetic markers. In contrast, the aesthetics
of the text Rashid shared consistently aligned with the clean, serious fonts of
contemporary art establishments.

Rashid flicked through clean navy slides with an elegant white serif font
(Georgia) that explained how to write artist bios, noting, "These should be in
the third person and give the reader a brief snapshot of who you are." As an
example, he showed the bio of the artist Hayv Kahraman, who is well known
in Middle East art circles and represented by one of Dubai's well-regarded

galleries, The Third Line. The otherwise empty blue slide had the following text perfectly centered:

> Hayv Kahraman's practice pulls on her personal experiences of migration to Europe (and then the United States) to create paintings, drawings, objects and performances. Her work engages the viewer, utilizing elements of Japanese style calligraphy, Italian Renaissance painting and illuminated Arab manuscripts to reflect on the placelessness and experience of diaspora, engaging aesthetic notions and codes of beauty to depict often psychologically brutal subjects. By developing a vocabulary of narrative and exploration the artist tries to contest and renegotiate boundaries found in the social and political third space between Western and Middle Eastern culture.
> *Bio courtesy of the Third Line, Dubai.*

Rashid emphasized that Kahraman's bio referenced three distinctive aesthetic influences, the different media in which she works, and a central conceptual issue: that of the diaspora and "space[s] between Western and Middle Eastern culture." The artist bio, Rashid instructed, should be three to four sentences maximum, and sharply focused on medium, influences or visual styles, and conceptual questions. Notably, these bios displayed no affective language. Even words like "brutal" were paired with terms like "psychologically" to sound more clinical and objective.

Rashid then included two images of Kahraman's work, again perfectly symmetrical on uncluttered navy slides, with captions in the following format:

Artist's Name
Title of work
Year work created
Media of work
Dimensions of work

The close-up, straight-on images of the works were aligned with the top of the slide, and neither had any glare, frames, or other visual data outside of the work. Rashid promoted symmetry and adherence to a grid, as well as an aesthetic of spaciousness, through these visual aids—borrowing the visual language of the white cube display and transferring it onto a slide.

In these sessions, Rashid defined the register of professional written representation of art and artists. The above format, which echoes the labels used by many museums around the world, encouraged artists to begin to think about their *own* work in these terms: to package their work as individual units with individual titles, and that the media used were relevant, as was the date of creation. Documenting these details would allow artists to communicate easily with exhibiting institutions, but this practice would also prove valuable should they ever have work up at auction and or need to establish provenance and authenticity, Rashid noted. The question of media used would be particularly useful for appropriate conservation, but also to ensure that the temperature, humidity, and light used to display the work in shows would not damage the work. This vein of thinking encouraged artists to consider the eventual presentation of their work and its display in gallery settings, not just the enjoyment of making it or whether it was visually appealing. The end goals for professional artists were market success and international visibility. These criteria were also reinforced during the cataloguing session, when Rashid encouraged artists to keep a comprehensive catalogue of all of their work including this information as well as dated photographs of individual works—essentially to keep tabs on their products and to always be thinking of the market.

To help artists draft bios that contained appropriate information, Rashid arranged an exercise where artists paired off and asked each other questions. He directed artists to respond to each of these prompts with a single sentence:

1. Who are you?
2. What is your artistic practice?
3. What is the main driving idea in your work?
4. What are your main influences?
5. What does your work aim to do?
6. Where have you exhibited? (Don't worry if you haven't)
7. What related experience do you have? (Also optional)

These questions narrowed the scope of an artist's self-definition, identifying core areas of focus. Rashid then took a moment to discourage inclusion of any phrases expressing "I have always loved art" or "Art is my passion." Effusive, messy, subjective language did not fit here. He noted that these were emotional statements and didn't convey any information about the artist's work. As an afterthought, he added, "No one is in art for the money, so we can safely assume anyone who is an artist is passionate about it." Rashid revealed to the class, "When artists write to me to share their portfolios and I see statements like this, I just delete the email. This kind of language indicates to me that they are not serious." I cast a quick glance around the room and saw panicked looks dart across several of the artists' faces as he said this. Some documents disappeared surreptitiously from the table, squirreled back into bags or covertly folded up.

The expunging of affective registers was one way that artists could convey their work as professional. In this case, the register of a professional artist was partly defined by absence: the absence of affective registers. Performing objectivity was meant to portray the artist's work as serious labor, rather than as a hobby, and could bolster framings of work as rational, objective or impersonal, and efficient (Harvey 2005; Hoag 2011; Weber 1998). The framing of art as work has also historically served to define art as labor, "signif[ying] serious, valuable effort" (Bryan-Wilson 2009, 15). The opposite of a professional artist was a "Sunday painter," implying that one had employment elsewhere and art was a hobby rather than a profession.[3] That Clarissa had described contemporary art as "cool" also applies here in a double sense, where "cool" means both trendy and unemotional or detached—as business purportedly is. Yet this seeming objectivity often works to depoliticize, by normalizing one approach or interpretation of a given context and denying all others. Donna Haraway argues in her classic essay on situated knowledges that there is no one, single, real objectivity: "Objectivity turns out to be about particular and specific embodiment . . . only partial perspective promises objective vision" (1988, 582–83). Using Haraway's concept of situated knowledges instead of objectivity allows us to recuperate the politics of these processes. In this instance, the term "professional" indexed objectivity and gravitas while obscuring—and thus depoliticizing—the inculcation of a particular register and mode of self-presentation, and its roots in a global neoliberal art market. That is, "professional" masked the erasures involved in cultivating these practices for a global market—erasures of aesthetics, differing terminologies, and alternative modes of understanding the role of the artist in society. By depoliticizing the adoption of these ways of being, the term "professional" also obscured how these processes legitimate and instantiate a global contemporary art aesthetic.[4]

In feedback sessions, Rashid and the artists in the class also discussed the topics in their artworks and how to convey them. For example, one artist I call Susan described her paintings of pomegranates as "reflecting on her fertility." Her style fell somewhere between Impressionist and Realist in its depiction of the fruit and was vaguely reminiscent of a still life. Rashid mused delicately, "So how would you frame your work in the kinds of terms that we saw in the artist bios and statements?" The examples he had shown focused on broader social themes and included the requisite sociopolitical critique (see Chapter 3), even when they incorporated individual experience. Rashid pushed Susan to think about why viewers would relate to her work: What kinds of exhibition themes would her work fall into? What were the big questions she was asking with this work? Rashid also drew on the work of two other students to illustrate his point: Newsha's work, which used paper structures, centered on migration and displacement, themes that were broadly relevant in the contemporary world, even as the work drew on her personal sense of feeling exiled from her homeland, Iran. Similarly, Mary's projects, which disassembled urban forms into patterns, focused on urbanism and the influence urban forms had on human experience, as a recent transplant to Dubai—this kind of topic, Rashid shared, could be relevant anywhere. He encouraged the artists to think and make artwork about themes in everyday life, but ensure they were stripped of affect and subjectivity. His main stress fell on the themes and critiques in the work, rather than the artists' chosen medium or aesthetic style.

By focusing on the artist statement and bio extensively in the early weeks of the course, Rashid encouraged students to think of presenting themselves and their work in writing within these genres, as opposed to whatever forms and registers in which they had previously articulated their work. To be taken as "professional" artists, Rashid indicated, these two forms of written self-presentation should be readily available and regularly updated. The artist statement and bio were critical means of presenting oneself as a professional artist. Any worthwhile project, exhibition, or residency program would want these documents, Rashid intimated, and would judge artists most rigorously on their mastery of these genres of self-presentation.

These prompts also pushed the participants to begin to conceive of themselves as artists in particular ways: firstly, to think that their work had to *mean* something, not just be visually pleasing, and secondly, to think of their art-making in terms of a unified or unifiable conceptual "practice." This identification is contrary to earlier historical modes of artists' self-identification, such as identifying as a painter or sculptor. First, the idea of "practice" transcends the creation of a single work, or even use of a particular medium (e.g., painting, sculpture, installation). This idea thus encourages artists to forge conceptual links between their individual works. It also furthers conceptions of professional art as a full-time job, cementing the prevailing definition of contemporary art as conceptual and critical. In Rashid's framing, artists "work on" issues or themes through various experiments. The construct of practice organizes artists as thinkers and social commentators first, and as makers of objects second. The works themselves become secondary, representative of a deeper intellectual or philosophical examination of an idea. Rather than making works by whim or inspiration, or in response to particular events or patrons' requests, Rashid told artists there must be a single animating idea (or a few) behind their practice. This focus on the concept as integral to the work, and pivotal to the artist's own understanding of what they do, echoes an international art world preoccupation with conceptual art.

A "practice" is also a specialized term, one belonging to the register of International Art English. International Art English has been frequently parodied in the English-language media as bombastic and vacuous, but it remains in widespread use and is a distinct register (Rule and Levine 2012). International Art English relies on a select set of terms that are theoretical and often vague, and which are considered erudite. Especially as English has become "the global language of contemporary art" (Dávila 2020, 87), artists' ability to deploy it successfully matters and can have material consequences. This register is aimed at facilitating global commerce and easy transnational legibility.

Artists needed to strike a delicate balance between using enough International Art English to come across as erudite and conceptual, but not go overboard into theoretical babble. Rashid cautioned artists not to be pompous in their self-presentation and to avoid convoluted theoretical jargon. Rashid's "Artist Statements to Avoid" slide read:

> "Drawing loosely on the image of the panopticon as evoked by Michel Foucault, my multidisciplinary practice invokes technologies of conflict that arouse an exploratory dimension in relation to Marxian and post-Marxian approaches that reference obtusely Baudrillardian conceptions of simulacra in contemporary society."
>
> *This is how a curator may write. It is great to have theoretical references but it best [sic] to use clear accessible language (at first). An artist can disguise a lack of substance with a strong coating of theory (not recommended).*

Not only does this kind of writing distort the message, he noted, it can actually make the artist look less intelligent (contrary to its intent) while also alienating audiences. Borrowing from another artist's sample statement, he encouraged the use of verbs like "investigate," "inquire," and "document" to emphasize to curators and funders the specialized work an artist was actively performing. Such verbs conveyed serious labor. In comparison, the syntax of "my work is about" was structurally weaker, as the verb "to be" in the form of "is" was less precise than these other verbs. In addition to the appearance of the text and its content, artists needed to use the register of professionalized art world terms.

After these sessions, Rashid assigned the students to draft or rewrite their bios and statements in order to get instructor feedback on them. Packing up their bags at the end of the session, the artists sitting near me chattered excitedly about the prospect of getting curatorial feedback on their writing, especially from someone with as many diverse experiences in the art world as Rashid. Over the course of the class, many artists shared with me that the opportunity to get curatorial feedback was a key reason why they had enrolled. One student, Mary, noted, "I keep getting rejections from open calls and I don't know why. Is it my work? Or maybe I'm just not presenting myself right." These comments also demonstrated that while artists understood they were being disciplined and inculcated into particular modes of self-presentation, they wanted this. All twelve students completed the class; no one dropped. They wanted an insider to help mold them.

Mastering self-presentation was one component, but the register was complicated for some members of the UAE arts community. Many students spoke English as a second or third language; the UAE was a polyglot hub. The most-spoken languages in the UAE include Malayalam, Urdu, and Tagalog. In the course, for example, Newsha spoke Farsi as a first language. Newsha often described herself and her work in more colloquial terms—the dialect of English in which she felt most comfortable expressing herself. She was not as familiar with the register of International Art English, so even the clarification the course offered in codifying a register was helpful to her. A number of the artists in the course expressed that previously, for these reasons or others, they had not presented themselves in the registers required for curators and contemporary art world elites to see them as professional artists.

Another session of the class focused on the aesthetic grammar of a professional display, promoting a white cube style that was largely interchangeable between museums and commercial galleries. All of the images used in Rashid's slideshow, again featuring the navy blue background, were of white cube displays that reiterated the white cube: Works were not crowded on walls, but separated out with space and invisibly mounted on the wall in straight lines. Rashid encouraged the use of software to design the gallery grid, allocating the works throughout the gallery with precision. All artworks were affixed to walls except sculptures or installation pieces. With the exception of one image, all the gallery walls in Rashid's presentation were white; the floors in each image were either polished concrete or wood. The gallery spaces, all designed expressly for exhibiting art, were also spacious, some with benches in the center of the rooms to allow visitors to sit and contemplate the works. This spatial aesthetic appeared in well-respected art spaces in the UAE like the Sharjah Art Foundation and the Third Line Gallery.[5] In this way, Rashid transmitted an iteration of what constituted proper curatorial practice to the artists, but he also gave them key terms and practices with which they could demonstrate their knowledge to future curators and ensure that their work was exhibited in ways that conveyed their professionalism. The images of the spaces shown throughout the course performed their own kind of work, inculcating artists into the aesthetic of global contemporary art exhibitions and what acceptable display looked like.

While Rashid's instructions helped students navigate the prevailing art world hierarchy, they also established a limited linguistic, behavioral, and aesthetic grammar for an artist's self-presentation and validated particular definitions of what constitutes art and who counts as an artist. They also provided a codified, approved register in which artists describe, make, and exhibit their work, privileging legibility to an international art market. A few months after the class concluded, one of the artists, Connie, shared at our interview, "The class basically shared the unwritten rules of the art world so it was very helpful." Susan approached me at an exhibition a few months after the course, sharing that she attributed her recent successful application to an open call exhibition to the knowledge she had acquired in the course. The course provided a register of International Art English, key genres of writing and self-presentation, and practices to signal professionalism to others in the field—thereby reiterating these elements as important insignia of the profession and establishing the codes and behaviors of "professional vision" for art (Goodwin 1994). While many of the artists understood that these were disciplining practices that obviously limited their ability to speak and present their work, they also expressed appreciation for, as one participant framed it, "knowing the rules of the game." They sought out opportunities for mentorship with curators because they wanted to be successful in an international art world and recognized curators as important gatekeepers in this process. And once artists understood the linguistic and visual aesthetic grammar curators looked for, they felt they were better equipped to perform it and get their work on display. Having work visible on display was crucial to another art world process: collecting. An artist needed to be visible on the market so institutions and individual collectors could buy their work. Collectors too were inculcated into the aesthetic grammar of professionalism, albeit in different modes than artists were.

Cultivating Collectors' Eye for Aesthetics

Collectors have gained significant heft in recent years: In fact, Gerardo Mosquera labels this a "private collector's age," wherein collectors are primary "legitimizers, promoters and gatekeepers" (2003, 61). Much as Rashid trained artists for entry into a market, my interlocutors also trained those who collected artwork, recognizing collectors as key to a thriving art community. I met Josie, a former auction staffer, at an empty café in a strip mall in Dubai for our final interview to discuss her experience setting up a branch of an auction house in the UAE. Auction houses play a critical role in a global art world, "determin[ing] *who* becomes perceived as successful at a global level. And they substantially shape the cross-border discourse about *what* constitutes value in contemporary art" (Buchholz 2022, 94). I was curious to see how auction house staff like Josie understood their role and work in setting up franchise offices. We sat outside in the pleasant warmth of a February afternoon, enjoying iced coffee under the generous shade of trees fed by a hose carelessly buried in the loose sand. In addition to the public, "it's also the clients, you know," Josie said.

"The clients?" I asked her. Josie had first began coming to the Emirates to assist with auctions prior to moving there, and she noted, "I was fully aware the [auction house staff] were not really familiar with how an auction was run. But"—she chuckled and arched one manicured eyebrow—"neither were the clients who had been purchasing works, some of them had been purchasing for a long time. So, it was also the clients." Josie's professionalizing efforts were thus twofold: to train her staff, but also to train her clients. In essence, she was to make her market.

Aware that those wealthy enough to afford to buy artwork at auction would not want to appear ignorant, Josie's organization began hosting small seminars for prospective local collectors. Much like Rashid's class taught artists an aesthetic grammar, Josie taught her prospective collectors a code of aesthetics, terms, and practices to buy art from professional organizations. According to Josie, these seminars were

> a sort of attractive manner in which to ask questions. So we set up a small group of seminars where we invited maybe five or six clients at a time to join us. I would do a presentation, under the guise of a lecture. So I'd do something like, the history of photography in a particular place. . . . That way, they weren't at a preview asking me, oh by the way, what's a buyer's commission exactly? And what does this symbol mean? It gave them an opportunity to ask questions.

Josie's work in professionalizing her clients was to surreptitiously and invisibly train them in the processes of the auction, to familiarize them with the names of important artists (whose work presumably would show up at auction . in the near future), and to impart the specialized register of terms and behaviors to enable them to participate in auctions. Roxy, a gallerist, reported similar events in the early days of her gallery. Significantly, presentation of a select few artists' work—in this case photographers—also established an aesthetic, simply by virtue of being selected and shown in this context.

Part of Josie's work included *not* saying certain things to prospective collectors as well. She related,

> In advising the client on what to purchase, [there is] what you should say, and what you shouldn't say. It was glaringly shocking for me. [My former coworkers] would be like, you should buy this because it'll be worth more in X number of years . . . and I'd be like, you cannot say that to a client. Cause actually in the UK they can legally sue you if you give them that advice.

Much like artists were to avoid emotional language, art sellers were to avoid making guarantees about economic value. Paradoxically then, to demonstrate cultural capital, one could not talk explicitly about the value creation, echoing Olav Velthuis's findings that art dealers and their artists "would not . . . demean themselves to what is called commerce" (2005, 1). Part of value production involved denial of economic interest.

Josie's training allowed clients to perform the requisite expertise at auctions. It is noteworthy that auction houses were keen to train clients, partly to prevent clients' potential embarrassment. Yet, for someone to be embarrassed, they would have to be at auction with people who knew the codes of accepted behavior in Sotheby's and Christie's auctions. That is, this training was oriented at buyers who aspired to be part of an established international market.[6]

Auction houses and galleries were not the only places training would-be collectors in professional contemporary art world practices. Another interlocutor, Habib, ran an informal, independent, sporadic series of events for prospective collectors; he also regularly published exhibition reviews. Habib had been an artist in his early twenties before leaving the art world for a more stable corporate career. His collectors' group was a way for him to bridge his interests: Still very interested in art, he had begun buying it instead of making it himself.[7] With his long experience in the scene, Habib had fairly fixed opinions on the UAE's arts venues, although he did attend shows at venues he did not rate highly. I asked him how he selected shows to feature in his reviews. He said, "It's selective unselection. If four shows opened last night and I review three of them, that's my critique. The fourth one wasn't worth writing about." Considering the politics of critique in the UAE, I consider Habib's choices— of which exhibitions to review, of which galleries to include in his collectors' group meetings—as intentional statements of value, not accidental or meaningless. Much as Rashid's slides and visuals consecrated, in Pierre Bourdieu's terms (1993, 51), certain aesthetics, so too did the venues Habib chose to feature. All the venues we visited together on his monthly collection tours were white cube, conceptually oriented spaces.

After we met, Habib invited me to tag along for the next session of his collectors' group. Drawing on his extensive network in the art world, Habib asked the director of one of Dubai's most prestigious galleries, located—as most of Dubai's galleries are—in a spacious and sparse warehouse with white walls and a polished concrete floor, to give our group a tour. When we arrived at eleven o'clock on a Saturday morning, the gallerist Clarissa had croissants, coffee, and orange juice laid out. The gallery was one large room, a white cube with black tracks for lighting suspended from the cathedral ceilings. A few black benches were arranged in the center of the room. Our group included a stylishly dressed young couple, a mother pushing a snoozing infant in a pricey stroller, a woman I recognized as a former education manager at a local art foundation, and myself. The show featured prints by internationally recognized Arab artists, including Kamal Boullata and Dia Azzawi. Azzawi's works were more modernist, akin to Picasso, in dark moody colors; Boullata's works were *ḥurufiya*, or letterism, a meditation on Arabic calligraphy.

The works were geometric repetitions of Arabic words printed in robin's-egg blues, sea-foam greens, and salmon pinks.

Clarissa imparted background information about the artists and their practices seamlessly, without it being obviously educational. She pointed out that because the works were prints, they were less expensive than paintings, allowing fledgling collectors to "dip a toe in" before committing substantial money. As she walked us through the show, rather akin to a museum tour, Clarissa described the style and particular medium used in each work and placed the work in the artist's life trajectory (e.g., "Kamal was working in silkscreens a lot during this period," etc.). She described the works not in subjective terms (e.g., pretty) but specialized, scholarly ones that exuded a professional expertise (such as process, symmetry, bold use of color, expressive, limited-edition print). Describing the works in "formal ways and in relation to dominant art tendencies" works to situate these artworks within a global art scene, a critical way in which gallerists created financial value for artworks (Dávila 2020, 147). Afterward, Clarissa handed us each a copy of the glossy catalogue of the show and stationed herself unobtrusively by the front desk, encouraging us to peruse the pieces at our leisure but remaining available for questions. Clarissa used the consecrated linguistic register and white cube display aesthetic to create value for the works and justify the price, and she provided a comfortable sales experience. She worked to educate prospective buyers in a way that covered any gaps in their knowledge so they did not feel ignorant, and she made them feel like they were purchasing an important work of art. Despite gallerists' adamant statements to me that galleries were different from museums, the crossovers of display styles, professionalized behaviors, and even the didactics of gallery tours were extremely similar, revealing the hybridity of commercial and noncommercial practice as well as the market-centric nature of arts practice generally.

One of our group members did buy a work that day. Habib acted as a go-between, facilitating the negotiations. He encouraged the prospective buyer, praising their selected work, while also asking the gallerist to give the buyer the best price for the print ("It's their first purchase ever!"). When the negotiations were completed, Habib smiled and said, "Congratulations!" Everyone in the group congratulated the buyer, even though the financial transaction had not taken place yet nor had the buyer taken possession of the work—that would happen once the show came down. The buyer and gallerist had only made a verbal contract.

The aesthetic grammar of professionalism did encompass such verbal contracts. These contracts were considered binding, and an important part of professional patron etiquette was to follow through on such commitments to the gallerists. These practices, and one's performance of them, were other modes of establishing oneself as someone in the know. When I toured Art Dubai with Habib and Sam, a curator, they were both drawn to a series of colorful geometrical drawings by an emerging British artist. The gallery had displayed the framed drawings in two rows of eight against the white walls: From a distance, the drawings almost looked like real objects, but had been abstracted just enough to be illegible. Habib and Sam each claimed a few, the gallerist calmly noting the sale commitments on her iPad. Later, Habib took us to the VIP Lounge area, where we drank free champagne to toast their purchases. Sam lamented, "I just spent 4,000 dirhams I don't have" (roughly $1,000 USD). I asked, half suggesting and half curious, "Can you back out of buying the artworks?" Both Habib and Sam raised their eyebrows and exchanged a knowing glance. "No," Sam said. "The gallery would blacklist you if you did that. They can sell works quickly during fairs, so if they hold a piece for you and then you back out, you're costing them a sale." So you would never be invited to the VIP day again, I followed up. "Probably not," Habib laughed. "Gallerists talk!"

In addition to transmitting and cultivating appropriate behaviors and practices for art collectors, Habib's tours also took the group to not-for-profit exhibitions, so his emerging collectors could learn about current trends in art and "develop their eye." These visits established a white cube aesthetic and validated a particular roster of artists who all identified as conceptual. But Habib's efforts were not always appreciated, largely because of the group's unapologetic focus on the commercial. He recounted sharing an overview of the prospective collectors' series to a classroom full of local artists and curators: "My presentation fell on *aggressively* deaf ears—'why was I helping galleries, organizations, not the artists?' My thoughts were, if you have no one to sell to, you have no patronage." For Habib, as for my gallerist interlocutors, a professional art world included not only artists but also those who could sustain them. Because of the history of problematic imbrication with money, such overt connections were not encouraged, an attitude that was a vestige of a bygone episteme where "pure" art remained a separate sphere from commercial interest (or at least, purported to). Educating buyers and encouraging potential collectors were also ways to support the art world while delineating its limits; reinforcing a register of terms, a canon of behaviors, and an aesthetic grammar of display as professional; and ultimately encouraging standardizing practices that focused on alignment with a global commercial art world. Professionalism facilitated legibility across difference, marking the rising influence of capital on artists' and collectors' practices.

Competing Aesthetics

Inside the old fort, the small room was cool despite the shimmering heat outside. The room had few windows, and the walls were made of coral and mud.[8] I was standing in the small regional museum where an organization I call the Foundation for the Northern Emirates (FNE) was hosting its annual arts festival. The museum was a historic fort; from the cobblestone parking lot, the beige coral walls of the fort rose imposingly against the electric blue sky. Four cannons pointed out facing the parking lot. To get to the room I was standing in, I had ducked through the carved wooden doors and through a dark, cool hallway that smelled of slightly damp sand to enter a bright courtyard, surrounded by the square fort encasing it. In the center of the courtyard, under the shade of some ghaf and mango trees, my colleagues were at work depositing bubble-wrapped works of art they unloaded from the trunk of a van backed up to a rear entry. The museum caretaker emerged at one point and handed us a giant sheaf of keys to open the individual rooms. The keys were not labeled, so we painstakingly tested each key to find the right ones.

Nancy, who was supervising the installation, asked another coworker, Brenda, and me to select which works would go in which room. "And don't forget," she reminded us, "we can't install anything on the walls of the fort. Only on the easels. Nothing that would damage the building. And don't take the bubble wrap off the works yet—the museum staff is going to go through and clean all the rooms, so we don't want to expose the works to any damage."

Brenda and I stared at the tables with artworks to be divvied. We had no artist statements, descriptions of the art, or even labels by which to categorize the works, and the exhibition did not have a theme or curator. Thus the decisions about where to situate works were fully up to our discernment. I flashed to Rashid's exhortation to design a gallery grid—there would be no software involved in this layout. Brenda, who had worked under Nancy at last year's festival, whispered, "She likes to arrange them by frames." By frames? I asked. "Yeah," Brenda said. "Nancy likes it when all the frames of the same kind are in the same room together. So all the wood frames, all the gold, Baroque-y ones together, the unframed photos together, you get the idea." We began to put the works into groups by frame style, peeling back a layer of bubble wrap to see each frame. After we had a series of potential groupings, Brenda fetched Nancy to give her approval. Nancy eyed the stacks. "We should have a 'moody room' with all the dark colored works," she said. Brenda sucked air between her front teeth; I could see her mentally tabulating the works that would need to be moved. "Even if the frames don't match?" she asked. Nancy nodded: "Even if the frames don't match." Brenda and I turned and wordlessly began to re-sort.

Once we managed to create acceptable piles for Nancy, we began to put the works into the individual rooms. I had installed one room, and Nancy came running up: "That work can't go there!" I looked at her, confused. Nancy pointed to the *barjil* wind tower above the work. "Pigeons roost up there. Last year they pooped on a work and the artist got really mad. So don't put any works under the air shafts for the wind towers," she said. Peering up into the dark for prospective pooping pigeons, I shimmied the easel over a few feet so it was no longer in range.

This show radically diverged from the standards of display, expectations of artists, and privileging of conceptual art that dominated many other arts organizations I worked with in the Emirates. The aesthetics of the fort—packed dirt floors and easels, artworks without any accompanying text—jarred with white cubes, polished concrete floors, and spaciously, symmetrically wall-mounted works of the gallery halls in the southern emirates like Dubai and Abu Dhabi. The proximity of natural elements like dirt, trees, and pigeon feces stood in stark contrast to the antiseptic industrial warehouse gallery model.

The show opened six weeks before I left the UAE, so by this point, I was well-inculcated into what the community's standards of "professional" display were. I felt stuck: I recognized that challenging the organizer's choices meant reiterating the standards of a global contemporary art world—the ones I have just critiqued in this chapter. At the same time, I worried that the artists involved in the show wouldn't benefit from the time they had put in, or that they could be judged negatively by their peers, as the UAE art community derided many of these practices of exhibiting without a theme or text, or curating by any metric other than meaning and concept. In a small way, this experience replicates that of my artist interlocutors, including their dilemmas recognizing the limitations inherent in adopting international contemporary art world standards—and the invisibility that resulted if they did not. I noted that only two of the seven artists I knew attended the opening, which was held on a workday at a time that would have been difficult for anyone residing in Abu Dhabi or Dubai to attend given rush hour traffic.

Above all, making a "professional" contemporary art world included training artists and teaching would-be patrons and collectors, instantiating a white cube display aesthetic and select terms and practices on the spectrum from art-making to art consumption. The aesthetic grammar of professionalism constituted visual, linguistic, and practice hierarchies, which all reiterated the supremacy of the market in the art world and the easy transfer between different nodes of contemporary art centers. These tenets disciplined the community into a unified appreciation for a white cube minimalist aesthetic, which decontextualized the diversity and specificity of the arts organizations in the Emirates. Flattening this diversity allowed artists and arts organizations to be globally translatable. Commercial and market practices, rather than overtly nationalist goals, were influential in defining the register of professionalism, another way the market exhibitionary complex has come to dominate twenty-first century art and museum practice.

Just as artists and collectors learned to perform this aesthetic grammar of professionalism, my interlocutors also cultivated audiences for future museums. While earlier museum organizers attempted to use museums and art as tools of public reform and edification, these processes were framed largely in classist terms, within one nation (Bennett 1995; Duncan 1995). With transnational migration and multicultural populations, museums and arts organizers must now orient to a global community rather than to the various classes of a singular one: Andrew McClellan notes that "making the world's museums truly cosmopolitan would be a noble goal for the global twenty-first century" (2008, 274). Museums and arts organizations in the UAE labored to cultivate exhibitions worthy of a diverse and cosmopolitan audience.

IN THE GALLERY V   **Rain of Light**

IN JANUARY 2020, I went to the Louvre Abu Dhabi for the first time (Figure G5.1). It was a rare gray day in the Emirates, unfamiliar clouds strewn across the sky. Upon exiting the highway, I was surprised by the sudden emergence of a wide boulevard with manicured landscaping on both sides that had appeared since my last visit to the construction site in 2018. After parking my rental car under a shade sail, I approached the low gray dome of the museum, walking along a white wall emblazoned with "Louvre Abu Dhabi" written in English/French and Arabic script. A gray metal sign near the entrance read, "Welcome to the

FIGURE G5.1. Exterior view of the Louvre Abu Dhabi.
Photo by Hakanyalicn (Shutterstock).

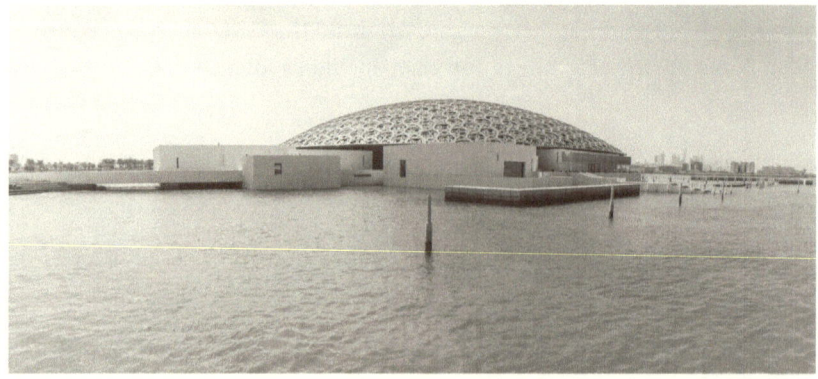

Louvre Abu Dhabi. Get ready to see humanity in a new light." In bold, the sign enjoined: "Respect each other. Respect the artworks. Respect where you are. Ask questions. Take your time." Under each injunction, a few sentences elaborated. Inside the entry corridor, one large window was stenciled with a verse in Arabic, English, and French: "Art is the shortest path from man to man" (*Al-fan huwa āqṣar tāriq baīn al-ānsān wa al-ānsān; L'art, c'est le plus court chemin de l'homme a l'homme*). Through the window, I could see the electric teal of the Gulf waters stark against a charcoal-toned construction site farther down the coastline. Another window by the entrance to the galleries bore the following stenciled quote: "Superficial differences between men conceal a profound unity" (*Al-ākhtilāfāt al-saṭhīya baīn al-bashr tukhfī warā'hā rūwābt 'āmiq; Les différences superficielles entre les hommes recouvrent une profonde unité*). Such phrases submerged difference in the name of universal inclusivity, setting the tone for the gallery narrative to follow. I entered the galleries. A large wall text in front of me described the visit to come as "twelve chapters" in a broader story. Notably, the path through the museum consisted of twelve galleries strung together in a narrative arc in a single pathway, each gallery leading to the next. The wall text noted, "The thematic presentation of the works draws attention to the similarities and particularities of our forms of artistic expression, surpassing any geographic limitations." Even here, the messaging focused on global translatability.

This invocation of unity aligned with the Louvre Abu Dhabi's overall branding, but the museum's layout is also a response to a major critique of the Louvre Paris: Scholars since Carol Duncan and Alan Wallach (1980) have often pointed out that the Louvre Paris's organizational schema, with the art of non-Western groups in the basement and French art on the higher floors, creates a physical hierarchy of artworks with French civilization at the apex. Given that the Louvre Paris was previously a royal palace and was converted to a museum dedicated to French empire, this organization represented a colonial, imperial logic of progressive evolutionism. The Louvre Abu Dhabi organizers, a team drawn from Agence France Musées and the Abu Dhabi Tourism and Culture Authority, laid out the Abu Dhabi museum differently, marshaling all communities everywhere onto a single timeline, organized first by chronology and then given a theme. The twelve permanent galleries of the Louvre Abu Dhabi articulated a universal, global (and globalizing) history: Beginning with *First Villages* and *First Great Powers*, which displayed prehistoric artifacts, the visitor would then walk through *Civilizations &*

Empires, Universal Religions (around the advent of Christianity), *Asian Trade Routes* (seventh century CE), *From the Mediterranean to the Atlantic* (eleventh century), *Thinking the State* (1500–1700 CE), *Early Modern Globalization* (focusing on the rise of European imperial powers), and *A New Art of Living* (the eighteenth century and industrial revolution). In *Thinking the State*, the wall text read:

> Between the 16th and 18th centuries, relations between rulers strengthened and progressively consolidated the codes of international representation. Introduced shortly after the great voyages of exploration, policies of territorial and commercial expansion brought radical change to the exercise of power. From Qing China to the conflicts in the Americas, from Mughal India to the Ottoman empire, the dividing up of territories required the creation of strong networks to ensure stable governance in the new empires.

Such euphemisms for colonization—"territorial and commercial expansion" and "great voyages of exploration"—mask the violence enacted by mostly, although not exclusively, European powers in particular. In this gallery, emblems of empire were on display. A gouache print of a Mughal emperor, dating from 1670, hung next to a steel lance blade from India. One glass case held an elaborate gold-trimmed coffee and tea set emblazoned with the insignia of Russian emperor Paul Petrovich. A marble tabletop of the Florentine de Medici family was on view, as was a large bronze neoclassical statue series of a man fighting a snake and two juveniles.

The gallery also contained a commemorative head of an *oba*, a king of Benin (dated 1800–1850), alongside a life-size bronze sculpture of Philip V of Spain mounted on his horse (dated 1702–1705). Between the two was a Beninese copper statuette of a rooster. The label for the object described it only as an "altar sculpture of a rooster" from the Edo culture (dated 1700–1800). While I found the object itself beautiful, there was no interpretive text or material to link it to the theme of rising states and empires; it seemed placed there not because it fit the theme, but because it fit the time period and, as an object from Edo, acted as counterbalance to the many European oil paintings of nobility hanging on the walls. In an attempt to diversify the timeline and assert coevalness, in this case, the curators sacrificed coherence, instead appearing to select artifacts to ensure global coverage, privileging inclusivity first and foremost. The displays often juxtaposed objects like African masks with Impressionist paintings, for example (Figure G5.2).

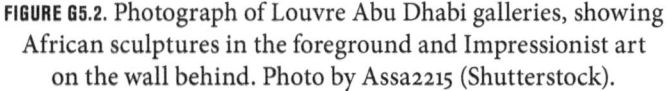

FIGURE G5.2. Photograph of Louvre Abu Dhabi galleries, showing African sculptures in the foreground and Impressionist art on the wall behind. Photo by Assa2215 (Shutterstock).

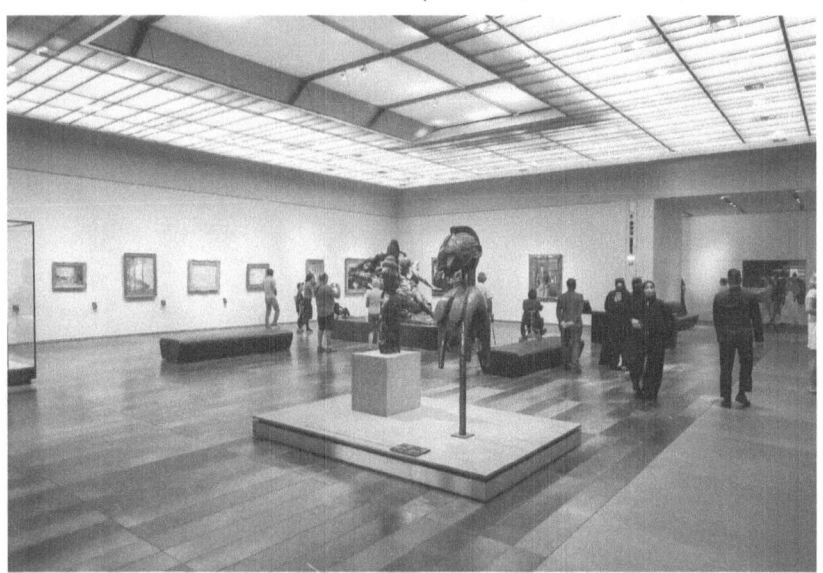

The final galleries outlined more recent histories: *A Modern World?* (the nineteenth century), *Challenging Modernity* (the twentieth century), and then, in conclusion, the *Epilogue* room.[1] The wall text for the *Epilogue* gallery read, "When entering this space, visitors . . . embody the universal ambition of the museum and thus partake in both a unique and a collective experience, reflecting the human condition." Passing through the *Epilogue* gallery transitioned visitors from this universal art historical narrative to the main hall, under the much-touted "rain of light," an intricate lattice of steel. A final display juxtaposed ancient Arabian stones with Cy Twombly's abstract contemporary art, the wall text describing both pieces as focused on memory, signs, and a universally human experience (Figure G5.3).

The "rain of light" (Figure G5.4) is the central gathering point of the museum, where all the supporting buildings come together under the dome into a long axial corridor. It is also selfie central. The ends of the hall are open, so visitors can walk out to the Gulf waterfront on several sides. Lifeguards in bright red-and-yellow outfits patrol water access; it is rare for a museum to have lifeguards on staff. I had seen splashy images of this space so many times:

FIGURE G5.3. Cy Twombly's paintings hung on the wall with ancient Arabian stone carvings in the foreground, installed at the Louvre Abu Dhabi. Photo by Assa2215 (Shutterstock).

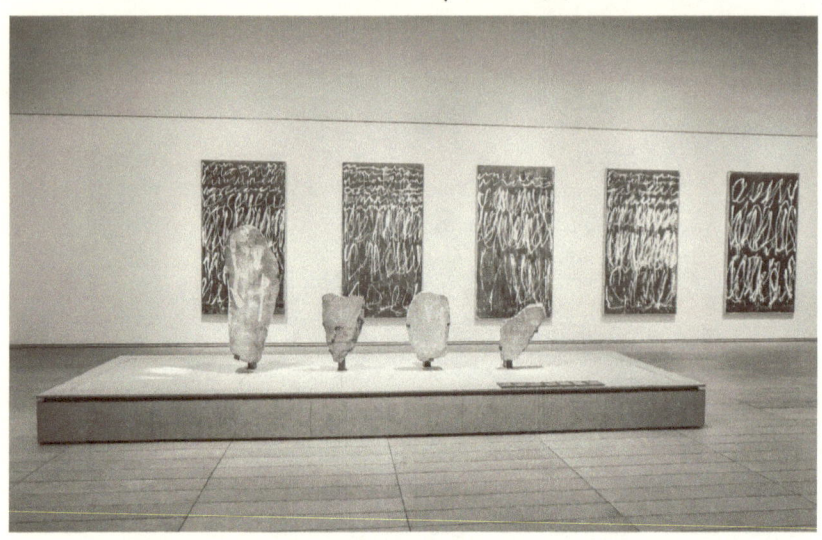

FIGURE G5.4. View of the central hall of the Louvre Abu Dhabi under the "rain of light," with Jenny Holzer's *For the Louvre Abu Dhabi* (2017) and Rodin's *Walking Man on a Column* (1900) in fore. Photo by Caroline Ericson (Shutterstock).

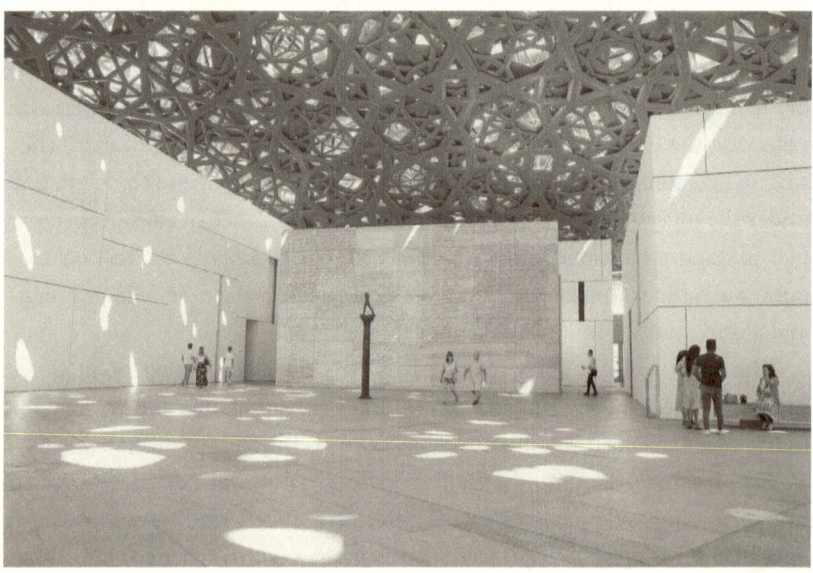

in plans for the Louvre Abu Dhabi, which had been announced in 2006; in maquettes, news articles, and renderings; and then on Instagram when the museum opened in 2017. Jean Nouvel designed the space to engineer awe, and it worked. The bright Gulf sun blazed through the lacy overlaid geometric shapes of the dome overhead, leaving tiny shards of light on the floor below.

On one side of the corridor, a Jenny Holzer installation (visible in Figure G5.4) claimed a large wall: *For the Louvre Abu Dhabi* (2017) consisted of a marble relief of a Sumerian and Akkadian cuneiform text from 1250 CE, a play on Holzer's text-centric art practice. Instead of words traveling in bright bands of neon across a gallery wall, her usual aesthetic, these words were indecipherable for modern audiences: One side of the work is written in ancient Sumerian and the other in Akkadian. The accompanying tombstone noted "these stone reliefs . . . reflect on the origins of civilization, the recording of history, and the dynamics of cross-cultural exchange." The final line notes, "The process of transcription, translation and transmission is part of a tradition which can be traced back to the birth of writing in Mesopotamia." The installation thus highlights the centrality of the Middle East to the creation of language, as well as a long history of intercultural exchange, given that the reference piece is actually a Rosetta stone of sorts, again emphasizing cross-cultural legibility and communication across difference. Spaced toward the middle of the hall in front of Holzer's piece stood Auguste Rodin's sculpture *Walking Man on a Column* (1900), the deep brown metal striking against the ecru wall installation behind it. These works from different time periods and geographies all contributed to the tableau. A small silver plaque on one wall displayed a quote attributed to French president François Hollande: "In tribute to the sincere friendship between our two countries, the United Arab Emirates gifts the Louvre Abu Dhabi Museum to mankind as a sign of hope for world unity and as a beacon of heritage and mutual respect." The message of a unified humanity, a unified civilization, suffused my first visit to the Louvre Abu Dhabi in works, layout, texts, and the very walls themselves.

As detailed in Chapter 2, organizers drew strategically on artists' status to project tolerance. But it was not just artists. Arts and museum organizers also cultivated visitors into these discourses—partly through wall texts and layouts, as the Louvre Abu Dhabi shows. They also schooled audiences, too.

FIVE

"Complementary Not Competitive": Scaffolding Publics and the Art of Tolerance

ART MUSEUMS AND EXHIBITIONS as tools of "civilizing" or edifying publics is a well-established phenomenon. Nineteenth-century reformers of museums wanted them to "function as a space of emulation in which civilized forms of behavior might be learnt and thus diffused more widely through the social body," especially through the working classes (Bennett 1995, 24). The museum targeted bodily comportment as a site of reform through prohibiting swearing, brawling, spitting, gambling, and dirty footwear (Bennett 1995, 27) and enforcing other "rules forbidding eating and drinking, outlawing the touching of exhibits and, quite frequently, stating—or at least advising—what should be worn and what should not. In this way, while formally free and open, the museum effected its own pattern of informal discriminations and exclusions" (Bennett 1995, 100). Museums as discipling institutions, above and beyond the processes of distinction-making amongst the artworks (Bourdieu 2000; Lena 2019), have often been tools of class-making. Eileen Hooper-Greenhill established that "the public museum was shaped into being as an apparatus with two deeply contradictory functions: 'that of the elite temple of the arts, and that of a utilitarian instrument for democratic education'" (cited in Bennett 1995, 89). This schismic binary, of simultaneously reinforcing elite culture while also purporting to support a wide public education (Cameron 1972; McClellan 2003; Rader and Cain 2014), remains at the crux of audience cultivation today, further complicated by museums' growing recognition that they must appeal to a broad, inclusive public (Dávila 2020; Levitt 2015). Forging inclusive publics has been a challenge for museums everywhere, but the exceptionally diverse population of the Emirates poses a particular challenge, both in terms of the number of nationalities present as well as vast income inequality. As rising numbers of people live outside their country of documented affiliation, the Emirates' museums and arts organizations offer insight into how twenty-first-century museums respond to such diverse publics and the ways they navigate a capitalist imperative toward tolerance and multiculturalism.

Throughout my fieldwork, I saw a number of institutions endeavoring to build art-appreciating, museum-going publics of all ages through a variety of channels both formal and informal. These programs targeted middle- and upper-class residents of the Emirates, regardless of citizenship background. Aside from some movie nights in Sharjah, I did not see any programming targeted at manual laborers, the Emirates' most precarious residents. Universities ran college classes on art criticism; art centers and museums offered informal courses, talks series, tours, and workshops. Even commercial endeavors like art fairs held trainings, reflecting the blurring of commercial and noncommercial in a twenty-first-century museum paradigm: Art Dubai held the Global Art Forum, a set of curated talks coeval with the commercial fair, as well as Campus Art Dubai, a Saturday program that ran for several months in the lead-up to the fair for emerging artists in the region. Abu Dhabi Art hosted talks throughout the fair, often focused on the upcoming museums and led by their staff. These staff also developed year-round exhibition programming. One museum's education manager ran trainings for staff and collected program evaluations that focused on audience development and segmentation. These varied endeavors included how to see art, how to talk about it, and how to define a museum.

Local museum workers carefully developed and staged these experiences, believing that art could encourage tolerance and change minds without overt conflict. Dina, who oversaw the development of education and outreach programming for a major museum, told me:

> The first segment you need to reach out to is the children, the kids, because this is where you create, you implement that awareness about art, heritage, and museums. And you try really to build the citizens of the future. Today, when you educate the kid, you educate the family. And you know that by really reaching out to kids, you know that you are changing a system, you're changing a society, you're changing a mentality.

In 2013, Dina spoke with me in her bright, well-appointed office in an Abu Dhabi skyscraper, and she described the great emphasis she and her team placed on cultivating younger audiences. She tied this project not only to civic goals ("the citizens of the future") but also framed children as gateways to shifting mindsets within the family unit and society more broadly. A key part of Dina's work was to translate museums for a local audience, and she noted, "the vision [for Saadiyat] is great, but the reality is very different." Cultivating cultured publics who would visit Saadiyat museums was essential to the long-term success of the UAE art scene, in the eyes of Dina and others. Dina told me, "Museums can't be sustainable if the community is not intrinsic, is not involved in the process." The museums' financial and social viability were therefore reliant on the community to sustain them. There was, in a way, a paradox, in that the community—and especially local artists—was intrinsic and necessary, but it also needed to be shaped, echoing a lengthy historical practice of museums molding their visitors (Bennett 1995; Duncan 1995; Hooper-Greenhill 1992, 1994; Mathur and Singh 2015; McClellan 2003; Rydell 1984).

The belief that art and museums promote tolerance parallels a definition of tolerance as a mode of flattening difference, of "tam[ing]" and "regulat[ing]" under a "conceit of neutrality" (Brown 2006, 7). Many of the museum and arts workers in the Emirates espoused a view that the arts could instill tolerance of multiculturalism and diversity, which were important traits for the society to gain respect of peer nations and to root the legitimacy of the Saadiyat museums. While tolerance is itself a relatively new term in its current connotations as a positive phenomenon (Brown 2006, 2), it is often ill-defined and amorphous (Brown 2006; Dzenovska 2018), frequently defined by what it is not rather than by what it is. Often glossed as openness and inclusivity, tolerance becomes institutionalized in different ways, through bureaucratic programs (Dzenovska 2018) or the performing arts (Dağtaş 2020).[1] In the UAE, amongst my interlocutors, tolerance appeared to mean the absence of conflict or disagreements, and generally not reacting toward difference.

The main thrust of the efforts to cultivate UAE publics aimed at tolerance, largely through preemptively removing potential conflicts and minimizing, if not altogether flattening, difference. Preemptive erasures were founded on a belief that art could change minds without conflict, avoiding the friction endemic to globalization (Tsing 2005). Universalisms, such as a single global timeline of cultural production or the idea of universally tolerant Emirati population, claim to "transcend difference," requiring "mechanisms to *process* [differences between people]" (Li 2020, 14). In addition to tolerance discourse, one mode of removing prospective conflict and processing that my interlocutors often undertook was to emphasize visual description over formal, contextual analysis, a move that often depoliticized or blunted politics by "minimizing the topics and issues guiding the work" (Dávila 2020, 147). Arlene Dávila observed similar whitewashing strategies in her study of Latinx artists. Meanwhile, such flattening made art and museums universal, easily legible to everyone and therefore maximally marketable. Difference was often eliminated—or commodified, any potential friction removed to be accessible to global audiences and, most importantly, to global markets.

Such tolerance discourse emerged consistently. In the opening to a Louvre Abu Dhabi exhibition catalogue, one official described "the spirit of universalism, an exploration of commonalities over centuries, is what . . . this museum hope [*sic*] to offer not only to the people of the United Arab Emirates, but also to the world" (Al Nahyan 2013, 13). Much like the twinned narrative that supported contingent citizens, here again the UAE is isolated from and simultaneously paired with a broader global audience. Another official penned a preface entitled "A Bridge to the World," writing that Emirati leaders' vision for the museums of Saadiyat ensures "future Emiratis . . . will grow and develop as true global citizens" (Al Muhairi 2013, 14). He continued, "They have envisioned the Saadiyat Cultural District as a bridge to the future, to connect knowledge and civilization" (Al Muhairi 2013, 14). The idea of art and culture as a bridge is not new, of course (Lena and Johnston 2015; Meskell 2018; Yúdice 2003). Such bridges are critical, per the writer, as "politics of identity . . . are emphasized to create difference and conflict, rather than celebrate diversity" (Al Muhairi 2013, 14). Mubarak Hamad Al Muhairi continues that "we" cannot accept "the rise of such intolerance" (2013, 14). He then poses the Louvre Abu Dhabi as the antidote to intolerance:

> Our universal museum will celebrate and advance intercultural dialogue— so profoundly needed in the modern world—and will be a place where people can connect with each other through the universal languages of the arts. We believe that such exchanges will allow us to rewrite the future of human civilization. (2013, 15)

So how precisely do museums work to promote these values? A director in Abu Dhabi's culture ministry highlighted art's transformative nature: "[These works] each participate in an aesthetic and cultural dialogue that expands minds. The works . . . cause us to question our own identities, whatever our nationality, background, or ethnicity, both within a global and historical context and from the standpoint of a particular time and place" (Aoun-Abdo 2013, 21). These experiences "are rich in discovery and grounded in acceptance, understanding and empathy" (Aoun-Abdo 2013, 21). Such discourses encouraged safe experimentation—a sanitization of difference for visitors to engage with, but in ways that were not bracing and which avoided direct conflict.

As part of their work to produce tolerant subjects, arts organizers evacuated difference and preemptively erased conflict, either discursively or through a focus on visual analysis over formal context. This erasure of difference emphasized universalism instead, appealing to an Enlightenment humanist ideology. In this chapter, I trace these attempts to cultivate frictionless, diverse audiences in children's and youth workshops, a college course, and, finally, a public talk.

Molding the Citizens of the Future Through Preemptive Erasure

Manarat Al Saadiyat (hereafter Manarat), a venue opened in 2010 on Abu Dhabi's Saadiyat Island, hosted a number of arts-related events prior to the opening of Saadiyat's headliner museums, including Abu Dhabi Art Fair and exhibitions jointly staged with the teams building the new museums. As an entity, Manarat was a partnership between the Tourism Development and Investment Company (TDIC), a public-private developer, and the Abu Dhabi cultural ministry. Exhibitions at Manarat were co-branded, such as the *Birth of a Museum* exhibition, which was cohosted by Manarat Al Saadiyat and the Louvre Abu Dhabi in 2013. At this stage, Abu Dhabi's cultural ministry, Tourism and Culture Authority Abu Dhabi (TCA Abu Dhabi), housed teams working on the development of the Louvre, Guggenheim, and Zayed National Museum collectively. The Guggenheim Abu Dhabi, Zayed National Museum, and the Louvre Abu Dhabi were not, at this time, open to the public, as their buildings were in various stages of planning and construction. The attempts to create audiences and pave the way for Saadiyat's museums were not hidden: One brochure noted, "Through exhibitions like *A History of the World in 100 Objects* . . . TCA Abu Dhabi aims to place the Zayed National Museum story into the context of the Middle East and the wider world" (Abu Dhabi Tourism and Culture Authority 2014, 3). Such exhibitions were one way not only to seed audiences, but also to build an entity's brand and identity in advance of the actual brick-and-mortar institution itself. These early exhibitions and the extensive roster of collateral events that accompanied them were important place-making tools.

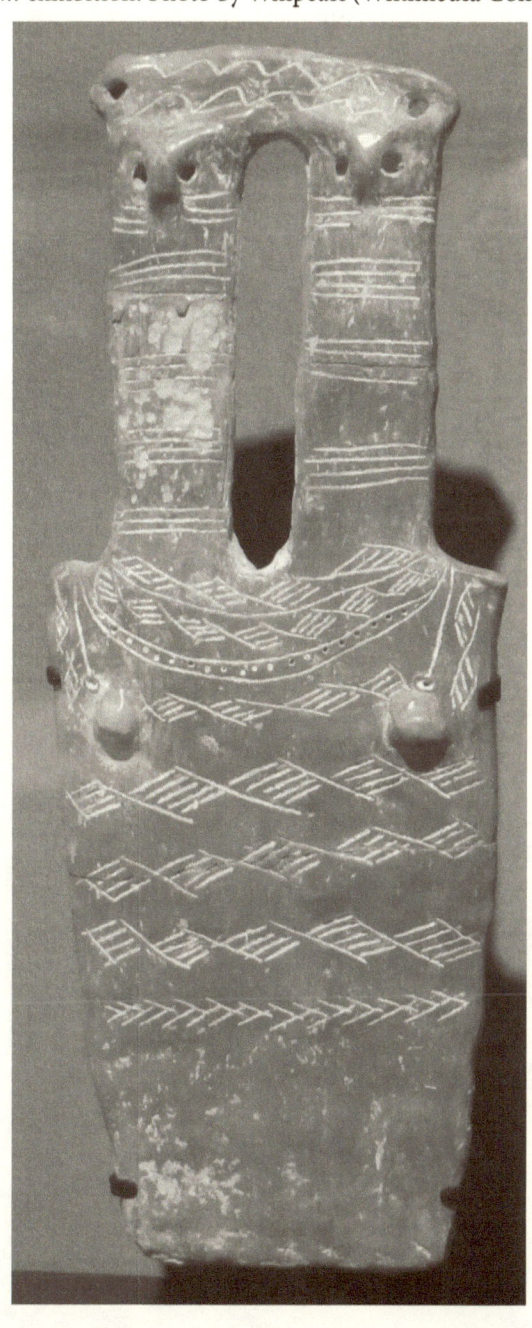

FIGURE 5.2. A photograph of a similar Bactrian princess figurine in the collection of the Louvre (Paris), 2016. Photo by Rama (Wikimedia Commons).

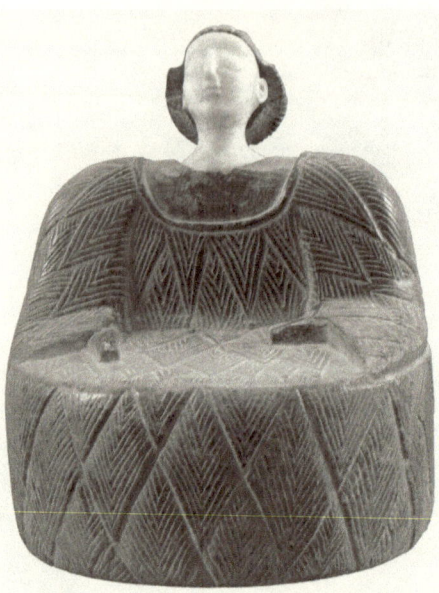

FIGURE 5.3. A gallery in the Louvre Abu Dhabi in 2023, with Yves Klein's *Anthropometry* (1960) on the rear wall on the right. Photo by Tatiana Diuvbanova (Shutterstock).

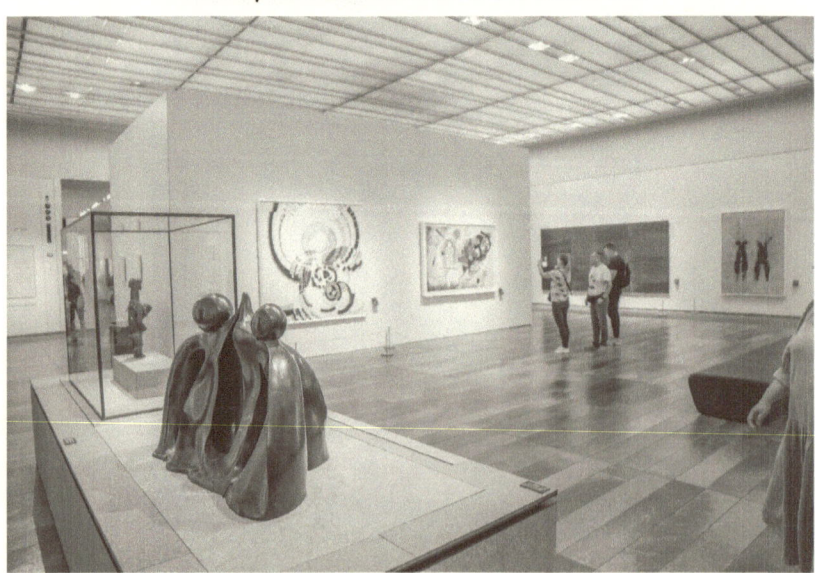

One senior cultural ministry employee on a museum team, Yusur, was herself Arab. Yusur had noted the importance of these workshops in our conversation. Referring to the juxtaposition of three figurative objects in an exhibition then on display at Manarat (Figures 5.1, 5.2, and 5.3), she said,

> I'll give you one tangible example. If you see the Bactrian Princess next to the Cypriot idol and the Yves Klein [*Anthropometry*, 1960] . . . when you look at this, it's already a big statement, because you are shown the human figure. And as you know, in Islam, the figure is not something that is part of the culture.

> These workshops are mainly for children two to five years old. They create a Bactrian Princess or Cypriot idol, so they are in direct contact with a human figure. So it's built into their subconscious in their life, the understanding of what is a human figure, so it doesn't become a taboo.

> So you can go every day in school and tell them that it's not a problem to show the human figure. But this doesn't work. *It will always be theory.* But when you get the child manually being in contact with art, you create codes and references that will be part of his knowledge.

There are several key ideas packed into these comments: a recentering of the European art historical mode of analyzing works, an assertion of aniconism and a presumptive chasm among viewers of these works, assumptions about what hands-on learning can do, and a future-oriented stance. First, in this instance, Yusur reproduced a widely accepted sociological framework of art as a series of codes. Pierre Bourdieu and Alain Darbel have noted that "as symbolic goods, works of art only exist for those who have the means of appropriating them, that is, of deciphering them" (1991, 39). They also argued that aesthetics are a "dimension of the . . . ethos of class," and that to appreciate artworks and understand them, "the uncultivated visitor can only invoke the quality and quantity of the work put into them, with moral respect taking the place of aesthetic admiration" (Bourdieu and Darbel 1991, 47). That is, if one does not possess the codes to appropriately decipher art, one's only appreciation of it can be—essentially—technical.

Interestingly this staff member had selected a particular widely held belief, that figuration is forbidden in Islam. Wendy Shaw refers to this widespread belief as an "unsubstantiated assertion of . . . 'a religiously based disdain for works of art that involved the portrayal of human forms'" (Trigger cited in

Shaw 2003, 40). In fact, where it does exist, "the opposition to figuration in Islam is not based on Qur'anic scripture but on various Traditions of the Prophet, the Hadith" (Flood 2002, 643). Proscriptive aniconism, or the absence of figural representation, thus depends on the particular school of Islam one adheres to and the *hadith* (oral traditions) legitimated by that school. Aniconism is not—despite popular misconception—universal among Muslims. Such concerns, however, are often among the Orientalist ones raised by critics of museums in the region. I was startled to see this idea pushed by someone who knew the region intimately, but she may have also selected this anecdote based on her reading of me as a white American academic. Alternatively, this framework could also have been the sanctioned narrative within the organization. At any rate, the targeting of such a particular trope was noteworthy, as was the idea that even such sensitive topics could be counteracted by the instilling of codes.

Yusur placed an overwhelming weight on hands-on learning, that such activities would outweigh formal education and familial and cultural socialization. The idea that hands-on learning at a very young age, before formal schooling, would prevail played into a theory of subconscious absorption. This tactic makes a few assumptions. First, it adopts unquestioned the manufactured, Orientalist perspective that assumes Muslim audiences in the Emirates believe figural representation to be forbidden, essentially reifying widespread Euro-American ideas about the region. Secondly, the tactic is essentially a preemptive one: Rather than changing someone's mind after a belief had become normalized, these museum organizers wished to imprint on young minds before they formed such opinions. Rather than directly addressing the presumed conflict head-on, and the potential "intolerance" it represented, some organizers aimed to preclude it, preventing the supposed conflict from coming into existence. This mode neutralizes conflict before it happens, erasing potential conflict to present tolerance. It was therefore a future-oriented strategy, and one that discouraged—and largely fully removed—any space for debate. Such top-down impositions of perspective run counter to prevailing ideas about the liberal democratic values that arts and museums are meant to foster in society.

In the summer of 2014, the director of the cultural authority granted me permission to attend and help out at that summer's workshops at Manarat. These workshops focused on different objects in the *History* exhibition that represented a wide swathe of present-day communities around the globe, including a Jomon pot (Japan), the Royal Game of Ur (Iraq), an Indus seal (Pakistan), a Colima dog vessel (Mexico), Viking jewelry, Chinese blue-and-white porcelain, and woodcuts (Germany). Art teachers taught workshops in three age tranches: children (six to eight years old), junior (nine to twelve years), and adult and teen (thirteen years old and above).[2] In preparation for supporting these workshops, I read a guide that the cultural ministry made for educators specifically for the exhibition in which museum organizers offered tools for a deeper analysis of the object. On the left page, a close-up, high-resolution image of the object appears on a black background, centered at the top of the page. Beneath the image, in left-aligned text, the name of the object is italicized. Under the name, each tidbit of information had its own line: Underneath "Arabian Bronze Hand," it read: "100–300 CE, Yemen, 1983,0626.2" (presumably the British Museum's accession number for the object, although this information was never clarified nor its relevance to research articulated), and listed the dimensions of the object. In addition to echoing the aesthetic grammar of professionalism described in the previous chapter, by appearing here this information is reinforced to visitors as necessary to look for, influencing how the visitor sees and interprets the object. On the facing page, a brief paragraph titled "About the Object" introduced it:

> This bronze hand is a devotional object made to honour a god named Ta'lab Riyam. . . . Local gods with specific duties were common in pre-Islamic Arabia, but the arrival of Judaism, Christianity, Zoroastrianism, and *ultimately Islam led to their obliteration*. This hand appears to have been cast from life, since it has unusual spoon-shaped nails and a broken little finger. (Abu Dhabi Tourism and Culture Authority 2014, 43; emphasis mine)

This information is followed by a paragraph offering historical context on the incense kingdoms of ancient Yemen.

Given Yusur's comments, I was not surprised that the text commented on the pre-Islamic period, which is called *Jāhilīya* (the time of ignorance) in Arabic. Muslim state actors can be wary of invoking *Jāhilīya*, hesitant to condone pre-Islamic pagan practices or, in some cases, even acknowledge them and thereby appear to condone them.[3] The careful phrasing of the text offered a possibly controversial fact in very smooth, banal framing, and also credited Islam with vanquishing pre-Islamic pagan deities. This framing, and Yusur's, tried to quietly assert facts without appearing to challenge Islam or mainstream interpretations of the pre-Islamic period. It avoided conflict, largely by refusing to acknowledge contradiction or irreconcilable difference. Para-doxically, then, in the name of tolerance, certain perspectives or beliefs are not tolerated. To perform tolerance in the museum, some perspectives are intolerable.

The educators' workbook also included a list of questions for the visit:

During your visit

Observation questions

- Look closely at this object, describe what you see.
- What material do you think it is made of?
- How do you think it was made?
- What do you think the inscription might say?
- What purpose do you think an object such as this would have been made for?
- Where do you think this *Arabian Bronze Hand* comes from? (Abu Dhabi Tourism and Culture Authority 2014, 43)

Many of these questions emphasized the importance of paying close atten-tion, encouraging curiosity, and using visual cues to extrapolate data. These prompts did not entice viewers to develop subjective responses to the objects; this mode of approach favored older models of formal analysis and connois-seurship in art history rather than a more contextualized, socially linked ver-sion that is typically practiced today. The "Post-Visit Discussion Questions and Suggested Activities" section of the educators' guide included a single prompt: "Research and discuss the use of religious offerings and protective rituals across different cultures. What sort of beliefs do each of the cultures carry? What are their similarities and differences?" (Abu Dhabi Tourism and Culture Authority 2014, 43).[4] By couching individual practices within a broad scale of cultures and even the topic of religion itself, the specifics of *Jāhilīya*-era practices seem less distinctive and noteworthy, just one era among many. This approach evacuates the specific in favor of a universal.

While public workshops did not include the same educators' guides and activities, preemptive flattening occurred in other ways. One summer after-noon, I arrived early at Manarat to help set up the large, cathedral-ceilinged white cube gallery space that doubled as a classroom. Nura, the artist running the workshop and a ministry employee, sighed in relief when she saw me walk through the door—her assistant had called in sick. The day's activity centered on the Arabian Bronze Hand. The adult and teen workshop attendees were going to make plaster casts of their own hands. She asked me to help divvy up strips of Modroc, a mesh covered with dry plaster globules, into even piles on each of the six round white tables in the classroom. Then we filled water jars and allocated paintbrushes on the tables. The participants would take the Modroc and lay the strips over one hand, painting them with water to activate and spread the plaster. By layering the strips, they would slowly create a hand sculpture. Once the Modroc dried and their hand casts were complete, they would be able to paint their own hand sculptures.

When the workshop started, Nura began by welcoming everyone, mostly teens and some parents who stayed with them. The twelve attendees were mostly white British, French, and American youth, although two Arab and two Japanese teens were also present. I was reminded of an exasperated comment by one education manager at the ministry: "We know right now our workshops only touch expats. We want to change that!" These workshop attendees seemed to align with the manager's take on their regular audiences. Nura then described the object, the bronze hand figurine from ancient Yemen. Then she directed each table to go to the rear of the room, by the sinks and storeroom, to get a smock to protect their clothing. After everyone had put on smocks, Nura called us together. "When we go into the exhibition," she told the group, "I want you to pay attention to the details. I'm going to ask you about them!" Then, with her at the front of the line and me at the back, we filed out of the classroom and took the participants into the exhibition to see the object.

Once we returned to the workshop, Nura directed a few questions at the participants, mainly the teenaged ones. One younger teen girl raised her hand: "It was yellowy." Good, Nura responded, the hand was made of bronze, a yellowy metal, anything else? A boy commented tentatively, "There were symbols on it." Excellent, Nura told them. These symbols were part of how archaeologists could tell what time period the hand was made in, because the symbols were actually an ancient Arabian language. "This was their alphabet," Nura explained, "so scientists know that this object was made around 100 to 300 CE. That is about two thousand years ago. What else?" The teens looked around, and Nura eventually prompted, "What did you notice about the fingers? Anything strange?" "Oooh!" One boy's hand shot up. "The fingernails looked kinda weird."

Yes, Nura affirmed. "We think this object was made from a real person, because the nails are not perfect and the little finger looks broken. So what we're going to do today is understand one way to make a hand like this, and once you make a copy of your hand and it dries, you can paint it with whatever symbols you like—just like the original maker did."

Nura's focus on the object encouraged looking closely for details, which could then extend the viewer's understanding of the work. Details like the *Musnad* alphabet (though Nura did not specify its name) and the idiosyncrasies of the hand anatomy helped to contextualize the objects for the participants. In the workshop for teens and adults, Nura did not discuss the religious significance of the hand, nor did she broach the topics of *Jāhilīya*, religion, or ritual at all. By not bringing up these topics in the workshop, Nura also avoided dredging up points of friction that might be considered political, opting instead for more universalizing information, like the date of creation, the alphabet, and the physical particularities of the maker. Incidentally, this information reinforced the professionalism discourses described in the previous chapter. Similar to the Klein piece, organizers avoided head-on engagement with potential conflict, attempting neutralization through preemptive erasure.

Other materials to cultivate junior publics flattened difference in the name of inclusive harmony in additional ways. Artist Alia Al-Shamsi illustrated the young person's guide to the exhibition *But We Cannot See Them*, the exhibition held at NYU Abu Dhabi Art Gallery in 2017.[5] The opening spread reads, "This exhibition is about a community of artists from around the world who made art together in the UAE" (Al-Shamsi 2017, 2). The guide, like the exhibition, lightly marks national origin: While the cartoons carry almost no trace of racialization, the only mentions of artists' belonging are offered in their introductions, and only for the two non-Emirati artists: "I'm Jos Clevers and I'm from the Netherlands. I arrived in the UAE in 1994. . . . I'm Vivek Vilasini and I come from India" (Al-Shamsi 2017, 6). The cover of the guide is black and white, showing the faces of five figures, their eyes calmly closed; all the noses are simple lines down the center of the face, and the cartoons do not depict mouths. The depictions are fully deracinated and meant to be universally legible. One appears to be a woman in a hijab; the other four are coded male. Aside from the marking of Ebtisam Abdulaziz's hijab and eyelashes, there are few distinguishing markers on the faces, often relegated to small distinctions like the shape of their hair, a moustache, or their glasses. One of the characters holds a flashlight, which illuminates an area in white where the title of the exhibition is written in a typewriter-like font. On first spread, the guide invites the young person to draw their own face on alongside the artists' faces.

The booklet de-emphasizes national, racial, or ethnic belonging in an ode to multicultural tolerance. It also establishes from the outset that the UAE is a peaceful place for all to come and make art together. The message is: All are welcome. In the classroom, one professor adopted a similar tactic to evacuate potential conflict, proposing the idea of art as simultaneously universal and singular, existing together without conflict. The way to reach broad audiences was to flatten difference—to make it neutral and palatable.

Ways of Seeing

On a sunny February morning, I woke up and prepared to head to class: An artist I had met at an Abu Dhabi art center, and who I call Ustaz Khalil, taught art at the Ladies' Campus of Emirates National University (ENU; a pseudonym), and he had invited me to attend a new class he was teaching, Art Criticism. The class had an art prerequisite, so the students were meant to have some exposure to studio art—and therefore some important vocabulary—beforehand. The class was designed to teach students how to consume art, and how to respond to it. After walking into the nondescript concrete building and up a flight of steps, I carefully checked the classroom number before entering. I walked to the back of the class and sat down, hoping to be inobtrusive and failing. All conversation around me chittered to a halt.

Ustaz Khalil strode in at the start time, carrying a precarious stack of papers and his laptop. Once he had started up a PowerPoint presentation, he introduced me to the class as a visiting researcher and said that I was observing his teaching for my work. He began by asking about a recent field trip, polling the twenty-eight female students, "Is this the first time you visited an art gallery?" A few students raised their hands. He nodded: "Our purpose was *scientific*"—he paused for emphasis—"when we went to the gallery. Some of you did very well on the assignment. I was surprised how much confusion there was, though," he said, shaking the stack of papers at the students. Description was simply naming what you see—the objects, the colors, the different elements of the artwork—and there was too much of this, Ustaz Khalil told them. He wanted more analysis of the forms, composition, and style elements. "*Takwīn ṣūra*," he said, translating the term "composition" into Arabic (and his only instance of using Arabic; the remainder of the class was conducted in English). Using the term "scientific" also reiterated a professionalized, dispassionate labor, as described in the previous chapter. Ustaz Khalil then introduced an activity to clarify the distinction between analysis and description; he handed out a paper to small groups. Students unzipped backpacks to extract pencils and pens.

Ustaz Khalil clicked the PowerPoint to advance the slide: "This is a classic. What year? What time was this painting done?" Some of the students whispered amongst themselves; one bold student piped up: "That's Da Vinci. It's Renaissance." Ustaz Khalil clicked through slides showing several works by male European painters Leonardo da Vinci, Pablo Picasso, Salvador Dalí, and Vincent van Gogh, asking students to name the painters, their nationality, and anything about the style the painter represented. The professor rattled off the paintings' dates of creation and the materials used. Then he paused and said: "When it comes to interpretation, see, this is different [from description]. First question, what is the theme or the subject matter? Is there a message, idea, a concept—something hidden? This is not a description. It's an explanation. To look at the hidden meaning. What's your immediate reaction to the artwork: How does it make you feel? Happy, sad?" Ustaz Khalil instructed the small groups to each take an image and then apply the list of questions he had shared on the handout. "Discuss them quietly in small groups," he said. "Exchange your views, and respect each other's views. When we come back together from our small group discussions, one or two will share, and the class will listen. Examine the works carefully." These guidelines—to focus, to be respectful and tolerant of others, to speak softly while looking at art—all echo the rules laid down by galleries. One activity guide instructed junior visitors to "use a quiet voice when sharing your ideas" (Manarat et al. 2014). These prescriptions also asserted that art had the capacity to broaden minds without conflict, and that the art museum was a depoliticized space. Even one's speaking demeanor was to be gentle and nonabrasive.

When the class regrouped, one group of students had examined Dalí's *The Persistence of Memory*. One student, Marwa, took the lead: "I felt confused by the work. It is clearly a work of fantasy."

Ustaz Khalil nodded. "Why was it confusing?"

"Well," Marwa started, "it's not organized. Stuff is not connected together." Another student, Mina, said, "It's like a dream. You don't see skies like this in real life."

Ustaz Khalil responded, "A dream? Or a nightmare?"

Mina's eyes flashed in recognition. "Yes, a nightmare. It's hot, and melting."

Ustaz Khalil pointed to the overhead. "Do you think the work represents anxiety in modern life, where people feel that way?"

Marwa raised an eyebrow. "Maybe because he was stressed about time, so he made the clocks look like they're melting, so they'd not be as strict." She gulped. "I don't like it."

Ustaz Khalil nodded again. "That is possible. That is a good reading." Then he continued, as if to encourage other students' ideas, "The artwork does not hold a single interpretation. We can come with multiple interpretations. We read it differently, we react differently." Here he emphasized the harmonious coexistence of multiple interpretations. He went on, "Do you feel this work represents something cultural, that isn't in Arab or Islamic culture?"

Mina looked confused. "There isn't anything cultural in here."

Ustaz Khalil tried again. "Would you say this work reflects Islamic or Arab elements?"

Mina shook her head no.

"So then it's not *a*cultural," Ustaz Khalil said, emphasizing the *a*.

Marwa jumped in: "I'd say it's more European because of the style of the clock, I guess."

Ustaz Khalil agreed, noting, "When we look at the artwork we need to identify the cultural context. This is not an Asian or Arabic or African work of art. It represents Western ideas, notions, form, taste." Ustaz Khalil encouraged students to look closely and pay attention to reference points in order to decode the deeper message of the artwork. In addition, the reference points reveal the views and positionality of the artist. Similar to the Manarat workshop, by casting one object or artwork within a broader universe of artistic production, the politics of that object and its maker diminish. Interestingly, such a view also accepts categories of Asian, Arabic, and African as distinct from "Western," creating another category of consumable boxes, which are, of course, not homogenous themselves. Such a move also, by giving overwhelming primacy to the visual as a source of data and the mode of art historical analysis, flattens and reifies difference. This strategy is interestingly in direct conflict with the impetus for artists to have conceptual, critical practice— where critique is necessary. Critique, it seems, is desirable in the creation of artwork but not in its consumption. These limitations reveal the limits of desirable novelty and difference, versus what is "too political" (Derderian 2020; see also Dávila 2020).

Ustaz Khalil's focus on technical elements and his comment about the "scientific" mission of visiting the gallery and examining artworks reinforced a savvy, informed way of looking at and reading artworks. Ustaz Khalil gave the students an entry point to analyze works, by not only looking at description, but also considering the ways that works made them feel or noting the content and cultural affiliation depicted in the works. This encouragement to put themselves into the work and share their feelings about it was similar to the *But We Cannot See Them* guide, and again differed from the prescriptions for artists in the permissibility of affective terms. By reassuring students that multiple interpretations were possible, Ustaz Khalil told them, in essence, that there were many right answers, giving them room to play and feel comfortable expressing opinions. He had also reiterated the need to "respect each other's views," again raising the specter of potential disagreement but reiterating the validity of multiple perspectives and the necessity of allowing them to exist. Because there is no one right answer, there can be no conflict. As Wendy Brown enjoins, tolerance is not accepting difference or even meaningfully engaging with it; it means just putting up with it—or, as the title of her book reads, tolerance is "regulating aversion" (2006). Here we see the limits of a framework of tolerance as merely the absence of conflict—these performances and enactments of tolerance not only flatten difference, they also subvert debate and meaningful engagement with difference.

In addition to classes at museums and colleges, there were also events oriented to a broad public—Quoz Fest, Art Week, Galleries Night, and talks. In particular, the talks accompanying Abu Dhabi Art were noteworthy because they were a blend of commercial and noncommercial interests, and they drew from serious resources that reached a wide audience, given their status as the wealthiest emirate in the UAE, as well as the seat of the capital and the president of the federation. These events abounded with tolerance talk, promoting tolerance as anti-conflict and positing art and museums as incubators of multicultural harmony.

Museums and the Stories They Tell

On my way to Manarat one afternoon, I noticed a series of high walls straitjacketing the exit ramp off the freeway. These temporary walls blocked the rampant construction with views of sun-bleached renderings of future attractions: Saadiyat Island Beach, Saadiyat Golf Club, and, of course, the planned

Guggenheim, Louvre, and Zayed National Museum (ZNM). These images prepare one well for arriving at Manarat, a picture-perfect oasis (Figure 5.4). I approached Manarat from a small cobblestone parking area, walking parallel to the building. Manicured boxy bushes sat atop miraculously green grass. Magnolia trees and triangular beige sails covered the walkway from the parking to the entrance, offering merciful protection from the blanching midafternoon sun. Manarat's exterior was clothed in gray metal grating, decorated with geometric tessellation. The metal plates were attached three feet from the beige walls of the structure, with another swoop of a gray metal extending over the front doors, a phalanx of tinted glass. As visitors entered Manarat to attend Abu Dhabi Art, above them was suspended a work that appeared to be a cloud with wooden spears protruding from it. Another work was installed above the café kiosk: The word *shukrān*, meaning thank you in Arabic, was outlined in colorful knives plunged into the wall. The careful, neat curation of the landscape and the aesthetics of the building established an atmosphere of sophistication and gravitas, picking up the vision of Saadiyat from the billboards and promoting these art spaces as peaceful, tolerant oases.

FIGURE 5.4. The entrance to Manarat Al Saadiyat in 2015.
Photo by PixHound (Shutterstock).

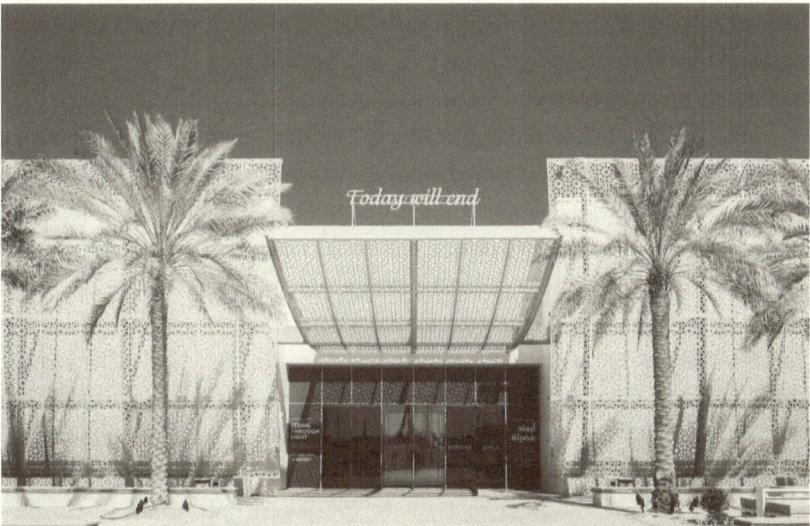

A Filipino attendant clad in a black polo shirt and black pants confirmed my e-registration and waved me into the auditorium. The late afternoon talk featured five white Euro-American experts, none of whom resided in the UAE. Sonya, an international art journalist, moderated a German philosopher I call Hans in conversation with senior personnel from the three museums on Saadiyat: George, Joe, and Alain. The talk with these art-world stars was part of the programming around Abu Dhabi Art. Unlike other commercial art fairs, this one had significant programming about museums, an early hint of the cultivation of an arts audience, as well as offering a polite riposte to critics by reiterating several tropes about tolerance and multiculturalism.

As I entered the auditorium, I could see the first several rows were marked as reserved, so I selected a beige plastic folding chair about five rows back. Many of the people sitting in the reserved section I recognized as cultural authority staff, some of whom I had worked with during preliminary field-work. Five black leather tulip chairs sat on the stage, each with a clear plastic modular side table aside it, bearing the branding for Abu Dhabi Art pasted on the front. Each side table had a bottle of Al Ain water and a glass. Spotlights flooded the stage, and dimmer coral lights partially illuminated the audience seating area. Between the dramatic lighting and leather chairs, the stage looked rather posh.

Seven minutes after the official start time, the panelists took the stage, filing up the steps and into their chairs. Sonya, the only woman, sat in the center, flanked by two older white men on each side. She looked the part of a European art expert, perfectly at home in museums and the kind of person to be engaged in philosophical conversations at dinner parties while swirling a glass of wine: Her crisp white tunic over blousy black silk pants and black strappy sandals matched her thick-framed eyeglasses and short, practical haircut.

She briefly noted a change to the program: The Director of Louvre Paris couldn't be here because of "terrible violence" in Paris, referring to the November 13, 2015, ISIL attacks in Paris, but Sonya shared that Alain would speak on his behalf. She also introduced Agence France Musées (AFM), which she described as an "organization into which . . . how many?" She turned to her colleague, who confirmed off-mic, and then Sonya continued, "Twelve French museums are pouring their expertise and also their loans for the museums you'll be getting shortly here."

Sonya first gave the floor to Hans to speak generally about the history and meaning of museums in shaping the contemporary world. He offered a historical overview that would have fit in an undergraduate museum studies lecture. Hans's accent softened and elongated the English words: "The museum as we know it is a quite late phenomenon in the history of mankind. It came up to the bourgeois era, it belongs strongly to the period of the French Revolution, when the monarchy's wunderkammern were opened to the public." Offering a brief snapshot of the history of the development of the modern public art museum, he continued to expound.

Hans then said rather poetically, "Time is the daughter of the storehouse, the storehouse is the big sister of the museum." As the audience looked slightly askance at each other, as if to verify that no one understood this family tree, he continued, "Modern museums are made as containers for the belief in value." In fact, one of the primary reasons that the Emirates had elected to build the museums was precisely this question of value. Aware that oil was a finite resource and equally aware of the government's dependence on it, the Emirati authorities had attempted to diversify the Emirati economy. One way to do so was to become a tourist hub. Hans droned on: "To make value visible. This visibility of the value, the revelation, can be transferred in our days by almost industrial techniques from proven works of art that have run through the test of history for centuries and are taken as granted masterpieces." Hans's talk emphasized the market and focused on a very European historical lineage of the museum.

Sonya tucked a stray hair behind her ear, and said without hesitation, "Professor Hans is quite right, museums have this magical quality." Yet she did not pick up the question of museums and value, a longstanding intellectual debate about separating art and museums from overt financial interests (Amariglio et al. 2009; Benjamin 1969; Bourdieu 2000; Buchholz 2022; Horkheimer and Adorno 2002; Lena 2019; Rectanus 2002; Velthuis 2005; Wu 2002; Zarobell 2017). Then she segued, "So the British Museum is not going to be present in the Emirates, but it has played a role and continues to play a role, I think, the creation of a very great museum you're building at the moment, the Zayed National Museum." With that, she effortlessly transitioned to George.

George noted that the British Museum, "to our great honor, has been invited to advise on how the Zayed National Museum can be shaped." The British Museum was thus providing more consultants in a long history of British cultural experts hired to shape cultural institutions on the Arabian Peninsula, from colonial officials in Aden in the 1930s and Kuwait in the 1950s to later UNESCO consultants. These longstanding connections also play into tolerance discourses by collapsing us/them, metropole/periphery distinctions and reiterating a universalizing humanity. The British Museum director had signed the 2002 Declaration on the Importance and Value of Universal Museums (republished in Karp et al. 2006, 247–49), which affirmed a universalist, global view to justify the continued display of looted artifacts by major Western museums. Unsurprisingly, George downplayed differences or distinctions between the local and the global, asserting them as both/and, not either/or:

> This is a museum about values. A local community is always part of a world community. This connection between the Emirates and the rest of the world goes back thousands of years. It's what we're trying to do, is argue that this narrative of being an Emirati, there has always been part of a much bigger narrative. It is local, it is global. And it's the purpose of a national museum to make that connection graspable to anybody . . . for a national museum, it has to be designed and developed in the context of public discussion, public debate. And so there have already began [sic] a series, *Multaqas*, where questions, issues, can be raised in the museum . . . more of these will take place to talk about the role of women, the conservation of the natural world, and so on.

George reiterated the idea of the museum as a depoliticized space where challenging issues could be discussed without conflict, a forum with depoliticized debate. That the forum (*multaqā*) conversations named *Multaqas* by the ZNM, were held prior to the opening of the museums, and as design and curatorial decisions were coalescing, reveals a concerted attempt to gather community input (or, at minimum, a desire to appear to do so). This structure seemed designed to preempt critiques and concerns, both from local audiences and international ones, partially by conscripting their participation in the design process and making the community feel engaged. Secondly, while calling for debates, museum organizers held back from addressing controversy directly. For example, George used very neutral language here to depoliticize two rather controversial topics: the role of women in Muslim societies, long a preoccupation of Euro-American audiences (Abu Lughod 2013), and climate change, a scientific reality denied by some religious and political groups.

George also connected two concerns: first, the relationship between the local and the global. On one side, the press termed these museums as Xanadus (Fattah 2007) in "the middle of the desert" (Rappolt cited in Brown 2013), contributing to a pervasive exceptionalization of the Gulf (Kanna et

al. 2020) as a place with no history and culture. In the midst of these circu-
lating discourses, George attempted to situate the Emirates within a broader
global scale. He also addressed the question in many critics' minds: Who
are these museums for? The ZNM needed to be "graspable" to anyone. Part
of that was connecting the local community to the museum and encouraging their input. Here George took pains to point out the Multaqa forum
series, hinting at the museum's engagement with the local community and
harkening back to a longstanding debate in museum studies: the museum
as temple or forum (Cameron 1972). Yet he did not translate "multaqa" for
the audience—his passing reference assumed an audience already familiar
with the talk series, or at least one who would understand the Arabic term
without translation and be able to gather in general what he was talking
about. These kinds of elisions contributed to making the talk feel more like
an internal hype meeting for cultural ministry staff rather than a talk for
the general public.

Continuing the erasure of difference by asserting universalism, Sonya
then asked George a question about a quote attributed to Shaykh Zayed, the
founding father of the Emirati nation: "Shaykh Zayed said the world is one
civilization, so how could there be a clash of civilizations? Do you feel that a
museum can actually help create this understanding, that we are not all just
little separate pockets?" This framing was exceptionally well-designed: By
citing a well-loved Emirati figure, Shaykh Zayed, many audience members
would likely give credence to the idea at the outset. It also drew from and
reiterated longstanding ideas that museums are symbols of civilizational at-
tainment, storehouses for humanity, and sites for the promotion of tolerance,
which Jessica Winegar has traced back to thinkers like Kant through early,
proto-anthropologists like Edward Tylor and Lewis Henry Morgan, who considered art as a sign of advanced civilization in their evaluation of so-called
primitive communities (Winegar 2008, 658–60). The idea that art is a "bridge
of understanding" relies on an assumption "that art is a uniquely valuable and
uncompromised agent of cross-cultural understanding" (Winegar 2008, 652),
despite that the canon is political and that historically thinkers and makers
from the Global South have been excluded from the category of art (Brzyski
2007; Dávila 2020; Iskin 2017; Karp and Lavine 1991; Karp et al. 1992, 2006;
Myers 2002; Price 1989, 2007; Smith 1999; Winegar 2006). Thus it is imperative to note that "when art is used to show Middle Easterners' humanity or
to advance certain views of Islam, a very particular and politicized 'bridge

of understanding' is created that obfuscates, and perhaps refuses, other understandings which might be less comfortable to America's secular cultural
elites" (Winegar 2008, 653). In this instance, thoroughly depoliticized language served to downplay potential conflicts.

George affirmed instantly: "I think our museum, this museum, is perhaps
the best place possible for that idea to be made graspable to a very wide public.
That idea that all civilizations are about the same values can be made very
clear through objects. And it can be very clear through comparative narratives
of different cultures, and different civilizations." He continued,

> This group of museums represents a unique opportunity, really, in the world
> to answer or affirm that statement. There is nowhere outside Europe and
> America at the moment that attempts to tell a story of the whole world. The
> only museums where that *can* be done are in cities in Europe and North
> America. *This will be the first opportunity, the first attempt to do that for the
> world outside.* (emphases mine)

George underscored here the question of global audience—global reach, universal humanity. He also pointed to the challenge—there was a long history of
museums being Eurocentric, this was a chance to change that.[6] This framing
also supports an argument that European and American museums do not
need to repatriate, because they are "sharing" their collections with a global
audience (see also the Declaration on the Importance and Value of Universal
Museums, republished in Karp et al. 2006, 247–49). Yet such a universalizing
prescription conflates an institution under one nation's rules, laws, and historical trajectory with the responsibility of managing humanity's collective
artistic accomplishment, erasing the arbitrary lines of national affiliation. It
also ignores the colonial extraction that permits these metropolitan museums
to hold such collections.

Pulling another primary critique into the conversation, Sonya asked,
"Contemporary art is . . . a construct of the West. So how does one set up a
museum outside the West aiming to fill it full of art from the rest of the world
without imposing on it a certain Western idea of what the art ought to be?"
She turned to Joe, who deferred slightly, defining contemporary art as that
which is "made at the moment, and it's made everywhere." This definition
was not region- or history-specific, but a chronological, temporal definition
pegged to modernity. However, he continued, just because contemporary art
was made everywhere did not mean it was valued evenly:

I think that whatever obstruction there might be is superimposing preordained values on what it is you're looking at. So contemporary art exists in a very broad way. Do we allow it intellectually to flourish in a broad way? That's the challenge. It's not as if there weren't great artists working around the world for hundreds of years. The problem is, the challenge is, our ignorance and our prejudices against those expressions.

In this framing, the lack of recognition of artists from Southwest Asia and the Middle East was not a problem of the artists or the Arab world, but a problem of perception only—a framework that minimized the structures of academic racism, uncomfortable histories and legacies of colonialism, and thorny questions of standards and canons. Projects that promote tolerance have often depoliticized, as they often "rende[r] racism and other forms of marginalization as matters of attitude rather than structural injustice" (Dzenovska 2018, 11). This concept, that the issue was not substantive but a mere matter of reception, denies these colonial histories and the systemic racism entrenched in the art world (Oguibe 2004). Joe's remarks link to the way Ustaz Khalil spoke with his students in his exhortation to acknowledge the cultural biases in artworks, particularly in their referents. They both emphasized the importance of how to read art, and how art's legibility impacted the creation of artistic canons.

Sonya then turned to Alain. He noted that most importantly, the future Louvre museum needed to be able to welcome artists, reaffirming a construct of a symbiotic relationship between museums and artists. Alain said a second goal was to develop audiences and enhance the ways visitors are welcomed. He referenced a few various initiatives undertaken by the Louvre in Paris, including the Petite Galerie children's initiative. He also emphasized that the majority of the Louvre Paris's visitors were not French, leaving unspoken that the Emirati population was also majority-foreign, the implication being that the Louvre staff were well-versed in reaching and meeting the needs of diverse, international audiences.

Sonya told Alain, "You're going to be the first," referring to the Louvre Abu Dhabi's opening date. "What is the correlation between the three museums?" Yet another critique has been the number and scope of Saadiyat Island plans, with three major museums. Would they compete? Again minimizing any potential conflict, Alain deftly noted the differences: one is a contemporary art museum, one is a national museum, one is a universal survey museum. He concluded, "So you have this critical mass, and each of us will have a part to play." Joe chimed in that he saw the museums as "complementary to one another, not redundant." This "complementary not competitive" discourse, common in my fieldwork, asserted a tolerant coexistence and a denial of conflict and friction.

Sonya then invited Hans back into the conversation, and he spoke about religion briefly. This tangent also seemed to direct the conversation to yet another critique and trope about the museums that outside commentators focused on: How would a museum like the Louvre Abu Dhabi function, for example, given that imagery of nudity is not permitted in the Emirates (which is often attributed to religious precepts in Islam)? Other critics have noted concerns about the museums, given the lack of freedom of speech and the prohibition of homosexuality, and the general fit of liberal, secular social institutions in an illiberal Muslim context (see Krieger 2008; Vora 2018). George took up the question, responding that the ZNM's task was "to try to articulate the long narrative of human existence here. And that obviously has been largely shaped by religion." Many of the objects on display, he said, would either be representative of how people have lived in the past, or

> will be works of art shaped by religious tradition. And that's perfectly normal . . . that would be a very easy basis to move from that understanding of human experience to the Louvre, and to look at the same phenomenon across other cultures, in a comparable way but through a different filter, and then in the twentieth century. The works at the Guggenheim will be exploring the same fundamental questions of the relationships between the individual, the society, and the cosmos.

Asserting the normalcy of religion, his answer sublimated the question of religion into a human universal, rather than respond directly to the critiques of the Emirati government or to concerns about religious fundamentalism. Here again, the speaker downplayed difference in the name of tolerance.

Sonya chimed in, "I just wanted to say . . ." Here she paused. "When I heard that museums were going to be created in this part of the world, I rejoiced. I thought this was an absolutely wonderful and illuminating decision. And fortunately the people in Europe who complained about it have ceased to complain about it." She continued, "Cause I think we're beginning to realize, the more diverse we are, the more we are capable of resisting fanaticism like that of ISIL [Islamic State of Iraq and the Levant], which is so very close to you, and to us." She then concluded, "So I'd like to thank you all, thank you very much."

Such frameworks support Alexandre Kazerouni's assertion (2015, 2017) that the Gulf rulers see these museums as cultural rapprochements with the "West" (*l'Occident*). These awkward comments at the end—the links to ISIL, references to religious fanaticism—and the injunction that religion was "natural" and that diversity can inoculate against fanaticism served to rebut critiques proffered by international media that draw from a longtime pseudo-intellectual clash of civilizations narrative advanced by the academic Samuel Huntington and others. At no point was it acknowledged that the UAE already had a diverse population.

Sonya had, perhaps unintentionally, opened and closed the panel with references to Islamic extremism, opening with ISIL attacks in Paris and closing by noting the proximity of ISIL to "you," the audience. The book-ending of the talk in this way reiterated the polemic of art versus terror, that a tolerant, multicultural art world could salve the violence. Violence and extremism emerge as the specter of intolerance. These references spoke to debates about the Gulf's museum projects in an Anglophone sphere, per-haps, but not those in the local community. Sonya's comments inadvertently reveal the politicization of these art and museum projects which is specific to the Arab and Muslim context. Despite Sonya's assertions that ISIL was close, I never heard any other references to the organization during my fieldwork, nor were militant groups of any ilk ever referenced again. These speakers offered a sanitized version of Islam, a "good" Islam versus a "bad" one to borrow a framework from Mahmood Mamdani (2004), using art and museums to preempt problematic and difficult Orientalist stereotypes (Said 1978; Shaheen 2001). The refusal to engage in such conversations also kept topics light.

Seeing Through Light

A month after the talk, I attended *Light Show* at the Sharjah Art Foundation. Just as it sounds, the show featured artists who worked with light. As I walked through the exhibition, I reached Carlos Cruz-Diez's *Chromosaturation*. A nearby sign indicated that visitors must remove their shoes or wear the pro-vided blue plastic shoe coverings to enter the installation, which included a series of three consecutive rooms branching off a small hallway. From outside the installation, the rooms appeared to be fairly generic rainbow shades of blue, orange, and green, consecutively.

As I entered the first room, I was immersed in a cerulean light. Looking down the hallway connecting the rooms, I saw the following room was a deep orange, much darker than it had looked from the entry. After waiting a few moments to allow my eyes to adjust to the saturated light, I stepped into the orange room. But it was a rosy lavender now! From here, the green room went from forest green to a neon sea-foam. And as I returned from the green to the orange, the orange now assumed a coral color. The concept imparted itself seamlessly, wordlessly—our perspective changes depending on where we are standing. And it moves with us.

One interlocutor reported that *Light Show* was one of the Foundation's most popular exhibitions. They attributed this popularity to the easy legibility of the show: Everyone understands light, and light is pretty. Light works afford an engagement with the visible, a passive embrace of a known entity that minimizes class differences by diminishing the capital and education required to appreciate the works. It is also easy to engage in visual analysis, rather than contextual analysis, with light artworks. And the underlying concepts of most of the works were, for lack of a better term, light—they were not about war, poverty, or suffering. They were not cloaked in heavy intellectual language that made a viewer feel uneducated or ignorant, and thus they were palatable to broad audiences. Furthermore, the Arabic word for light, *nūr*, is synonymous with enlightenment or illumination; in Islam, Allah is also the source of light, and therefore light holds special resonance for Muslim visitors. Light as a theme for a show met many of the goals of these arts organizations—to allow easy entrée, to get visitors in the door, and to stage an exhibition that was an easy fit for the museum in the UAE context, avoiding any seeming contradictions.

Light remains a popular and accessible theme for Gulf art institutions. In late 2014, the burgeoning Guggenheim Abu Dhabi staff had staged *Seeing Through Light* at Manarat Al Saadiyat. Around the same time, Sharjah's Islamic Art Festival put on their annual show, the 2015 theme being *Noor* (Light). The annual Noor Riyadh Festival launched in 2021, breaking Guinness World Records for "largest light art festival" among others in 2022 (Kaddoura 2022). Such shows allow for a broad, purportedly unproblematic engagement, crossing linguistic and cultural lines to form the perfect example of a bridge of understanding, the perfect example of tolerance and universalism in a twenty-first-century museum paradigm.

IN THE GALLERY VI   Gulf Futures

UPON LANDING IN ALULA, Saudi Arabia, in late November 2023, my artist friend Anne and I waited an hour and a half to get through passport control. Our flight from Dubai was full of tourists, all needing visas, and we overwhelmed the limited customs officers on site. Once through, I turned on my eSIM card in order to open Google Maps and navigate to our hotel. Anne and I had come to check out AlUla for a long weekend, and we were staying in a caravan of vintage Airstream trailers outside of town. Driving north out of the airport, we mused how our visit would have been quite different even in 2017. At that time in Saudi Arabia, women couldn't drive and were required to cover their hair in public. Saudi ruler Mohammed bin Salman, or MBS, changed the laws in 2018 to permit women to drive and to stipulate that head coverings were not required. Western media often portrayed these changes, along with the reopening of movie theaters, as the Saudi state wooing prospective tourists, and as the kingdom "opening up."

Once we reached the southern part of AlUla's Old Town, my GPS began to stutter, repeatedly telling me to make a U-turn on a road with cement barrier down the middle. It seemed the route had been recently reworked from a one-way street to a two-way street, with the cement barriers preventing turns in any direction. The merging of two one-way roads into a single road with one lane running in each direction allowed for the Old Town to be converted to a pedestrian zone. Later, we experienced a similar conundrum: To find the Pink Camel bakery, located in the Daimumah (*Dīmūma*) oasis, my GPS told me to turn right where there was a sandy track, but no paved road. Anne and I both took a deep breath as the wheels of our sedan, decidedly not a 4WD, navigated the sand. "Is this right? This can't be right," I muttered. "Let's keep going a little bit," Anne responded optimistically. She was right; after swishing

FIGURE G6.1. A Lihyanite tomb at Hegra, AlUla, Saudi Arabia, 2023. Photo by author.

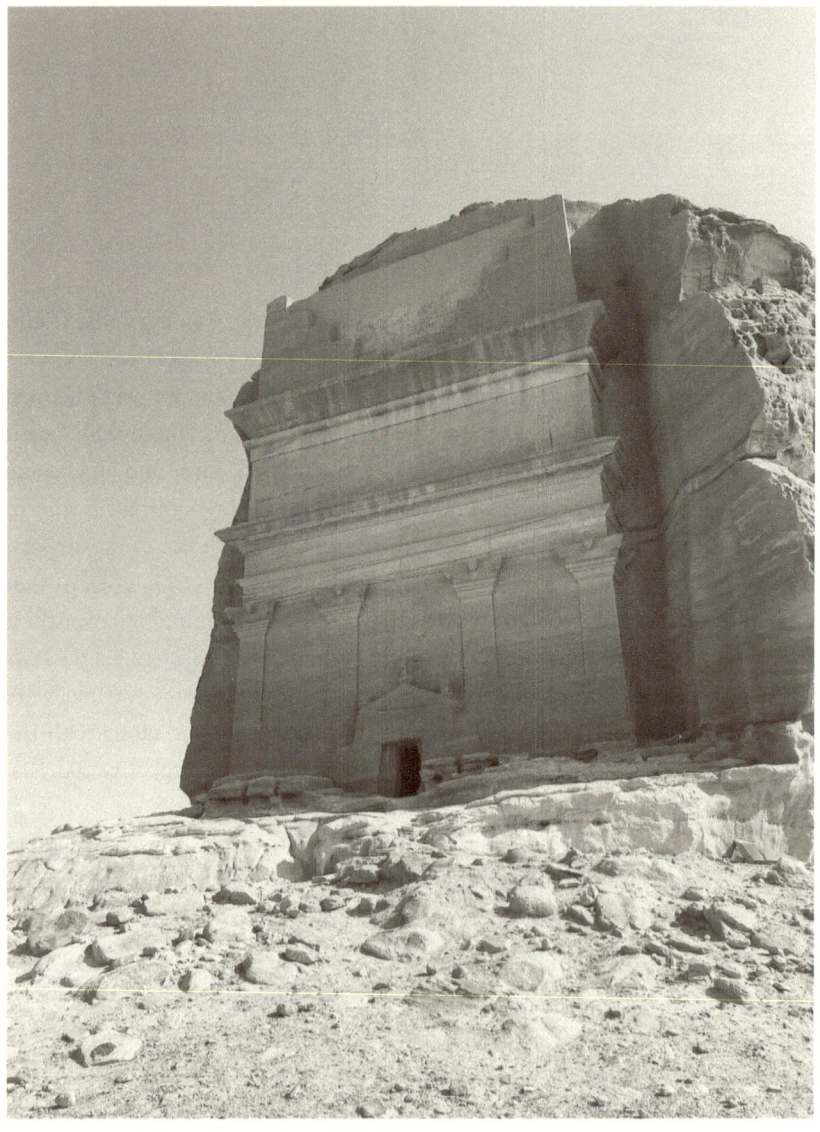

FIGURE G6.2. Downtown AlUla, Saudi Arabia, 2023. Photo by author.

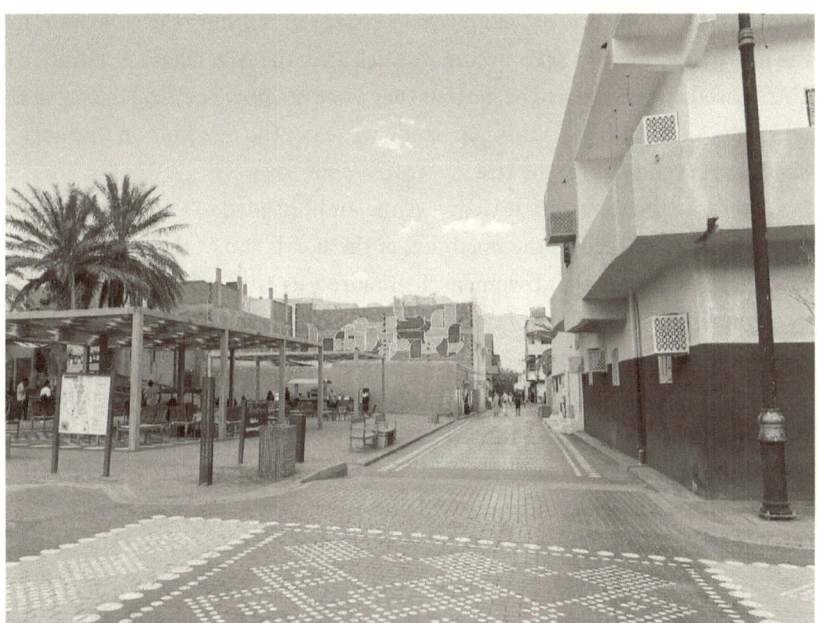

our tires a few times in some loose sandpits, we eventually made it to the Pink Camel. Google Maps was still updating what now constituted a road and what wasn't anymore. Things in AlUla were changing fast.

Starting in 2020, images of AlUla had started showing up on my Instagram feed: The town was host to the Desert X biennial that year and again in 2022. Images of the picturesque sandstone cliff formations, visitors frozen midair on trampolines installed in-ground, and mind-bending images of a building entirely covered in mirrors, which reflected back the splendor of the valley, littered my social media. An oasis town in the Medina Province, AlUla is home to breathtaking Nabataean, Lihyanite, and Dadanite ruins (Figure G6.1). In 2017, the Saudi government created the Royal Commission for AlUla (RCU) to protect and develop these historical sites—and to "invest in education and learning for AlUla's next generation and create training and employment opportunities for its people" (Royal Commission 2023). In early 2023, Saudi officials announced they would be opening a contemporary art museum in AlUla, in partnership with France's Centre Pompidou. Many of my UAE interlocutors had been invited to AlUla in conjunction with its various arts initiatives, and at a dinner for Abu Dhabi Art in 2023, I sat with two curators from Saudi Arabia, one of whom was in charge of building the collection for the new contemporary art museum. A week after the Abu Dhabi Art dinner, a UAE-based curator mused to me that they were no longer getting the same attention—"now, with everything in Saudi, we're not the new kids on the block." Saudi's art scene was on the rise.

After touring the ruins at Hegra, Anne and I headed to Old Town (Figure G6.2). Visitors parked in the north lot, at the north end of the one-way road, and then young men and women chauffeured us in a golf cart to the start of the walking zone. One of our drivers, a Saudi woman I guessed to be in her twenties, spoke to us in English and talked about her two sisters, both of whom were studying in England. She shared she was excited for the jobs, and the tourists, that the town's projects were attracting. Billboards along AlUla's roads showed images of smiling families walking through oases, under palm trees or sitting in plazas strung with lights, renderings of a future to look forward to—reminding me of my early visits to Saadiyat Island and the similar images of Saadiyat's future museums straitjacketing the roads and walkways. After being ferried to the pedestrian area, we strolled past a pottery shop and innumerable kiosks selling sweatshirts for the sharp temperature drops after sunset. In the pedestrian-only area, many people I assumed to be locals based on their clothing were meeting in the gathering dusk to sit in cafés and plazas strung with lights, or to enjoy an ice-cream cone from a bright yellow food truck. There were some, but not many, tourists like us. At one end of the pedestrian zone, we saw signs showing the licensure for the renovation of the Old Town, an active archaeological zone. One roundabout bore a sign stating that licenses for construction were obtained earlier that year.

As we headed back to the parking lot, we saw a plain beige building with *Yayoi Kusama* written on the side in elegant, spare font, and an attendant in a *khandūra* standing by the door. "*Maftūḥ?*" I asked—is it open? He gestured toward the doors behind him. Inside, another attendant explained the well-known Japanese artist's "The Brilliance of the Souls" work we would soon enter, one of her *Infinity Room* series. A fully enclosed mini room was installed in the larger room: The attendants asked us to follow the queue marked out by stanchions even though there was no one else in line. We dutifully walked to the left and circled the room instead of walking directly up to the mini room. The infrastructure was there for a nonexistent, but anticipated, crowd. A third attendant opened the door to the mini room and pointed out the walkway inside: A small series of tiles took us to the center of the little room; the rest of the floor was water, and the attendant enjoined us not to step off the walkway. Then she closed us in. All around us hung small globes of varying sizes painted in vibrant teals, limes, mustards, and fuchsias, which slowly transitioned from color to color. The walls were covered in mirrors, so everywhere we looked, the suspended globes blinked, an infinity space of electric colors shining in the darkness and our dim figures in the center. This series reflects the way Kusama experiences the world: Coping with abuse as a child led to hallucinations in which dots blocked out her entire vision. Visitors walk into her mind in these works, moving from a space of individualism to a space that transcends the singular human experience, becoming but shadows in a realm of never-ending color and light. Kusama installations are Instagram gold; her name is well known in contemporary art circles. The installation at Old Town was clearly an effort to link AlUla to a broader, respected contemporary art scene, and it used light, a theme that neatly skirted potential conflicts.

The ubiquitous construction, the billboards teasing an art mecca soon to be, the abrupt presence of massively famous artists, the awkwardness of road directions and instructions for tourists that weren't quite worked out yet, even the delays in getting through passport control at AlUla airport when we arrived—all of these phenomena felt achingly familiar, reminding me of my first experiences in Abu Dhabi beginning in 2012. Then, too, big plans were afoot. There was a palpable sense of a brighter future yet to be. A new world was on the way, not yet realized.

Openings and Closings

AMID ALL DUE POMP and circumstance, the Louvre Abu Dhabi opened to the public on November 11, 2017, no longer an intangible spectacle but a real museum of concrete and steel, eleven years after its announcement. Press had been allowed in on November 6 and then "VVIPs" on November 7 and 8, after which articles and photos began to spill out into social media, flooding Instagram and Twitter. *The Atlantic* published a photo of the back of an *abaya*-clad woman contemplating two European paintings—a favorite tactic that obviates permissions and protects anonymity, while also presenting a seeming contradiction: the religious woman opposite the hallmarks of a purportedly secular, intellectual Enlightenment civilization.[1] These images feed into Orientalist stereotypes while also presenting the UAE as a tolerant space, devoid of friction.

Another picture captured Moroccan king Mohammed VI standing in front of "Whistler's Mother" (Arrangement in Grey and Black No. 1), and French president Emmanuel Macron and his wife, Brigitte, were photographed congratulating Dubai's ruling shaykh and the UAE's vice president, Shaykh Mohammed bin Rashid Al Maktoum, alongside then–Crown Prince Mohamed bin Zayed Al Nahyan (Taylor 2017). It seems even the museum's opening was itself a tool of diplomacy. CNN's report, by local arts writer Anna Seaman, was entitled "Louvre Abu Dhabi: Why All Eyes Are on the Middle East's New Billion Dollar Museum" (Seaman 2017). The article proclaims the Louvre's ongoing expansion: It will someday be home to a children's museum, as well as a research center. While the Louvre

Abu Dhabi opened after years of delays, the remaining Saadiyat museums remain unfinished. The island's future state is still under construction.

The buzz around art from the Gulf did not diminish after the Louvre Abu Dhabi's opening, nor was the Louvre Abu Dhabi the last cultural megaproject underway in the region. The following month, the museum announced it would house Leonardo da Vinci's painting *Salvator Mundi*, which had made headlines after selling for a record $450.3 million at auction.[2] The beginning of construction on the Guggenheim Abu Dhabi, announced in 2007 alongside the Louvre but mired in delays, was announced in April 2019. The Gehry-designed Guggenheim building alongside the new Zayed National Museum were scheduled for completion in 2025 (Cascone 2021; Kershoff 2023). Elsewhere in the UAE, Dubai's new contemporary art center, the Jameel Arts Centre, opened in 2019 to great fanfare and has quickly become the epicenter of contemporary art in Dubai; the Barjeel Art Foundation's exhibition *Taking Shape: Abstraction from the Arab World, 1950s–1980s* toured a number of U.S. college campuses and made an argument for a definitively Arab canon of artwork. New artist- and curator-led initiatives have also popped up across the UAE, such as Bayt al Mamzar, Bayt 15, and Dirwaza Curatorial Lab.

Other entities around the region continue to invest significant capital in arts and culture projects, sparking media attention and occasional ire. Qatar's new National Museum opened in 2019; the Art Mill Museum, a museum of modern and contemporary art, is set to open in 2030 (Qatar Museums 2025). Saudi Arabia in particular has been in the U.S. media spotlight, its newly announced cultural initiatives seen to clash with the brutal killings of dissidents and journalists like Jamal Khashoggi. Funded by the Saudi oil giant Aramco, the King Abdulaziz Center for World Culture (Ithra) opened in Dhahran in 2017, a massive ellipsoid structure containing a theater, cinema, museum, children's museum, and archives, alongside other cultural facilities. In January 2018, Saudi's crown prince, MBS, inaugurated the Misk Art Institute, holding the international program launch at MoMA, the Museum of Modern Art, in New York City, perhaps a hint at its intended audience and diplomatic intentions. Misk had big collaborations in mind, proclaiming partnerships with commercial art fairs as well as educational exchanges for Saudi students abroad. In May 2019, Saudi Arabia participated in the Venice Biennale after an eight-year hiatus. The New York–Arab World Art and Education Initiative of 2018 and 2019, although partially canceled, was a series of events and exhibitions that "aims to build greater understanding between the United States and the Arab world" and included organizations like MoMA and UNESCO. Hayy Jameel, a Riyadh-based art center in the Art Jameel network, opened in December 2021. As previously noted, Saudi officials are planning a contemporary art museum with the Centre Pompidou for AlUla. AlUla was reportedly chosen as a site for such expansion for two reasons: because its built heritage places Saudi Arabia at the crossroads of exchange for centuries, dispelling persistent myths of the Arabian Peninsula as an uninhabited tabula rasa; and secondly, because the Nabataean, Pre-Islamic site of Hegra/Mada'in Saleh could associate the Kingdom with something other than Islam. Art, it seems, is not only a bridge between East and West, but is also key to a tolerant, multicultural capitalist future. That so many megaprojects are in the Gulf could be read as a recentering of a colonized industry, a decolonization of museums achieved by relocating them. Time will tell. But in the meantime, the crowds keep coming.

Performing Arts

It is productive to think of these launches, press releases, and spectacular plans as a kind of Austinian performative speech (Austin 1962). For John Austin, an act of performative speech is an utterance that does the act it describes; the most famous example being how saying "I do" in a marriage ceremony constitutes the act of wedding. Considering the announcement of plans for Saadiyat Island museums as performative utterances allows us to take seriously the work these proclamations do and the very real changes that these utterances enact and enable. Legislative acts perform and create cultural bureaucracy in the UAE: Royal decrees have birthed and formed the Emirates Fine Arts Society (EFAS), the Abu Dhabi Authority for Culture and Heritage (ADACH) turned Tourism and Culture Authority (TCA), and the informal Dubai cultural council turned Dubai Culture and Arts Authority. Words have made material structures. The UAE's many cultural bureaucracies themselves are products of performative sovereign speech. Because these announcements are partially performative, they suspend the present, rendering it a liminal space where these institutions are partially realized and effecting changes, and partially unrealized, a future as yet incomplete.

The language of the region's arts initiatives is often declarative, performative, and future-oriented. The boundary between the real and the surreal, the mirage and the museum, disappears in the unrealized and imaginative projections of the Gulf's cultural planners. In her ethnography of dreamers in Cairo, Amira Mittermaier describes how, for her interlocutors, "the imagined . . . is not inherently unreal, but it is present and absent at the same time" (2011, 19). Similarly, the performative speech of the Gulf's cultural bureaucrats describing a desired future cultural scene calls it into being. This imagined utopian artistic future is absent and present simultaneously, its material reality second to its presence in the communal imagination. Organizations held events, developed audiences, and built a presence before their brick-and-mortar facilities existed, before they had a dedicated organization, HR department, or payroll office. Such futures and aspirations are not neutral (Bocast 2019), as futures and potentialities are "vehicles for politics," inflected by the political economic context (Taussig et al. 2013, S5). They also determine where art worlds go from here, what Pierre Bourdieu has termed the "social conditions of possibility" (1995, 236). That is, that which is radical, avant-garde, or new is only so in relation to what is currently in existence. The structures, concepts, and aesthetics of the present "define and delimit the universe of the thinkable and the unthinkable" (Bourdieu 1995, 236). The seeds of future museum and representational paradigms lie dormant in the flowering of arts and museum practice today.

But how long is the present, and how far away the future? What is the horizon? The calling into being of a desired future casts the present as a liminal state. Just as Mandana Limbert's Omani interlocutors referred to the "dreamtime" of oil (2010), a liminal state suspended between the past before the discovery of oil and the unknowable future when oil will vanish, my interlocutors in the UAE seemed suspended in the dreamtime of high culture. This suspension allowed for deferral of responsibility: After all, the Saadiyat project is not *yet* complete, the Louvre Abu Dhabi still has elements under construction, and there is no Guggenheim or Zayed Museum *yet*. This is perhaps the ultimate neoliberal capitalist obfuscation of final accountability, and the capitalist need to constantly make more space for more work to be done, more profit to be made, more markets to be created. What can we make of all these delays and postponements? Will the overly hyped Saadiyat, with its four shiny, spectacular museums, ever fully appear? Perhaps this is not the right question, as it defines success on the terms of physical structures yet to be. Perhaps it does not matter if a maritime museum (which has fallen from view), or even the Guggenheim Abu Dhabi itself, ever opens. This book details the immense and important changes made real since the performative speech of the Saadiyat museums' announcement. Their announcement made them real, and this set in motion changes across the UAE's art scene, showing a new paradigm of museums in globalization: one where capital, rather than the state, takes precedence; where pressures to be inclusive for a global market transform museums and arts organizations, art makers, and their publics— changes so definitive and sweeping that in some ways, it does not matter if the Louvre had ever opened. Its announcement changed the shape of futures imagined, and those yet to be.

Notes

Introduction

1. For more on these phenomena, see: Alexander 1996; Amariglio et al. 2009; Buchholz 2022; Bydler 2004; Gardner and Green 2016; Gerber 2017; Krauss 1990; Lind 2012; Stallabras 2004; Rectanus 2002; Quemin 2002; Velthuis and Brandellero 2018; Win 2014; Wu 2002; Zarobell 2017.

2. This robust body of work includes but is not limited to: Banks 2010, 2019; Benoit-Bryan et al., 2023; Buchholz 2022; Brzyski 2007; Carr 2021; Cooks 2011; Dávila 2020; Gardner and Green 2016; C. Harris 2012, 2014; Ho 2014; Ho Hing-Kay 2010; Iskin 2017; Joselit 2020; Levitt 2015; Lonetree 2012; McClellan 2003, 2008, 2012; Myers 2002; Oguibe 2004; Pegno and Brindza 2021; Price 1989, 2007; Sweeney et al. 2022; Winegar 2006.

3. See also Auerbach and Hoffenberg 2008; Barringer and Flynn 1998; Bennett 1995; Lonetree 2012; McAleer and Longair 2014; McAleer and MacKenzie 2015; Rydell 1984.

4. The connection between capitalization and difference, particularly racial difference, is not surprising. After all, "race is instrumental to capitalism" (Shankar 2015, 6), and scholars have persistently shown the ways in which racial and ethnic difference are commodified (see Hale 2005; Marable 2015; Melamed 2006; Oguibe 2004).

5. Hanieh uses this transliteration of *khalījī*, meaning of the Gulf, from the Arabic *khalīj*.

6. Mass production also challenged the construct of authenticity altogether by challenging "the very ideal of the original" (Krauss 1990, 6). In fact, one of the major critiques of the Louvre and Guggenheim planned for Abu Dhabi is precisely that they are not "original" or organic, but transplants—and therefore inauthentic. These hybrid enterprises profoundly interrogate the idea of an original through multiple production. Their franchised nature challenges preconceived notions of what major and national museums look like and who they represent.

7. While Reagan's cutback in 1981 was ultimately about 6 percent, he was reportedly aiming to defund the NEH entirely (Honan 1988). Controversies over NEH- and NEA-funded art and exhibitions erupted over Richard Serra's *Tilted Arc*, an exhibition by Robert Mapplethorpe, and others, leading conservative ideologues to question the use of taxpayer funds on art (Dubin 1999; Senie 2001).

8. Thank you to Lisa Monetti for this insight.

9. Despite various attempts otherwise, Magnus Resch argues that "20 artists make up over 50% of the value of the auction market for contemporary art" (quoted in Schultz 2024), showing that a few elite artists control much of the market.

10. Dubai and its sister emirate Sharjah are both the capitals of their pseudonymous emirates. While run by distinct governments and having different reputations, Sharjah and Dubai exist as a large urban metropolitan area, and artists and arts organizations in both routinely traverse between the two.

11. The state polices citizenship transmission. Some rulers naturalized individuals on a case-by-case basis and granted these individuals Emirati passports, although this practice was more common in the 1970s and early 1980s than it is today. In addition, because of more lax prior residency rules and policies, some families who immigrated to the UAE in the 1970s and '80s from other parts of the Arab world or Iran had acquired Emirati passports, but in neither of these instances do these individuals have *khulāṣat al-qaīd* and therefore are not recognized as citizens by the state, nor are they entitled to all state benefits. Given the changing history of citizenship regulation and the disparate adoption of citizenship by various family members in the 1970s, predicting someone's status was not always easy or obvious. My interlocutors reported that obtaining documents or benefits could be dependent on the individual administrator they were facing: While some administrators honored Emirati passports without requiring *khulāṣat al-qaīd*, others were more strict. Some administrators also discriminated against naturalized citizens, recognizing their foreign origin in their name.

12. While there have been some instances of citizenship being conferred on those with Emirati mothers and foreign fathers, or other one-off instances of citizenship conferral, these are extremely rare and not systematic. It must also be noted that benefits for citizens are not distributed evenly: Those in wealthier emirates, like Dubai and Abu Dhabi, and in urban areas receive more benefits than the rural and poorer northern Emirates of ʿAjmān, Fujairah, Ras al-Khaimah, and Umm Al-Quwain. For more analysis on the UAE's citizenship bureaucracy, see Lori (2019).

13. Two particular trends occurred between 2000 and 2020: First, the UAE government appeared to have an agreement with the Comoros Islands, where the Comoros issued passports to undocumented peoples (*bidūn*) who the UAE refuses to acknowledge as citizens (and who often have Iranian or Pakistani roots but have resided in the Emirates for generations). Many bidūn, lacking any state documentation, struggle to access health care, education, and jobs. While figures on the number of bidūn are difficult to come by, some estimates place this number at approximately 100,000 individuals, which would be a bit over 10 percent of the current UAE citizen population. Instead, families have been offered citizenship in the Comoros Islands—although in

the case of the UAE, it is unclear what the UAE government offered the Comoros in return. Second, there have been purges of those perceived to be Shiʻi—either because they are of Iranian descent or because of close ties to countries with significant Shiʻi populations like Syria, Lebanon, Iraq, and Yemen. In these expulsions, some individuals have been stripped of their Emirati passports, or had their residency visa renewals denied ("UAE's stateless acquire foreign passports," *Financial Times*, June 4, 2012). For an in-depth scholarly analysis of the issue of stateless peoples in the Gulf, see Lori (2019) and Beaugrand (2018).

14. Many families came from Iraq to the UAE to escape Saddam Hussein, the later invasion of Kuwait, and subsequent military conflict with the United States; Syrian and Lebanese communities relocated due to civil strife. It is worth noting the influence U.S. empire has on igniting, exacerbating, or prolonging these conflicts in Lebanon, Syria, Palestine, and Egypt (to say nothing of Yemen), and the subsequent refusals to accept refugees fleeing these conflicts and utter disavowal of U.S. responsibility.

15. For more on labor in the Gulf, see Gardner (2010), Le Renard (2021), Longva (1997); Vora (2013), Kanna (2011), and Wright (2021). Vora (2018) also addresses the racialization of professionalized labor in Qatar's universities.

16. In this chapter I borrow the terms used by my interlocutors to describe artists' backgrounds, largely to avoid confusion when drawing on examples from interviews or marketing language, although these terms and categories are problematic and often overly simplistic.

17. Among under-forty Arab artists, enrollment in private or government schools was also a matter of socioeconomic class. Those from wealthier emirates of Abu Dhabi, Dubai, and Sharjah often came from families who could afford private school more easily than those coming from the poorer, northern emirates. In this way, language proficiency reflected both a generational schism and also social capital.

18. Modernist and contemporary art are not a binary: Joselit argues that contemporary artist from the Global South often use heritage as a "kind of currency" to reorganize aesthetic hierarchies (2020, 2), seeing a constructive—or reconstructive—potential in heritage, while others have shown how expectations about identity and heritage have limited artists' freedom to self-define, with expectations that they make work about their heritage (Harris 2012; Myers 2002; Winegar 2006). There are certainly many instances in which heritage and contemporary art intersect; however, amongst my interlocutors, they explicitly defined themselves as working in or making contemporary art.

19. I had initially thought that art scenes in Kuwait, Bahrain, and Qatar would be relevant to understanding the UAE's art scene today, but my assumption was not borne out in my data. While Kuwaiti and Bahraini galleries and artists did attend Art Dubai, it was uncommon for my UAE-based colleagues to travel there. Neither Kuwait nor Bahrain had megaprojects similar to Qatar or the UAE. Both states have very different political realities from other GCC states: Bahrain is the only GCC state with a significant Shiʻi population, and Kuwait is the only GCC state with an elected parliament. The politics of expression therefore differ from what I describe in the UAE and merit study of their own. Oman is also distinct in developing or revamping its own

museums (Limbert 2010; Sachedina 2021) for a majority-citizen population, distinguishing it from many other GCC states. Saudi Arabia, as the most populous GCC state, also developed a number of arts initiatives during my fieldwork (Foley 2019), and I began to see interlocutors traveling to the kingdom as new spaces and art centers opened.

In the Gallery I

1. Documentation in Al Qasimi and Marta (2015, 143) lists a "Fourth GCC States' Plastic Arts Exhibition" held in Salalah, Oman, August 20–25, 1988. If this is the same series of exhibitions, it indicates a longer continuity.

Chapter 1

1. The GCC states agreed to institute VAT taxes in 2017, and in June 2023, the UAE began enforcing a business tax scheme. However, the new scheme continued to exempt businesses in economic free zones from this taxation (Barrington 2023).

2. Sheila Carapico (2004) invited scholars to consider the Arabian Peninsula as a region, yet much scholarship remains focused on the Gulf Cooperation Council (GCC) states while Yemen is treated separately.

3. One important way that museums conveyed these messages was through their architecture, which often reflected their early origins as princely collections, housed in palaces such as the Louvre in France (McClellan 1994) or the Hermitage in Russia (Maynard 2016; White 2018). As Duncan points out, "from the 18th through the mid-20th century [museums] were deliberately designed to resemble" temples, coopting the palatial style of buildings representing divine and sacred authority (1995, 7). These regal and sacred spaces disciplined visitors' behavior and reiterated the values of political elites (Bennett 1995); indeed, the museum emerged as a sort of civic temple (Cameron 1972) where citizens performed "civic rituals" (Duncan 1995).

4. Files documenting these museums are at the British Library and the National Archives Kew. The Aden museum also got a brief and unflattering mention in Markham and Hargreaves' *The Museums of India: A Survey* (1936).

5. His name is also spelled Selim Abdul Hak in various records. During protectorate and trucial administrations, the British controlled entry and exit to the region for all non-locals, including temporary workers in the pearl industry, foreign businessmen and archaeologists, and British themselves, hence they were able to facilitate the entry of British consultants and private firms. For more, see Onley (2007) and Alshehabi (2019). Abdul Haq's entry to Kuwait is recorded in the British Resident's Diary of Nov 24–Dec 28, 1959 (Jarman 1990b, 158).

6. The museum did not open until 1983, as the Dar al-Athar al-Islamiyyah (Bloom and Gould 2000). Dar al-Althar al-Islamiyyah (DAI) may be translated as House (Palace) of Islamic Antiquities. It is interesting that the DAI's official name reflects an Islamic focus rather than a national one; in the mid 2000s, Qatar drew attention for its bid to become a center of Islamic culture by building the Museum of Islamic Art, similarly avoiding an overtly nationalist nomenclature.

7. Rajab later studied art in England, and upon his return to Kuwait, created a private museum featuring valuable antiquities, the Tareq Rajab Museum, which opened in 1980 (Tareq Rajab Museum n.d.).

8. Flyers in Kuwaiti artist Khalifa Al Qattan's archives also note that the Atelier was transferred to the Ministry of Information in 1972, and that regulations were established for full-time artists in the Atelier.

9. While Qattan's personal archive, like any individual artist's, cannot be said to represent the entirety of the exhibitions held during these years, and it reflects the style, connections, and personality of Qattan, these documents bear testimony to a rising number of artists and exhibitions on the Peninsula, many of which were not staged in dedicated fine arts venues.

10. This report also mentions Cultural Caravans that toured rural areas showing films and taking part in festivals, as well as an annual "Cultural Season" featuring lectures by fifteen Arab intellectuals. I assume that these lectures were the programming of the Cultural Foundation, described by my interlocutors, especially since the report notes that a cultural center in Abu Dhabi was due to open in early 1980 (UNESCO 1982, 60).

11. The Cultural Foundation was temporarily closed in 2009 and reopened in 2018. While the Foundation was established in the early 1970s, it took nearly a decade to open: The Architects' Collaborative (TAC) won the international competition for its architectural design, and construction took place subsequently. The Foundation did not open to the public until 1981 (Cultural Foundation 2019).

12. Allison et al. note that Sharif was supervising these exhibitions, which began in 1975 (2017, 78).

13. I include the titles *shaykh* (masculine) or *shaykha* (feminine), which indicate an individual is a member of a ruling family, to help clarify which arts initiatives are affiliated with state entities or royal families.

14. Holding this type of biennial is contingent on securing funding, which not all locales are able to do; therefore, economics and class must be considered when studying biennials. It's also critical to acknowledge the fragmentation and destabilizing of labor that occurs with rising numbers of short-term contract jobs that do not offer benefits including healthcare or residency visas. For more on the politics of biennials, see Gardner and Green (2016) and Wu (2009).

15. It is worth noting here that U.S. arts organizations were not always nonprofits, but that that model emerged to fulfill elite interests in Boston in the late 1800s, per DiMaggio (1982; see also Lena 2019).

16. This model also arose in the U.S., although for different reasons; in the U.S., collectors donated to museums to offset their taxes. Corporations have also strategically sponsored art and art museums for tax exemptions (Rectanus 2002; Wu 2002) or for other reasons (Banks 2019).

17. Readers might rightly note the differences between individual emirate-level initiatives and federal ones, which is a topic deserving of study in its own right but for which I do not have space here. Acknowledging that they are distinct, I combine them

because my interlocutors moved easily between the emirates and they often experienced these different initiatives as multilayered and overlapping, rarely navigating one in isolation.

18. Briony's mention of Sharjah is here very telling—while Abu Dhabi is the capital of the UAE and the seat of the future megamuseums, my interlocutors often cited Sharjah as the true origin of arts and culture in the country.

19. This ratio has since changed.

20. Alserkal Avenue is another instance of the complex blending of the commercial and noncommercial: Alserkal began as a series of independent galleries who rented spaces near one another, and the landlord transformed into a cultural producer of its own around the time of my fieldwork, cultivating galleries and creative businesses as renters. One tenant reported that Alserkal had raised their neighbor's rent drastically, forcing them to vacate and find a new space; the tenant felt this decision was taken because the other tenant's business was not sufficiently creative nor did their storefront evoke the right aesthetic that the Avenue was cultivating. To further facilitate this new identity, Alserkal also created various lines of free public programming, from coordinating Galleries Nights to artist talks to events like Quoz Fest, a two-day festival on the Avenue. Alserkal also expanded in 2015, doubling its size (Gronlund 2015), opening a new exhibition space, beginning an artist residency program, and offering a roster of programming to complement Art Dubai. While the galleries located in Alserkal are commercial, the overall umbrella of the Avenue purports a noncommercial air.

21. Prior to 2023, businesses in the Emirates were required to have a local partner (an Emirati citizen or firm) own a 51 percent stake of the business; companies established in free zones could skirt these requirements, but there were restrictions on their businesses.

22. One might also question how these new operations that the British Museum and Louvre Paris undertook have changed their organizations at home, as well.

Chapter 2

1. I use the term "citizen artists" in this chapter as a shorthand for "artists who currently hold Emirati passports and family cards." Because many of my interlocutors would self-describe as "Emirati" or being "from the Emirates," whether they held citizenship or not, I try to avoid using this designation because I do not wish to reaffirm any single definition of who or what counts as Emirati (nor is it my place to do so). In addition, I describe the responses of artists together rather than parse by their citizenship status, again to avoid discursively reiterating a distinction they disavow. I specify "citizen artist" or "noncitizen artist" to elucidate the relative stakes of their engagement, and to convey the very palpable sense of social status and privilege that permeated social interactions, although I am wary of reinscribing their inequalities in doing so.

2. Another factor that reiterated the humanity game narrative in the UAE was the prevailing language ideology of positivity. It was socially unacceptable and often considered rude to express negatives directly (I expand on this in the following chapter as

well). Furthermore, Emirati slander laws were extremely vague and allowed citizens to sue for defamation over mere criticism; criticizing the Emirati state or its royal families was also illegal. In 2024, forty-three people were charged with life in prison for criticizing the government (Gambrell 2024). These factors encouraged the dissemination of positive comments, such as "the UAE is a highly tolerant nation," and discouraged dissent. After all, claiming the opposite could be perceived as criticizing the state, subjecting the speaker to various penalties including deportation or revocation of citizenship.

3. The inclusion of archaeology is interesting. Archaeological excavations in the UAE have uncovered evidence of pre-Islamic civilizations, and in one instance, evidence that a queen ruled parts of what is now the emirate of Sharjah (Ghazal 2016). These excavations have not been featured extensively in the (state-controlled) UAE press because they disrupt the current political regime's version of the region's history.

4. During my primary fieldwork (2015–2017), political tensions between the UAE, allied with Saudi Arabia in fighting in Yemen, led to increasing discrimination and expulsion of those based in the UAE who were perceived to have close ties with Iran and other Shi'i-majority communities (in Syria, Iraq, and Lebanon). This phenomenon is worthy of study in its own right, but I do not have space to cover it here.

5. Given Asma's concerns about confirming her status, I asked her to read this chapter prior to sharing it with others. Believing it to be sufficiently anonymized, she gave me permission to share her story. As of 2023, Asma's family has been informed their status is to be restored. Protracted cases like this were also common among Noora Lori's (2019) interlocutors; Lori analyzes delay as a bureaucratic technique of refusal.

6. It is also critical to note that many, like Eman and Layla, live in the UAE because civil war, exile, and U.S. imperialism have prolonged or exacerbated conflicts in their countries of documented belonging, leaving the UAE as a place of refuge for many middle-class Arab families. In many cases, this community does not have the option to go work elsewhere, so refusing to work in the UAE or boycotting the country for its labor record is not a feasible option.

7. Eman here refers to the fact that many Palestinian families moved to the Gulf in the decades following 1948, when the creation of the state of Israel forcibly evicted more than 750,000 Palestinian Arabs from their homelands in what is referred to in Arabic as "the catastrophe." While some Palestinians moved to neighboring states such as Egypt, Jordan, and Syria, the Gulf states took in Palestinians in high-level positions within the government and society, often employing them as middlemen given their Arabic fluency. The Gulf has been a place of refuge and exile for many Arabic-speaking and Muslim communities from the region since the 1970s. The protagonist of Susan Abulhawa's novel *Against the Loveless World* (2020) is a Palestinian woman who lives in Kuwait before migrating again and offers a fictionalized account of this tumultuous period. After the Iraqi invasion, many Palestinians had to leave Kuwait, even those who had obtained Kuwaiti passports, due to a belief that

Palestinians had supported the invading Iraqi forces. However, while the Gulf regimes were nominally pro-Palestine at the time of my fieldwork, they had not opened up broad paths for naturalization for Palestinians and thus Palestinians in the Gulf states were subject to the same rules other migrants experienced: They needed to be actively employed in order to remain in the Gulf countries legally. In addition, those with Palestinian documents who are not UAE residents could not enter the UAE on arrival; they had to apply for a visit visa in advance. This policy made it difficult for Gulf-based Palestinians to host visiting family members. The question of Palestine and the Gulf has grown increasingly more complex since I completed fieldwork: In September of 2020, the UAE normalized relations with Israel and prohibited the expression of pro-Palestinian sentiments online. Subsequently, several writers and activists were jailed for posting on social media in support of UAE-based Palestinians. During the Israeli assault on Gaza following October 7, 2023, and through 2024, however, a number of UAE-based organizations including those headed by members of royal families were publicly supportive of Gazans, revealing how Emirati support for Palestinians is a complicated issue.

8. During fieldwork, only those holding passports from the U.S., Canada, Western European countries, Australia, and a few other places could enter the UAE without a tourist visa arranged in advance. With a Lebanese, Syrian, Iraqi, Indian, or Pakistani passport, however, visas on arrival were not available. Thus some people who were born in the UAE could not visit their birthplace without applying for visas in advance.

9. The UAE's complex judicial system includes religious, civil, and criminal courts. Notably it does not operate on judicial precedent, and court proceedings—particularly family rulings—are not publicly recorded. Judges rule on individual cases before them, interpreting relevant federal or religious laws, but unbound to other similar or historical cases. This means that judges can rule very differently on similar cases, and rulings are not compared or unified through precedent. In addition, the anonymity policy means that lawyers and clients have no prior sense of a particular judge's ruling, unless they have defended in front of them before.

10. Since my primary fieldwork, the UAE has expanded its residency visa options and there are now some options for retirees without citizenship to reside in the UAE, including residency by investment and the golden visa program, among others.

11. The critiques of the treatment of workers in the UAE are valid and important—but I want to expand them geographically and historically. It is equally important to question the strategies of exclusion that have gone into building European and American museums, as their histories are not unlike the UAE's current strategies. In addition to condemning the labor practices employed by the Gulf states, it is important to acknowledge similar exploitation of laborers who built the Louvre in Paris—a castle erected in the twelfth century by (likely nonconsensual) poorly compensated, overexploited workers, or that Met accepted donated artwork from industry barons to afford them tax credits and expand the profits these men made off the backs of manual workers in the railroad, oil, and coal industries. So-termed contractual slavery is not unique

to the contemporary Arab Gulf, but is often part of narratives that exceptionalize the region (Kanna et al. 2020; Vora and Koch 2015).

12. These initiatives included the exhibitions *1980–Today: Exhibitions in the Emirates* (Sharjah Art Foundation); *But We Cannot See Them* (NYU Abu Dhabi Art Gallery); and *Is Old Gold?* (DUCTAC). My fieldwork fortuitously overlapped with the ten-year anniversaries of many UAE-based arts organizations. During this talk, the British Museum curator mentioned thirteen names of artists, including Mohamed Ahmed Ibrahim and Mohamed Kazem, both of whom fall into the *jīl al-ruwād* or pioneers' generation of UAE-based artists.

13. Their situation presents an interesting contrast to athletes recruited for national teams outside their countries of origin, who do technically become citizens in order to play for a national team, such as the Kuwaiti or Qatari soccer teams. In part, it speaks to the eligibility requirements put in place by international sports organizations that have no equivalent in the art world.

In the Gallery III

1. The UAE had maintained positive diplomatic relations with other members of the Gulf Cooperation Council (GCC), including Qatar, since the GCC's founding in 1981. The royal families of the Emirates and Qatar have also intermarried. Thus the UAE joining Saudi Arabia's blockade of Qatar in 2017 reversed course with a longtime ally seemingly overnight. Similarly, many of the GCC states had refused to acknowledge Israeli statehood ostensibly in solidarity with Palestine; there is a significant population of Palestinians in the UAE. When the UAE announced normalization of relations with Israel in 2020, it seemed to reverse a policy or unspoken understanding that had been in place since prior to the founding of the UAE in 1971.

Chapter 3

1. On the oppositional/avant-garde artist, see also: Drucker (2005, xiv); Kisin and Myers (2019, 320); Smith (2019, 78–79).

2. Katya Johanson et al. (2022) argue that the Venice effect is overexaggerated and does not significantly influence many of these metrics, but that the quality of exhibition opportunities improves for artists post-Venice.

3. The critic assumed an important role in the Impressionist period—as David Galenson and Robert Jensen argue, the dealer-critic system replaced the prior system for validating art, which had been the Academy and the state (2007, 139).

4. The oppositional aesthetic critique has not manifested in the same ways in all places: In China, according to David Joselit, it emerged instead as a socialist realist trend (2020, 63).

5. This litmus test also applies to academics and scholars—in peer reviews of my work, reviewers have often commented that I should explicitly state my disapproval of the Emirati state's policies on labor and migration or steered comments toward South Asian manual laborers, even though that is not a community in which I work. Such attention ensures every piece of writing about the UAE focuses on migrant labor; I

have not experienced similar policing of other issues, for example the effects of British or American imperialism in the region.

6. *The National*, the government-run news source, has publicized rather stringent legal resolutions to slander cases. In one case, a teacher was fined 500,000 AED (about $136,000 USD) for insulting her uncle on a private WhatsApp message (sent only to him). In another, a husband was deported after sending insulting private messages to his wife via WhatsApp. Lawyers have pointed out that taking photos without consent of the individual *or the owner of the object being photographed* is illegal and can be punished under UAE law, pointing out the case of an Australian woman who was jailed, fined, and deported for posting a photo of a car, license plates blurred, that was parked in a reserved accessible parking space.

7. Museums and archives also use absence to address the predatory histories of their collectors and collections, however they usually call explicit attention to the absence to do so. For example, a 2019 display of Indigenous ceremonial objects at the University of British Columbia's Museum of Anthropology were swathed in brown fabric, and a nearby plaque noted that "this is so the public can understand not everyone is meant to see these things." In June 2022, the Field Museum also had a display covered, and two small plaques included a letter from the Central Council of Tlingit and Haida Indian Tribes of Alaska. The other, which read, "Why is this display covered up?" explained to the viewer that the museum modified the display "by removing culturally sensitive objects from view." Similarly, anthropologist Kimberly Christen's "Digital Dynamics Across Cultures" website allowed visitors to learn about some aspects of Warumungu practice; when viewers clicked on links to restricted information, the website produced a black box with a note "restricted content" or images covered with duct tape to inform viewers that this knowledge is not appropriate for them (the website is now unfortunately defunct). In contradistinction to these absences in other contexts, however, the intent in UAE-based artists' practice of conspicuous omission is that these absences are legible as gaps *only* to limited audiences, rather than universally legible as omissions. In the two museum examples and web project mentioned above, absence is highlighted as a pedagogical tool and intended to be universally visible as an absence.

8. Artists also used other strategies, such as displacing their critiques geographically. Elsewhere, I describe the use of new media to deterritorialize such critiques from the UAE (Derderian 2023). In some instances, artists also chose to reside abroad and reserved their critiques until they were in other places, although the stridency of their critiques was often marked by concern for relatives still in the Emirates or plans to return.

Chapter 4

1. Krisztina Fehérváry's "aesthetic regime" refers to "politically charged assemblages of material qualities that have provoked widely shared affective responses" (2013, 3). I find this concept tremendously useful but wish to emphasize the language component. In some ways this bouquet of patterning echoes what David MacDougall

has described as a social aesthetic: "a wide range of culturally patterned sensory experience" (2006, 98). For MacDougall, the social aesthetic at his field site included "objects and actions" such as "the design of buildings and grounds, the use of clothing and colors . . . particular styles of speech and gesture, and the many rituals of everyday life" (2006, 98). MacDougall's framing comes close, in many ways, to Pierre Bourdieu's idea of habitus, while focusing on one sole site, which, unlike my field site, was under the purview of a distinct, delimited set of administrators across multiple institutions with their own respective brands.

2. Riwaq asked me to liaise with them and to offer writing feedback to participants in exchange for access to the class. In many organizations I worked with, offering my native English language skills was one way I could contribute to organizations that supported my research, as English language proficiency was in high demand. Whereas I tried to focus only on word choice (particularly for non-native English speakers) that reflected what speakers expressed to me, grammar, and the general guidelines Rashid had shared when I gave feedback, by offering feedback at all I felt complicit in the greater project of professionalization I am critiquing here. The artists in the class expressed a strong desire for this kind of feedback, although I struggled with this sense of complicity. Perhaps ironically, Rashid also failed to show up for several of the class sessions, putting me in the awkward situation of having to run the class, inculcating practices of which I was critical.

3. Another way my interlocutors downgraded the work of some artists was to dismiss them as "housewives," essentially those dependent on the residency visa of another to remain in the UAE.

4. Arlene Dávila (2020, 138–67) has also argued that presenting (Latinx) artists' work within this limited aesthetic range and only with reference to Western art historical canons constitutes a form of whitewashing.

5. For the most part, the commercial gallery booths at Art Dubai also maintained the white cube display, although two or three of the seventy-five booths each year might opt for a dramatic wallpaper to make a statement.

6. For more on collectors, see Davalos 2007; Dávila 2020; Plattner 1996, 164–93.

7. Museums have also created collectors' groups to encourage prospective collectors: Arlene Dávila notes the fee structures of such groups at El Museo Del Barrio and the Studio Museum (2020, 109). Habib's group was free to attend.

8. Coral was a traditional building material in the UAE because it allows the walls to breathe in the intensely hot and humid climate of the Gulf.

In the Gallery V

1. The titles and themes of galleries five through twelve were slightly different when I visited in 2023, but they were still organized in a universal, global timeline.

Chapter 5

1. Critically, even when artists recognize that discourses around the tolerance of multiculturalism are "a way of *managing* intergroup relations and accommodating the

interests of the ethnic middle class," as Fazal Rizvi found in Australia, the discourse itself can create "a range of symbolic resources around which they could organize themselves politically . . . to use its contested political terrain to push for greater equality and access of opportunity . . . and to contest the prevailing state ideology of multiculturalism" (2003, 230). That is, even as artists may recognize the weaponization of tolerance and multiculturalism discourses, they can at times find productive uses of such discourses.

2. None of these workshops appeared to be oriented at the two to five years old range Yusur had mentioned.

3. During my fieldwork, archaeological discoveries at the site of Mleiha indicated potential female rulers, although this fact was largely downplayed in the media (Ghazal 2016).

4. The guide also encouraged educators to brief students on gallery rules before their visit. The list of gallery rules was as follows: "Please do not touch the artworks for your safety and the safety of the artworks. Photography and video is not permitted within the exhibition. Please note that food, drinks and chewing gum are not allowed in the exhibition. Pencils can be used for writing or sketching. No crayons, pens, markers or wet materials are permitted in the galleries. Please do not lean on walls or cases and do not use them as writing surfaces. Please turn off mobile phones and please use a soft voice so that you do not distract other groups in the galleries. Running is not permitted within the exhibition so you do not hurt yourself or damage the artworks" (Abu Dhabi Tourism and Culture Authority 2014, 7). Such rules are in line with the hierarchies presented by the museum; after all, "public museums instituted an order of things that was meant to last" (Bennett 1995, 80). Eileen Hooper-Greenhill's noted paradox, of temple of the arts versus tool for public education, has peaked a few times, notably in 1972 when Duncan Cameron wrote his famous article, "Temple or Forum?" questioning whether the museum was meant as a temple, consecrating ideals and objects, or a public forum, a tool.

5. The guide is available for download at https://www.nyuad-artgallery.org/en_US/our-exhibitions/main-gallery/bwcst-archive/.

6. Did they in fact solve Eurocentrism in museums? Saloni Mathur (2005) argues no.

Openings and Closings

1. And a reminder of why Ariella Azoulay has termed photography a tool of imperialism (2008).

2. It had initially appeared that Saudi Arabia had purchased the painting and was later revealed that a Saudi royal had purchased the work on behalf of the Louvre Abu Dhabi.

Bibliography

Abdelkarim, Abbas. 1999. *Change and Development in the Gulf.* Macmillan.

Abdel-Nabi, Susie, and Alexandra Lester. 2019. "Defamation and Social Media in the UAE: Clyde & Co (En)." Clyde & Co., April 3. https://www.clydeco.com/insight /article/defamation-and-social-media-in-the-uae.

Abramian, Cleo. 2019. "Iraqi Performance Artists Use Silence as a Gesture of Dissent." *Hyperallergic*, November 22. https://hyperallergic.com/529421/iraqi -performance-artists-use-silence-as-a-gesture-of-dissent/.

Abu Dhabi Tourism and Culture Authority. 2014. *A History of the World in 100 Objects: Pre- and Post-Visit Materials for Educators (Primary to University).* Abu Dhabi Tourism and Culture Authority.

Abulhawa, Susan. 2020. *Against the Loveless World.* Simon & Schuster, Inc.

Abu-Lughod, Lila. 2013. *Do Muslim Women Need Saving?* Harvard University Press.

Abu-Lughod, Lila. 1990. "The Romance of Resistance: Tracing Transformations of Power through Bedouin Women." *American Ethnologist* 17 (1): 41–55. https://doi .org/10.1525/ae.1990.17.1.02a00030.

Abungu, Lorna. 2005. "Museums and Communities in Africa: Facing the New Challenges." *Public Archaeology* 4 (2–3): 151–54. https://doi.org/10.1179/pua.2005 .4.2–3.151.

Ajami, Fouad. 1978. "The End of Pan-Arabism." *Foreign Affairs* 57 (2): 355–73.

Alexander, Victoria. 1996. *Museums and Money: The Impact of Funding on Exhibitions, Scholarship, and Management.* Indiana University Press.

Allison, Maya, Bana Kattan, and Alaa Edris. 2017. *But We Cannot See Them: Tracing a UAE Arts Community 1988–2008.* Akkadia Press.

Al Muhairi, Mubarak Hamad. 2013. "A Bridge to the World." In *Louvre Abu Dhabi: Birth of a Museum,* edited by Laurence Des Cars. Abu Dhabi Tourism and Culture Authority/Musee du Louvre/Skira Flammarion.

Al Nahyan, Sultan bin Tahnoon. 2013. "Foreword." In *Louvre Abu Dhabi: Birth of a Museum*, edited by Laurence Des Cars. Abu Dhabi Tourism and Culture Authority/Musee du Louvre/Skira Flammarion.

Al Qadiri, Monira. 2025. "Info." https://www.moniraalqadiri.com/info/.

Al-Qasimi, Sultan Muhammed. 1988. *The Myth of Arab Piracy in the Gulf*. Routledge.

Al Qasimi, Hoor, and Karen Marta, eds. 2015. *1980–Today: Exhibitions in the United Arab Emirates*. National Pavilion United Arab Emirates la Biennale di Venezia.

Al Qassemi, Sultan Sooud. 2020. "Toward Abstraction: The Case of Kuwait in the 1960s." In *Taking Shape: Abstraction from the Arab World, 1950s–1980s*, edited by Suheyla Takesh and Lynn Gumpert. Hirmer Publishers.

Al Qassemi, Sultan Sooud. 2013. "Kuwait Art Museum Succeeds Where Others Have Failed." *HuffPost*, June 2. https://www.huffingtonpost.com/sultan-sooud -alqassemi/kuwait-art-museum-succeed_b_2996769.html.

Al Qassemi, Sultan Sooud, and Todd Reisz. 2021. *Building Sharjah*. Birkhäuser Verlag.

Al-Rashoud, Talal. 2019. "From Muscat to the Maghreb: Pan-Arab Networks, Anti-Colonial Groups, and Kuwait's Arab Scholarships (1953–1961)." *Arabian Humanities* 12. https://journals.openedition.org/cy/5004.

Al-Shamsi, Alia. 2017. "Youth Guide: But We Cannot See Them." New York University Abu Dhabi Art Gallery. https://www.nyuad-artgallery.org/en_US/about /publications/youth-guides/youth-guide-but-we-cannot-see-them/.

Alshehabi, Omar Hesham. 2019. "Policing Labour in Empire: The Modern Origins of the Kafala Sponsorship System in the Gulf Arab States." *British Journal of Middle Eastern Studies* 48 (2): 1–20. https://doi.org/10.1080/13530194.2019.1580183.

Amariglio, Jack, Joseph Childers, and Stephen Cullenberg. 2009. *Sublime Economy: On the Intersection of Art and Economics*. Taylor & Francis Group.

Anderson, Benedict. 2006. *Imagined Communities: Reflections on the Origin and Spread of Nationalism*. Rev. ed. Verso.

Aoun-Abdo, Rita. 2013. "Belonging to a Moment, Belonging to a Place." In *Louvre Abu Dhabi: Birth of a Museum*, edited by Laurence Des Cars. Abu Dhabi Tourism and Culture Authority/Musee du Louvre/Skira Flammarion.

Appadurai, Arjun. 1990. "Disjuncture and Difference in the Global Cultural Economy." *Theory, Culture & Society* 7 (2–3): 295–310. https://doi.org/10.1177 /026327690007002017.

Appel, Hannah. 2019. *The Licit Life of Capitalism: U.S. Oil in Equatorial Guinea*. Duke University Press.

Appiah, K. Anthony. 1994. "Identity, Authenticity, Survival: Multicultural Societies and Social Reproduction." In *Multiculturalism: Examining the Politics of Recognition*, edited by Amy Gutmann. Princeton University Press.

Apter, Andrew. 2005. *The Pan-African Nation: Oil and the Spectacle of Culture in Nigeria*. University of Chicago Press.

Art Dubai. n.d. "Campus Art Dubai—School for Artists and Designers." *Art Dubai* (blog). https://www.artdubai.ae/campus-art-dubai/.

Atshan, Sa'ed. 2020. *Queer Palestine and the Empire of Critique*. Stanford University Press.

Auerbach, Jeffrey, and Peter Hoffenberg, eds. 2008. *Britain, the Empire, and the World at the Great Exhibition of 1851.* Ashgate Publishing.

Austin, J. L. 1962. *How to Do Things with Words.* Harvard University Press.

Azoulay, Ariella. 2008. *The Civil Contract of Photography.* Princeton University Press.

Bahrain Authority for Culture and Antiquities. 2021. "Under the Patronage of H. E. Shaikha Hala Bint Mohammed Al-Khalifa, Director-General of Culture & Art, Bahrain Contemporary Art Association Inaugurated Its '50 Years' Golden Jubilee Exhibition." January 11. https://www.culture.gov.bh/en/mediacenter/news_center/2021/Jan2021/Name,19167,en.html.

Baia Curioni, Stefano. 2012. "A Fairy Tale: The Art System, Globalization, and the Fair Movement." In *Contemporary Art and Its Commercial Markets: A Report on Current Conditions and Future Scenarios,* edited by Maria Lind and Olav Velthuis. Sternberg Press.

Bani Hashim, Alamira Reem. 2019. *Planning Abu Dhabi: An Urban History.* Routledge.

Banks, Patricia Ann. 2019. *Diversity and Philanthropy at African American Museums: Black Renaissance.* Routledge.

Banks, Patricia Ann. 2010. *Represent: Art and Identity Among the Black Upper-Middle Class.* Routledge.

Barringer, T. J., and Tom Flynn, eds. 1998. *Colonialism and the Object: Empire, Material Culture, and the Museum.* Routledge.

Barrington, Lisa. 2023. "UAE Begins Corporate Tax Roll-out, with Free Zones Exempted." *Reuters,* June 1. https://www.reuters.com/world/middle-east/uae-begins-corporate-tax-roll-out-amid-diversification-push-2023-06-01/.

Beaugé, Gilbert. 1986. "La kafala: Un système de gestion transitoire de la main-d'œuvre et du capital dans les pays du Golfe." *Revue européenne des migrations internationales* 2 (1): 109–22. https://doi.org/10.3406/remi.1986.998.

Beaugrand, Claire. 2018. *Stateless in the Gulf: Migration, Nationality and Society in Kuwait.* I. B. Tauris.

Becker, Carol. 2002. *Surpassing the Spectacle: Global Transformations and the Changing Politics of Art.* Rowman & Littlefield.

Becker, Howard Saul. 1982. *Art Worlds.* University of California Press.

Belting, Hans, Andrea Buddensieg, and Peter Weibel, eds. 2013. *The Global Contemporary and the Rise of New Art Worlds.* The MIT Press.

Benjamin, Walter. 1969. "The Work of Art in the Age of Mechanical Reproduction." In *Illuminations,* edited by Hannah Arendt. Schocken Books.

Bennett, Tony. 1995. *The Birth of the Museum: History, Theory, Politics.* Routledge.

Benoit-Bryan, Jen, Diane Jean-Mary, and Mia Locks. 2023. "Workplace Equity and Organizational Culture in U.S. Art Museums." *Museums Moving Forward.*

Birkett, Whitney. 2012. "To Infinity and Beyond: A Critique of the Aesthetic White Cube." Master's thesis, Seton Hall University. Seton Hall eRepository (209).

Birnbaum, Daniel, and Isabelle Graw, eds. 2008. *Canvases and Careers Today: Criticism and Its Markets.* Sternberg Press.

Bishara, Fahad. 2017. *A Sea of Debt: Law and Economic Life in the Western Indian Ocean, 1780–1950*. Cambridge University Press.

Bloom, Jonathan, and Lark Gould. 2000. "Patient Restoration: The Kuwait National Museum." *Saudi Aramco World* 51 (5): 10–21.

Bocast, Brooke. 2019. "Toward a Bright Future: Politics of Potential in a Ugandan Village." *PoLAR: Political and Legal Anthropology Review* 42 (1): 1–16. https://doi.org/10.1111/plar.12279.

Boltanski, Luc, and Eve Chiapello. 2005. "The New Spirit of Capitalism." *International Journal of Politics, Culture, and Society* 18 (3/4): 161–88.

Bose, Sugata. 2006. *A Hundred Horizons: The Indian Ocean in the Age of Global Empire*. Harvard University Press.

Bourdieu, Pierre. 2000. *Distinction: A Social Critique of the Judgement of Taste*. Translated by Richard Nice. Harvard University Press.

Bourdieu, Pierre. 1995. *The Rules of Art: Genesis and Structure of the Literary Field*. Translated by Susan Emanuel. Stanford University Press.

Bourdieu, Pierre. 1993. *The Field of Cultural Production: Essays on Art and Literature*. Columbia University Press.

Bourdieu, Pierre, and Alain Darbel. 1991. *The Love of Art: European Art Museums and Their Public*. Polity Press.

Boyer, Dominic. 2003. "Censorship as a Vocation: The Institutions, Practices, and Cultural Logic of Media Control in the German Democratic Republic." *Comparative Studies in Society and History* 45 (3): 511–45. https://doi.org/10.1017/S0010417503000240.

Brown, Mark. 2013. "Qatar's Sheikha Mayassa Tops Art Power List." *The Guardian*, October 23. https://www.theguardian.com/artanddesign/2013/oct/24/qatar-sheikha-mayassa-tops-art-power-list.

Brown, Wendy. 2006. *Regulating Aversion: Tolerance in the Age of Identity and Empire*. Princeton University Press.

Bryan-Wilson, Julia. 2009. *Art Workers: Radical Practice in the Vietnam War Era*. University of California Press.

Brzyski, Anna, ed. 2007. *Partisan Canons*. Duke University Press.

Bsheer, Rosie. 2020. *Archive Wars: The Politics of History in Saudi Arabia*. Stanford University Press.

Buchholz, Larissa. 2022. *The Global Rules of Art: The Emergence and Divisions of a Cultural World Economy*. Princeton University Press.

Buffenstein, Alyssa. 2016. "Rana Begum Wins 2017 Abraaj Group Art Prize." *Artnet News*, October 6. https://news.artnet.com/art-world/rana-begum-abraaj-group-art-prize-2017-688598.

Bull, Malcolm. 2011. "The Two Economies of World Art." In *Globalization and Contemporary Art*, edited by Jonathan Harris. Wiley-Blackwell.

Bunzl, Matti. 2014. *In Search of a Lost Avant-Garde: An Anthropologist Investigates the Contemporary Art Museum*. University of Chicago Press.

Bydler, Charlotte. 2004. "The Global Art World, Inc: On the Globalization of Contemporary Art." PhD diss., Uppsala Universitet.

Cachin, Françoise, Jean Clair, and Roland Recht. 2006. "Les musées ne sont pas à vendre." *Le Monde.fr*, December 12. https://www.lemonde.fr/idees/article/2006 /12/12/les-musees-ne-sont-pas-a-vendre-par-francoise-cachin-jean-clair-et -roland-recht_844742_3232.html.

Cain, Abigail. 2017. "How the White Cube Came to Dominate the Art World." *Artsy*, January 23. https://www.artsy.net/article/artsy-editorial-white-cube-dominate-art.

Cameron, Duncan. 1972. "The Museum: A Temple or the Forum." *Journal of World History.* 14 (1): 189–202.

Carapico, Sheila. 2004. "Arabia Incognita: An Invitation to Arabian Peninsula Studies." In *Counter-Narratives: History, Contemporary Society, and Politics in Saudi Arabia and Yemen*, edited by Robert Vitalis and Madawi Al-Rasheed. Palgrave Macmillan.

Carr, Christina. 2021. "Board Age Diversity and the Future of Museum Leadership." *Curator: The Museum Journal* 64 (2): 237–52.

Carroll, Noël. 2007. "Art and Globalization: Then and Now." *The Journal of Aesthetics and Art Criticism* 65 (1): 131–43.

Cascone, Sarah. 2021. "After Delays, Protests, and a Pandemic, the Guggenheim Abu Dhabi Has a New Date for Its Debut: 2026." *Artnet News*, September 21. https:// news.artnet.com/art-world/guggenheim-abu-dhabi-2011351.

Castells, Manuel. 2000. *The Rise of the Network Society.* 2nd ed. Blackwell Publishers.

Cavanaugh, Jillian R., and Shalini Shankar, eds. 2017. *Language and Materiality: Ethnographic and Theoretical Explorations.* Cambridge University Press.

Chambers, Iain, Alessandra De Angelis, Celeste Ianniciello, and Mariangela Orabona. 2016. *The Postcolonial Museum: The Arts of Memory and the Pressures of History.* Routledge.

Chaudhuri, K. N. 1990. *Asia before Europe: Economy and Civilisation of the Indian Ocean from the Rise of Islam to 1750.* Cambridge University Press.

Chumley, Lily. 2016. *Creativity Class: Art School and Culture Work in Postsocialist China.* Princeton University Press.

Coffey, Mary. 2012. *How a Revolutionary Art Became Official Culture: Murals, Museums, and the Mexican State.* Duke University Press.

Cooke, Miriam. 2014. *Tribal Modern: Branding New Nations in the Arab Gulf.* University of California Press.

Cooks, Bridget. 2011. *Exhibiting Blackness: African Americans and the American Art Museum.* University of Massachusetts Press.

Corona, Lara. 2022. "Digitization for the Visibility of Collections." *Collection and Curation* 42 (3): 73–80. https://doi.org/10.1108/CC-06-2022-0024.

Coutin, Susan. 2007. *Nations of Emigrants: Shifting Boundaries of Citizenship in El Salvador and the United States.* Cornell University Press.

Cultural Foundation (Abu Dhabi). 2019. "Cultural Vision through a Cultural Foundation." https://culturalfoundation.ae/en/cultural-foundation.

Dağtaş, Seçil. 2020. "The Civilizations Choir of Antakya: The Politics of Religious Tolerance and Minority Representation at the National Margins of Turkey." *Cultural Anthropology* 35 (1): 167–95. https://doi.org/10.14506/ca35.1.11.

Davalos, Karen. 2007. "A Poetics of Love and Rescue in the Collection of Chicana/o Art." *Latino Studies* 5 (1): 76–103.

Davalos, Karen. 2004. "Exhibiting Mestizaje: The Poetics and Experience of the Mexican Fine Arts Center Museum." In *Museum Studies: An Anthology of Contexts*, edited by Bettina Messias Carbonell. 1st ed. Blackwell.

Davidson, Christopher. 2008. *Dubai: The Vulnerability of Success*. Columbia University Press.

Dávila, Arlene. 2020. *Latinx Art: Artists, Markets, and Politics*. Duke University Press.

Dávila, Arlene. 2012. *Culture Works: Space, Value, and Mobility across the Neoliberal Americas*. New York University Press.

Dávila, Arlene. 2004. *Barrio Dreams: Puerto Ricans, Latinos, and the Neoliberal City*. University of California Press.

Dávila, Arlene. 1999. "Latinizing Culture: Art, Museums, and the Politics of U.S. Multicultural Encompassment." *Cultural Anthropology* 14 (2): 180–202. https://doi.org/10.1525/can.1999.14.2.180.

Davis Ruffins, Fath. 1992. "Mythos, Memory, and History: African American Preservation Efforts, 1820–1990." In *Museums and Communities: The Politics of Public Culture*, edited by Ivan Karp, Christine Kreamer, and Steven Lavine. Smithsonian Institution Press.

De Cesari, Chiara. 2017. "Heritage between Resistance and Government in Palestine." *International Journal of Middle East Studies* 49 (4): 747–51.

Demerdash, Nancy. 2017. "Of 'Gray Lists' and Whitewash: An Aesthetics of (Self-)Censorship and Circumvention in the GCC Countries." *Journal of Arabian Studies* 7 (Sup1): 28–48.

Derderian, Elizabeth. 2024. "Visible Critique/Critical Visibility: Contemporary Artists and Conspicuous Omission in the United Arab Emirates." *American Ethnologist* 51 (2): 175–327.

Derderian, Elizabeth. 2023. "Covering Critiques: Film and New Media Artwork in the UAE." In *Reorienting with the Middle East: Film and Digital Media Where the Persian Gulf, Arabian Sea, and Indian Ocean Meet*, edited by Dale Hudson and Alia Yunis. Indiana University Press.

Derderian, Elizabeth. 2021. "Engendering Change: Charting a History of the Emirates through Women Artists." *Hawwa: The Journal of Women and the Middle East* 19 (1): 28–50.

Derderian, Elizabeth. 2020. "Challenging Terms: Contemporary Art and the Disciplining of Novelty in the UAE." *Museum Anthropology* 43 (2): 79–93. https://doi.org/10.1111/muan.12223.

Di Leonardo, Micaela. 2008. "Introduction: New Global and American Landscapes of Inequality." In *New Landscapes of Inequality: Neoliberalism and the Erosion of*

Democracy in America, edited by Micaela di Leonardo, Jane Collins, and Brett Williams. School for Advanced Research Press.

DiMaggio, Paul. 1982. "Cultural Entrepreneurship in Nineteenth-Century Boston: The Creation of an Organizational Base." *Media, Culture & Society* 4 (1): 33–50.

DiMaggio, Paul, and Francie Ostrower. 1990. "Participation in the Arts by Black and White Americans." *Social Forces* 68 (3): 753–78.

Diop, Abdoulaye, Trevor Johnston, and Kien Trung Le. 2015. "Reform of the Kafāla System: A Survey Experiment from Qatar." *Journal of Arabian Studies* 5 (2): 116–37. https://doi.org/10.1080/21534764.2015.1113681.

Drogin, Bob. 1991. "In 7 Months, Iraqis Stole 'the Very Soul' of Kuwait: Culture: Museums Were Looted, Zoo Animals Were Killed. And What Wasn't Taken Was Destroyed." *Los Angeles Times*, March 11. https://www.latimes.com/archives/la-xpm-1991-03-11-mn-145-story.html.

Drucker, Johanna. 2005. *Sweet Dreams: Contemporary Art and Complicity.* University of Chicago Press.

D'Souza, Aruna. 2018. *Whitewalling: Art, Race and Protest in 3 Acts.* Badlands Unlimited.

Dubai Airports. 2024. "Who We Are." https://www.dubaiairports.ae/corporate/about-us/history/.

Dubin, Steven. 1999. *Displays of Power: Memory and Amnesia in the American Museum.* New York University Press.

Duncan, Carol. 1995. *Civilizing Rituals: Inside Public Art Museums.* Routledge.

Duncan, Carol, and Alan Wallach. 1980. "The Universal Survey Museum." *Art History* 3 (4): 448–69. https://doi.org/10.1111/j.1467-8365.1980.tb00089.x.

Duncan, Sally, and Andrew McClellan. 2018. *The Art of Curating: Paul J. Sachs and the Museum Course at Harvard.* The Getty Research Institute.

Dzenovska, Dace. 2018. *School of Europeanness: Tolerance and Other Lessons in Political Liberalism in Latvia.* Cornell University Press.

Écochard, Michel. 1972. "Programme, Selection of Site and First Sketch for a Museum—Bahrain." UNESCO. UNESDOC Serial No. 2758/RMO.RD/CLP. https://unesdoc.unesco.org/ark:/48223/pf0000001658?posInSet=1&queryId=e97493da-d624-472b-9040-3c5ff7b13fbf.

Écochard, Michel. 1964. "Plans for a National Museum in Kuwait." *Museum* XVII (3): 146–51.

Écochard, Michel. 1954. *Casablanca, Le Roman d'une Ville.* Editions de Paris.

Eggeling, Kristin. 2017. "Cultural Diplomacy in Qatar: Between 'Virtual Enlargement,' National Identity Construction and Elite Legitimation." *International Journal of Cultural Policy* 23 (6): 717–31.

Elkins, James, and Michael Newman. 2008. *The State of Art Criticism.* Routledge.

Ellwood, Wayne. 2007. *The No-Nonsense Guide to Globalization.* 2nd ed. New Internationalist Publications Ltd.

Elyachar, Julia. 2005. *Markets of Dispossession: NGOs, Economic Development, and the State in Cairo.* Duke University Press.

Erskine-Loftus, Pamela. 2014. *Museums and the Material World: Collecting and the Arabian Peninsula.* MuseumsEtc.

Erskine-Loftus, Pamela, Mariam Al-Mulla, and Victoria Penziner Hightower, eds. 2016. *Representing the Nation: Heritage, Museums, National Narratives, and Identity in the Arab Gulf States.* Routledge.

Exell, Karen. 2018. *The Global Spectacular: Contemporary Museum Architecture in China and the Arabian Peninsula.* Lund Humphries.

Exell, Karen. 2017. "Utopian Ideals, Unknowable Futures, and the Art Museum in the Arabian Peninsula." *Journal of Arabian Studies* 7: 49–64. https://doi.org/10.1080/21534764.2017.1352163.

Exell, Karen. 2016. *Modernity and the Museum in the Arabian Peninsula.* Routledge.

Exell, Karen, and Trinidad Rico, eds. 2014. *Cultural Heritage in the Arabian Peninsula: Debates, Discourses and Practices.* Ashgate.

Farhat, Maymanah. 2009. "Imagining the Arab World: The Fashioning of the 'War on Terror' through Art." *Callaloo* 32 (4): 1223–31. https://doi.org/10.1353/cal.0.0556.

Fassin, Didier. 2017. "The Endurance of Critique." *Anthropological Theory* 17 (1): 4–29.

Fattah, Hassan. 2007. "Celebrity Architects Reveal a Daring Cultural Xanadu for the Arab World." *The New York Times*, February 1. https://www.nytimes.com/2007/02/01/arts/design/01isla.html.

Fechter, Anne-Meike, and Katie Walsh. 2010. "Examining 'Expatriate' Continuities: Postcolonial Approaches to Mobile Professionals." *Journal of Ethnic & Migration Studies* 36 (8): 1197–210. https://doi.org/10.1080/13691831003687667.

Fehérváry, Krisztina. 2013. *Politics in Color and Concrete: Socialist Materialities and the Middle Class in Hungary.* Indiana University Press.

Ferguson, James. 2006. *Global Shadows: Africa in the Neoliberal World Order.* Duke University Press.

Fernea, Elizabeth Warnock. 1965. *Guests of the Sheik.* Doubleday.

Fibiger, Thomas. 2017. "Potential Heritage: The Making and Unmaking of the Pearl Monument in Bahrain." *Journal of Arabian Studies* 7 (2): 195–210. https://doi.org/10.1080/21534764.2017.1405635.

Flood, Finbarr Barry. 2002. "Between Cult and Culture: Bamiyan, Islamic Iconoclasm, and the Museum." *The Art Bulletin* 84 (4): 641. https://doi.org/10.2307/3177288.

Foley, Sean. 2019. *Changing Saudi Arabia: Art, Culture, and Society in the Kingdom.* Lynne Rienner Publishers.

Foster, Robert. 2002. *Materializing the Nation: Commodities, Consumption, and Media in Papua New Guinea.* Indiana University Press.

Fraiberger, Samuel, Roberta Sinatra, Magnus Resch, Christoph Riedl, and Albert-László Barabási. 2018. "Quantifying Reputation and Success in Art." *Science* 362 (6416): 825–29. https://doi.org/10.1126/science.aau7224.

Fraser, Pamela, and Roger Rothman, eds. 2017. *Beyond Critique: Contemporary Art in Theory, Practice, and Instruction.* Bloomsbury Publishing.

Fuller, Nancy. 1992. "The Museum as Vehicle for Community Empowerment: The Ak-Chin Indian Community Ecomuseum Project." In *Museums and Communities:*

The Politics of Public Culture, edited by Ivan Karp, Christine Kreamer, and Steven Lavine. Smithsonian Institution Press.

Galenson, David, and Robert Jensen. 2007. "Careers and Canvases: The Rise of the Market for Modern Art in Nineteenth-Century Paris." In *Current Issues in 19th-Century Art: Van Gogh Studies 1*, edited by Chris Stolwijk. Waanders Publishers.

Gambrell, Jon. 2024. "Dozens of People Are Sentenced to Life in Prison in the UAE in a Mass Trial Criticized Abroad." *AP News*, July 10. https://apnews.com/article/uae -mass-trial-dissidents-2108263bffe49915a866eecc64d1b605.

Gardner, Andrew. 2010. *City of Strangers*. Cornell University Press.

Gardner, Anthony, and Charles Green, eds. 2016. *Biennials, Triennials, and Documenta*. Wiley-Blackwell.

Gerber, Alison. 2017. *The Work of Art: Value in Creative Careers*. Stanford University Press.

Ghazal, Rym. 2016. "Sharjah's Mleiha Archaeological Centre—A Step Back in Time." *The National*, April 6. https://www.thenational.ae/arts-culture/sharjah-s-mleiha -archaeological-centre-a-step-back-in-time-1.137537.

Giebelhausen, Michaela. 2006. "Museum Architecture: A Brief History." In *A Companion to Museum Studies*, edited by Sharon MacDonald. 1st ed. Wiley-Blackwell.

Gill, Harjant. 2017. "Censorship and Ethnographic Film: Confronting State Bureaucracies, Cultural Regulation, and Institutionalized Homophobia in India." *Visual Anthropology Review* 33 (1): 62–73. https://doi.org/10.1111/var.12122.

Glissant, Édouard. 1997. *Poetics of Relation*. Translated by Betsy Wing. University of Michigan Press.

Gomberg-Muñoz, Ruth. 2016. *Becoming Legal: Immigration Law and Mixed-Status Families*. Oxford University Press.

Goodwin, Charles. 1994. "Professional Vision." *American Anthropologist* 96 (3): 606–33. https://doi.org/10.1525/aa.1994.96.3.02a00100.

Graw, Isabelle. 2009. *High Price: Art between the Market and Celebrity Culture*. Sternberg Press.

Green, Nile. 2014. "Rethinking the 'Middle East' after the Oceanic Turn." *Comparative Studies of South Asia, Africa and the Middle East* 34 (3): 556–64.

Gronlund, Melissa. 2015. "Alserkal Avenue Expansion Means a Bigger Canvas for the Community." *The National*, November 14. https://www.thenationalnews.com/arts /alserkal-avenue-expansion-means-a-bigger-canvas-for-the-community-1.27817.

Guglielmo, Antoniette. 2021. "Unprecedented Leadership." *Curator: The Museum Journal* 64 (2): 209–12. https://doi.org/10.1111/cura.12424.

Guha-Thakurta, Tapati. 2004. *Monuments, Objects, Histories: Institutions of Art in Colonial and Postcolonial India*. Columbia University Press.

Guilbault, Serge. 1983. *How New York Stole the Idea of Modern Art: Abstract Expressionism, Freedom, and the Cold War*. University of Chicago Press.

Gulf Labor Artist Coalition. 2016. "Who's Building the Guggenheim Abu Dhabi?" https://gulflabour.org/.

Gupta, Akhil. 2012. *Red Tape: Bureaucracy, Structural Violence, and Poverty in India*. Duke University Press.

Hale, Charles. 2005. "Neoliberal Multiculturalism: The Remaking of Cultural Rights and Racial Dominance in Central America." "PoLAR:" *Political and Legal Anthropology Review* 28 (1): 10–28.

Hall, Carla. 1981. "Reagan Seeks 50% Cuts in Endowments' Budgets." *Washington Post*, February 18. https://www.washingtonpost.com/archive/lifestyle/1981/02/18/reagan -seeks-50-cuts-in-endowments-budgets/234f4737-a676-4b08-ba21-f46ea916ffd3/.

Hall, Stuart. 2000. "Conclusion: The Multicultural Question." In *Unsettled Multiculturalism: Diaspora, Entanglements, Transcriptions*, edited by B. Hesse. Zed Books Ltd.

Hanieh, Adam. 2011. *Capitalism and Class in the Gulf Arab States*. Palgrave Macmillan.

Haraway, Donna. 1988. "Situated Knowledges: The Science Question in Feminism and the Privilege of Partial Perspective." *Feminist Studies* 14 (3): 575–99. https://doi.org /10.2307/3178066.

Harris, Clare. 2014. *The Museum on the Roof of the World: Art, Politics, and the Representation of Tibet*. University of Chicago Press.

Harris, Clare. 2012. "In and Out of Place: Tibetan Artists' Travels in the Contemporary Art World." *Visual Anthropology Review* 28 (2): 152–63. https://doi.org/10.1111 /j.1548-7458.2012.01121.x.

Harris, Jonathan, ed. 2011. *Globalization and Contemporary Art*. Wiley-Blackwell.

Harvey, David. 2005. *A Brief History of Neoliberalism*. Oxford University Press.

Hazbar, Talin. n.d. "Accumulation—Talin-Hazbar." *Talin Hazbar* (blog). https:// hazbartalin.com/ACCUMULATION.

Heard-Bey, Frauke. 1982. *From Trucial States to United Arab Emirates: A Society in Transition*. Motivate.

Hicks, Dan. 2020. *The Brutish Museums: The Benin Bronzes, Colonial Violence and Cultural Restitution*. Pluto Press.

Hightower, Victoria Penziner. 2013. "Pearling and Political Power in the Trucial States, 1850–1950: Debt, Taxes, and Politics." *Journal of Arabian Studies* 3 (2): 215–31.

Hightower, Victoria Penziner. 2012. "'We Were Never Weak in the Old Days': Gender and Pearling in the Southern Gulf Emirates, 1870–1950." *Liwa: Journal of the National Center for Documentation & Research* 4 (8): 5–17.

Hindman, Heather. 2013. *Mediating the Global Expatria's Forms and Consequences in Kathmandu*. Stanford University Press.

Hinsley, Curtis M., and David R. Wilcox, eds. 2016. *Coming of Age in Chicago: The 1893 World's Fair and the Coalescence of American Anthropology*. University of Nebraska Press.

Ho, Engseng. 2006. *The Graves of Tarim: Genealogy and Mobility across the Indian Ocean*. University of California Press.

Ho, Oscar. 2014. "Under the Shadow: Problems in Museum Development in Asia." In *Contemporary Asian Art and Exhibitions: Connectivities and World-Making*, edited by Michelle Antoinette and Caroline Turner. The Australian National University Press.

Hoag, Colin. 2011. "Assembling Partial Perspectives: Thoughts on the Anthropology of Bureaucracy." *PoLAR: Political and Legal Anthropology Review* 34 (1): 81–94. https://doi.org/10.1111/j.1555-2934.2011.01140.x.

Ho Hing-Kay, Oscar. 2010. "Oscar Ho Hing-Kay." *Artforum* (blog), June 1. https://www.artforum.com/features/oscar-ho-hing-kay-194581/.

Honan, William H. 1988. "Book Discloses That Reagan Planned to Kill National Endowment for Arts." *The New York Times*, May 15. https://www.nytimes.com/1988/05/15/arts/book-discloses-that-reagan-planned-to-kill-national-endowment-for-arts.html.

Hooper-Greenhill, Eileen. 1994. *Museums and Their Visitors*. Routledge.

Hooper-Greenhill, Eileen. 1992. *Museums and the Shaping of Knowledge*. Routledge.

Horkheimer, Max, and Theodor W. Adorno. 2002. "Dialectic of Enlightenment." In *Dialectic of Enlightenment*, edited by Gunzelin Schmid Noerr. Stanford University Press.

Hull, Matthew. 2012. *Government of Paper: The Materiality of Bureaucracy in Urban Pakistan*. University of California Press.

Hussain, Muayad. 2012. "Modern Art from Kuwait: Khalifa Qattan and Circulism." PhD diss., University of Birmingham. https://etheses.bham.ac.uk/id/eprint/3909/.

Inda, Jonathan Xavier, and Renato Rosaldo, eds. 2008. *The Anthropology of Globalization: A Reader*. 2nd ed. Blackwell Publishers.

Iskin, Ruth, ed. 2017. *Re-Envisioning the Contemporary Art Canon: Perspectives in a Global World*. Routledge.

Jarman, Robert, ed. 1990a. *Political Diaries of the Persian Gulf*. Vol. 20: 1955–1958. Cambridge: Archive Editions.

Jarman, Robert, ed. 1990b. *Political Diaries of the Persian Gulf*. Vol. 22: 1959–1960. Cambridge: Archive Editions.

Johanson, Katya, Bronwyn Coate, Caitlin Vincent, and Hilary Glow. 2022. "Is There a 'Venice Effect'? Participation in the Venice Biennale and the Implications for Artists' Careers." *Poetics* 92 (101619): 1–14. https://doi.org/doi.org/10.1016/j.poetic.2021.101619.

Joselit, David. 2020. *Heritage and Debt: Art in Globalization*. The MIT Press.

Joselit, David. 2017. "An Allegory of Criticism." In *Beyond Critique: Contemporary Art in Theory, Practice & Instruction*, edited by Pamela Fraser and Roger Rothman. Bloomsbury Publishing.

Kaddoura, Mohammed. 2022. "Massive Light Art Festival in Saudi Arabia Breaks Six World Records." *Guinness World Records*, November 25. https://www.guinnessworldrecords.com/news/commercial/2022/11/massive-light-art-festival-in-saudi-arabia-breaks-six-world-records-726790.

Kanna, Ahmed. 2011. *Dubai, the City as Corporation*. University of Minnesota Press.

Kanna, Ahmed, Amelie Le Renard, and Neha Vora. 2020. *Beyond Exception: New Interpretations of the Arabian Peninsula*. Cornell University Press.

Karinkurayil, Mohamed. 2024. *The Gulf Migrant Archives in Kerala: Reading Borders and Belonging.* Oxford University Press.

Karp, Ivan, Corinne Kratz, Lynn Szwaja, and Tomás Ybarra-Frausto, eds. 2006. *Museum Frictions: Public Cultures/Global Transformations.* Duke University Press.

Karp, Ivan, Christine Kreamer, and Steven Lavine, eds. 1992. *Museums and Communities: The Politics of Public Culture.* Smithsonian Institution Press.

Karp, Ivan, and Steven Lavine, eds. 1991. *Exhibiting Cultures: The Poetics and Politics of Museum Display.* Smithsonian Institution Press.

Kazerouni, Alexandre. 2017. *Le miroir des cheikhs.* Presses Universitaires de France.

Kazerouni, Alexandre. 2015. "Musées et soft power dans le Golfe persique." *Pouvoirs* 152 (1): 87–97.

Kershoff, Estee. 2023. "Guggenheim Abu Dhabi: Top Museum's Opening Date and More [2023 Update]." *Time Out,* April 26. https://www.timeoutabudhabi.com /attractions/guggenheim-abu-dhabi-guide.

Keshavarzian, Arang. 2024. *Making Space for the Gulf: Histories of Regionalism and the Middle East.* Stanford University Press.

Khaire, Mukti, and R. Daniel Wadhwani. 2010. "Changing Landscapes: The Construction of Meaning and Value in a New Market Category—Modern Indian Art." *Academy of Management Journal* 53 (6): 1281–304. https://doi.org/10.5465/AMJ .2010.57317861.

Khalaf, 'Abd al-Hādī, Omar AlShehabi, and Adam Hanieh, eds. 2015. *Transit States: Labour, Migration and Citizenship in the Gulf.* Pluto Press.

Khalaf, Sulayman. 2005. "National Dress and the Construction of Emirati Cultural Identity." *Journal of Human Sciences* (11): 230–67.

Khalaf, Sulayman. 2000. "Poetics and Politics of Newly Invented Traditions in the Gulf: Camel Racing in the United Arab Emirates." *Ethnology: An International Journal of Cultural and Social Anthropology* 39 (3): 243–61. https://doi.org/10.2307 /3774109.

Khalidi, Rashid. 1998. "The 'Middle East' as a Framework of Analysis: Re-Mapping a Region in the Era of Globalization." *Comparative Studies of South Asia, Africa and the Middle East* 18 (1): 74–81. https://doi.org/10.1215/1089201X-18-1-74.

Khodr, Ali. 2017. "Revisiting Michel Ecochard's Master Plans for Beirut between 1941– 1964." PhD diss., MIT. https://dspace.mit.edu/handle/1721.1/111541?show=full.

Khouri, Kristine. 2014. "Mapping Arab Art through the Sultan Gallery." *ArteEast* (blog), April 15. https://arteeast.org/quarterly/mapping-arab-art-through-the -sultan-gallery/.

Kisin, Eugenia, and Fred R. Myers. 2019. "The Anthropology of Art, After the End of Art: Contesting the Art-Culture System." *Annual Review of Anthropology* 48 (1): 317–34. https://doi.org/10.1146/annurev-anthro-102218-011331.

Koch, Robert. 2002. "The Critical Gesture in Philosophy." In *Iconoclash: Beyond the Image Wars in Science, Religion and Art,* edited by Bruno Latour and Peter Weibel. MIT Press.

Krauss, Rosalind. 1990. "The Cultural Logic of the Late Capitalist Museum." *October* 54: 3–17. https://doi.org/10.2307/778666.

Kräussl, Roman. 2015. "Art as an Alternative Asset Class: Risk and Return Character-istics of the Middle Eastern and Northern African Art Markets." In *Cosmopolitan Canvases: The Globalization of Markets for Contemporary Art*, edited by Olav Vel-thuis and Stefano Baia Curioni. Oxford University Press.

Kreps, Christina. 2011. "Changing the Rules of the Road: Post-Colonialism and the New Ethics of Museum Anthropology." In *The Routledge Companion to Museum Ethics*, edited by Janet Marstine. Routledge.

Krieger, Zvika. 2008. "Has NYU President John Sexton Sold Out with an Abu Dhabi Ex-pansion?" *New York Magazine*, April 10. https://nymag.com/news/features/46000/.

Latour, Bruno. 2004. "Why Has Critique Run out of Steam? From Matters of Fact to Matters of Concern." *Critical Inquiry* 30 (2): 225–48. https://doi.org/10.1086/421123.

Lavine, Steven. 1991. "Art Museums, National Identity, and the Status of Minority Cul-tures: The Case of Hispanic Art in the United States." In *Exhibiting Cultures: The Poetics and Politics of Museum Display*, edited by Ivan Karp and Stephen Lavine. Smithsonian Institution Press.

Le Renard, Amelie. 2021. *Western Privilege: Work, Intimacy, and Postcolonial Hierar-chies in Dubai*. Stanford University Press.

Lena, Jennifer. 2019. *Entitled: Discriminating Tastes and the Expansion of the Arts*. Princeton University Press.

Lena, Jennifer, and Erin Johnston. 2015. "U.S. Cultural Engagement with Global Muslim Communities." *Grantmakers in the Arts Reader*. https://www.giarts.org/article/us-cultural-engagement-global-muslim-communities.

Lenssen, Anneka. 2018. "In Focus: Biennials and Arab Representation." In *Modern Art in the Arab World: Primary Documents*, edited by Anneka Lenssen, Sarah Rogers, and Nada Shabout. The Museum of Modern Art Press.

Levitt, Peggy. 2015. *Artifacts and Allegiances: How Museums Put the Nation and the World on Display*. University of California Press.

Li, Darryl. 2020. *The Universal Enemy: Jihad, Empire, and the Challenge of Solidarity*. Stanford University Press.

Li, Tanya. 2014. *Land's End: Capitalist Relations on the Indigenous Frontier*. Duke Uni-versity Press.

Limbert, Mandana. 2010. *In the Time of Oil: Piety, Memory, and Social Life in an Omani Town*. Stanford University Press.

Lind, Maria. 2012. "Preface: Contemporary Art and Its Commercial Markets." In *Con-temporary Art and Its Commercial Markets*, edited by Maria Lind and Olav Vel-thuis. Sternberg Press.

Lind, Maria, and Olav Velthuis, eds. 2012. *Contemporary Art and Its Commercial Mar-kets*. Sternberg Press.

Lionnet, Francoise. 2004. "The Mirror and the Tomb: Africa, Museums, and Memory." In *Museum Studies: An Anthology of Contexts*, edited by Bettina Carbonell. Blackwell.

Liscia, Valentina Di. 2020. "An Instagram Account Is Amplifying Anonymous Testi-monies of Racism in Museums." *Hyperallergic*, June 30. http://hyperallergic.com/574189/change-the-museum-instagram/.

Lloyd, David, and Paul Thomas. 1998. *Culture and the State*. Routledge.

Londoño, Johana. 2020. *Abstract Barrios: The Crises of Latinx Visibility in Cities*. Duke University Press.

Lonetree, Amy. 2012. *Decolonizing Museums: Representing Native America in National and Tribal Museums*. University of North Carolina Press.

Longair, Sarah. 2015. *Cracks in the Dome: Fractured Histories of Empire in the Zanzibar Museum, 1897–1964*. Ashgate Publishing.

Longair, Sarah. 2012. "'The Experience of a Lady Curator': Negotiating Curatorial Challenges in the Zanzibar Museum." In *Curating Empire: Museums and the British Imperial Experience*, edited by Sarah Longair and John McAleer. Manchester University Press.

Longva, Anh Nga. 1997. *Walls Built on Sand: Migration, Exclusion, and Society in Kuwait*. Westview Press.

Lori, Noora. 2019. *Offshore Citizens: Permanent Temporary Status in the Gulf*. Cambridge University Press.

Louvre Press. 2017. "Louvre Abu Dhabi, a New Cultural Landmark for the 21st Century, Opens to the Public on 11 November." *Espace presse du musée du Louvre*, December 22. https://presse.louvre.fr/louvre-abu-dhabi-a-new-cultural-landmark-for-the-21st-century-opens-to-the-public-on-11-november/.

Low, Michael Christopher. 2014. "The Indian Ocean and Other Middle Easts." *Comparative Studies of South Asia, Africa and the Middle East* 34 (3): 549–55.

Lulu, Tahiyya. 2012. "Abdulhadi Al-Khawaja and Bahrain's Political Prisoners." *Jadaliyya*, April 11. http://www.jadaliyya.com/Details/23894.

Lulu, Tahiyya. 2011. "Saudi Hegemony Stamps Out the Bahraini Spring." *Jadaliyya*, April 10. http://www.jadaliyya.com/Details/23894.

Macdonald, Sharon. 2006. *A Companion to Museum Studies*. 1st ed. Blackwell Publishing.

MacDougall, David. 2006. *The Corporeal Image: Film, Ethnography, and the Senses*. Princeton University Press.

MacGilp, Alexandra. 2016. "Curator's Foreword." In *Maraya in Residence 2015*. Maraya Productions.

MacLean, Matthew. 2016. "Time, Space & Narrative in Emirati Museums." In *Representing the Nation: Heritage, Museums, National Narratives & Identity in the Arab Gulf States*, edited by Victoria Penziner Hightower, Pamela Erskine-Loftus, and Mariam Al-Mulla. Routledge.

Mahmood, Saba. 2005. *Politics of Piety: The Islamic Revival and the Feminist Subject*. Princeton University Press.

Mamdani, Mahmood. 2004. *Good Muslim, Bad Muslim: America, the Cold War, and the Roots of Terror*. Pantheon Books.

Manarat Al Saadiyat, The British Museum, and Abu Dhabi Tourism and Culture Authority. 2014. *Activity Guide: A History of the World in 100 Objects*. Abu Dhabi Tourism and Culture Authority.

Marable, Manning. 2015. *How Capitalism Underdeveloped Black America: Problems in Race, Political Economy, and Society.* Haymarket Books.

Maraya Art Centre. 2023. "About Maraya Art Centre." https://maraya.ae/site/page/about-maraya-art-centre/11.

Markham, Sydney F., and Harold Hargreaves. 1936. *The Museums of India: A Survey.* Museums Association.

Marzio, Peter. 1991. "Minorities and Fine-Arts Museums in the United States." In *Exhibiting Cultures: The Poetics and Politics of Museum Display*, edited by Ivan Karp and Steve Lavine. Smithsonian Institution Press.

Massad, Joseph. 2015. *Islam in Liberalism.* University of Chicago Press.

Mathur, Saloni. 2005. "Museums and Globalization." *Anthropological Quarterly* 78 (3): 697–708.

Mathur, Saloni, and Kavita Singh, eds. 2015. *No Touching, No Spitting, No Praying: The Museum in South Asia.* Routledge.

Matthiesen, Toby. 2013. *Sectarian Gulf: Bahrain, Saudi Arabia, and the Arab Spring That Wasn't.* Stanford University Press.

Maynard, Audrie. 2016. "The Soul of the Nation: The State Hermitage Museum and the Quest for Russian National Identity." Master's thesis, Proquest Dissertations and Theses (10144655).

Mazzarella, William. 2013. *Censorium: Cinema and the Open Edge of Mass Publicity.* Duke University Press.

McAleer, John, and Sarah Longair, eds. 2014. *Curating Empire: Museums and the British Imperial Experience.* Manchester University Press.

McAleer, John, and John MacKenzie, eds. 2015. *Exhibiting the Empire: Cultures of Display and the British Empire.* Manchester University Press.

McClellan, Andrew. 2012. "Museum Expansion in the Twenty-First Century: Abu Dhabi." *Journal of Curatorial Studies* 1 (3): 271–93. https://doi.org/doi: 10.1386/jcs.1.3.271_1.

McClellan, Andrew. 2008. *The Art Museum from Boullée to Bilbao.* University of California Press.

McClellan, Andrew. 2003. *Art and Its Publics: Museum Studies at the Millennium.* Blackwell Publishing.

McClellan, Andrew. 1994. *Inventing the Louvre: Art, Politics, and the Origins of the Modern Museum in Eighteenth-Century Paris.* Cambridge University Press.

McElhinny, Bonnie. 2010. "The Audacity of Affect: Gender, Race, and History in Linguistic Accounts of Legitimacy and Belonging." *Annual Review of Anthropology* 39: 309–28.

McLeod, Malcolm. 2004. "Museums Without Collections: Museum Philosophy in West Africa." In *Museum Studies: An Anthology of Contexts*, edited by Bettina Messias Carbonell. Blackwell.

Melamed, Jodi. 2006. "The Spirit of Neoliberalism: From Racial Liberalism to Neoliberal Multiculturalism." *Social Text* 24 (4): 1–24.

Menger, Pierre-Michel. 2014. *The Economics of Creativity: Art and Achievement Under Uncertainty.* Harvard University Press.

Menger, Pierre-Michel. 1999. "Artistic Labor Markets and Careers." *Annual Review of Sociology* 25: 541–74.

Meskell, Lynn. 2018. *A Future in Ruins: UNESCO, World Heritage, and the Dream of Peace.* Oxford University Press.

Mezaina, Hind. 2017. "Bayn: The In-Between." *Tea with Culture* podcast.

Minutillo, Josephine. 2008. "Thomas Krens, Guggenheim's Controversial Leader, Steps Down." *Architectural Record.* https://www.architecturalrecord.com/articles/4264-thomas-krens-guggenheim-s-controversial-leader-steps-down.

Mittermaier, Amira. 2011. *Dreams That Matter: Egyptian Landscapes of the Imagination.* University of California Press.

Moghadam, Amin. 2021. "Iranian Migrations to Dubai: Constraints and Autonomy of a Segmented Diaspora." Ryerson Centre for Immigration and Settlement—Working Papers Series, January 1. https://www.academia.edu/45007353/Iranian_Migrations_to_Dubai_Constraints_and_Autonomy_of_a_Segmented_Diaspora.

Molho, Jérémie. 2021. "Putting the City on the World Art Map: Star Curators and Nation Branding." *International Journal of Politics, Culture, and Society* 34: 455–70.

Mosquera, Gerardo. 2003. "Alien-Own/Own Alien: Notes on Globalization and Cultural Difference." In *Complex Entanglements: Art, Globalization, and Cultural Difference*, edited by Nikos Papastergiadis. Rivers Oram Press.

Murphy, Keith. 2017. "Fontroversy! Or, How to Care about the Shape of Language." In *Language and Materiality: Ethnographic and Theoretical Explorations*, edited by Jillian R. Cavanaugh and Shalini Shankar. Cambridge University Press.

Murray, Grace. 2017. "Emerging Art Center: Doha, Qatar." In *Art and the Global Economy*, edited by John Zarobell. University of California Press.

Muslic, Hana. 2017. "A Brief History of Nonprofit Organizations." Nonprofit Hub, October 27. https://nonprofithub.org/a-brief-history-of-nonprofit-organizations/.

Myers, Fred R. 2002. *Painting Culture: The Making of an Aboriginal High Art.* Duke University Press.

Myers, Fred R. 1994. "Beyond the Intentional Fallacy: Art Criticism and the Ethnography of Aboriginal Acrylic Painting." *Visual Anthropology Review* 10 (1): 10–43. https://doi.org/10.1525/var.1994.10.1.10.

Nye, Joseph. 2004. *Soft Power: The Means to Success in World Politics.* Public Affairs.

O'Doherty, Brian. 1986. *Inside the White Cube: The Ideology of the Gallery Space.* 1st ed. Lapis Press.

Oguibe, Olu. 2004. *The Culture Game.* University of Minnesota Press.

Ong, Aihwa. 2006. *Neoliberalism as Exception: Mutations in Citizenship and Sovereignty.* Duke University Press.

Ong, Aihwa. 1999. *Flexible Citizenship: The Cultural Logics of Transnationality.* Duke University Press.

Onley, James. 2007. *The Arabian Frontier of the British Raj: Merchants, Rulers, and the British in the Nineteenth-Century Gulf.* Oxford University Press.

Onley, James, and Gerd Nonneman. 2020. "The Journal of Arabian Studies and the Development of Gulf and Arabian Peninsula Studies." *Journal of Arabian Studies* 10 (1): 1–50.

Özyürek, Esra. 2006. *Nostalgia for the Modern: State Secularism and Everyday Politics in Turkey.* Duke University Press.

Pegno, Marianna, and Christine Brindza. 2021. "Redefining Curatorial Leadership and Activating Community Expertise to Build Equitable and Inclusive Art Museums." *Curator: The Museum Journal* 64 (2): 343–62.

Pieprzak, Katarzyna. 2010. *Imagined Museums: Art and Modernity in Postcolonial Morocco.* University of Minnesota Press.

Plattner, Stuart. 1996. *High Art Down Home: An Economic Ethnography of a Local Art Market.* University of Chicago Press.

Polite, Smita. 2002. "Qatari Construction Industry Seeing 'Best of Times.'" *Middle East News Online*, July 15.

Price, Sally. 2007. *Paris Primitive: Jacques Chirac's Museum on the Quai Branly.* University of Chicago Press.

Price, Sally. 1989. *Primitive Art in Civilized Places.* University of Chicago Press.

Prior, Nick. 2002. *Museums and Modernity: Art Galleries and the Making of Modern Culture.* Berg.

Pritchard, Stephen. 2020. "The Artwashing of Gentrification and Social Cleansing." In *The Handbook of Displacement*, edited by P. Edey. Springer International Publishing.

Qatar Museums. 2025. "Art Mill Museum." https://qm.org.qa/en/about-us/art-mill -museum/.

Quemin, Alain. 2002. *L'Art Contemporain International, Entre les Institutions et le Marché: Le Rapport Disparu.* Artprice.

Rader, Karen, and Victoria Cain. 2014. *Life on Display: Revolutionizing U.S. Museums of Science and Natural History in the Twentieth Century.* University of Chicago Press.

Rectanus, Mark. 2002. *Culture Incorporated: Museums, Artists, and Corporate Sponsorships.* University of Minnesota Press.

Reisz, Todd. 2021. *Showpiece City: How Architecture Made Dubai.* Stanford University Press.

Relyea, Lane. 2013. *Your Everyday Art World.* MIT Press.

Rey, Virginie, ed. 2020. *The Art of Minorities: Cultural Representation in Museums of the Middle East and North Africa.* Edinburgh University Press.

Rice, Michael. 1977. "National Museum of Qatar, Doha." *Museum XXIX* (2/3): 78–87.

Riding, Alan. 2007. "France Frets as Louvre Looks Overseas." *The New York Times*, January 1. https://www.nytimes.com/2007/01/01/arts/design/01louv.html.

Rizvi, Fazal. 2003. "Looking Back and Looking Forward: Policies of Multiculturalism and the Arts in Australia." In *Complex Entanglements: Art, Globalization and Cultural Difference*, edited by Nikos Papastergiadis. Rivers Oram Press.

Robinson, Megan, and Jennifer Novak-Leonard. 2021. "Refining Understandings of Entrepreneurial Artists: Valuing the Creative Incorporation of Business and

Entrepreneurship into Artistic Practice." *Artivate: A Journal of Entrepreneurship in the Arts* 10 (1): 1–19. https://doi.org/10.1353/artv.2021.0002.

Rogers, Douglas. 2015. *The Depths of Russia: Oil, Power and Culture After Socialism*. Cornell University Press.

Ross, Andrew, ed. 2015. *The Gulf: High Culture/Hard Labor*. OR Books.

Royal Commission for AlUla. 2023. "Royal Commission for AlUla, About RCU." https://www.rcu.gov.sa/en/about-us/about-rcu/.

Rule, Alex, and David Levine. 2012. "International Art English." *Triple Canopy*, July 30. https://www.canopycanopycanopy.com/issues/16/contents/international _art_english.

Rydell, Robert. 1984. *All the World's a Fair: Visions of Empire at American International Expositions, 1876–1916*. University of Chicago Press.

Sachedina, Amal. 2021. *Cultivating the Past, Living the Modern: The Politics of Time in the Sultanate of Oman*. Cornell University Press.

Said, Edward. 1978. *Orientalism*. 25th anniv. ed. Vintage Books.

Salamandra, Christa. 2004. *A New Old Damascus: Authenticity and Distinction in Urban Syria*. Indiana University Press.

Schielke, Samuli. 2020. *Migrant Dreams: Egyptian Workers in the Gulf States*. American University of Cairo Press.

Schultz, Abby. 2024. "Art Economist Magnus Resch Wants to Convert Art Lovers into Art Buyers." *Barron's*, February 14. https://www.barrons.com/articles/art -economist-magnus-resch-wants-to-convert-art-lovers-into-art-buyers-808bd81f.

Seaman, Anna. 2017. "Louvre Abu Dhabi: Why All Eyes Are on the Middle East's New Billion Dollar Museum." *CNN*, November 9. https://www.cnn.com/style/article /louvre-abu-dhabi-museum-opening/index.html.

Seaman, Anna. 2016. "Melting the Sky: Opens Tonight in Dubai." *The National*, September 26. https://www.thenationalnews.com/arts-culture/art/melting-the-sky -opens-tonight-in-dubai-1.221222.

Seligson, Joelle. 2008. "Can Museums Buy Happiness?" *Museum* Nov/Dec: 46–53.

Senie, Harriet. 2001. *The Tilted Arc Controversy: Dangerous Precedent*. University of Minnesota Press.

Shaheen, Jack. 2001. *Reel Bad Arabs: How Hollywood Vilifies a People*. Olive Branch Press.

Shankar, Shalini. 2015. *Advertising Diversity: Ad Agencies and the Creation of Asian American Consumers*. Duke University Press.

Shaw, Wendy. 2003. *Possessors and Possessed: Museums, Archaeology, and the Visualization of History in the Late Ottoman Empire*. University of California Press.

Simpson, Audra. 2014. *Mohawk Interruptus: Political Life across the Borders of Settler States*. Duke University Press.

Sindelar, Melanie. 2017. "Land Art as a Means to Negotiate Natural and Cultural Heritage in the United Arab Emirates." *Český Lid* 104 (2): 213–30.

Smith, Linda Tuhiwai. 1999. *Decolonizing Methodologies: Research and Indigenous Peoples*. 2nd ed. Zed Books Ltd.

Smith, Sarah-Neel. 2019. "Cengiz Çekil's Dual Practice: Conceptual Installations and Authoritarian Monuments, 1983–91." *Art Journal* 78 (4): 76–97. https://doi.org/10.1080/00043249.2019.1684111.

Smith, Terry. 2009. *What Is Contemporary Art?* University of Chicago Press.

Stallabras, Julian. 2004. *Art Incorporated: The Story of Contemporary Art*. Oxford University Press.

Stoby, Aisha. 2017a. "Bayn: Between." In *Bayn: The In-Between*, edited by Warehouse 421. Maraya Productions.

Stoby, Aisha. 2017b. "Modern Art Pioneers: An Introduction to Artist Communities in the GCC." In *But We Cannot See Them: Tracing a UAE Art Community 1988–2008*. Akkadia Press.

Sultan, Shaykh Zayed bin. 2016. "Foreword." In *Al Haraka Baraka: In Movement There Is Blessing*. Maraya Productions.

Sweeney, Liam, Deirdre Harkins, and Joanna Dressel. 2022. "Art Museum Demographic Survey 2022." *Ithaka S&R*. https://sr.ithaka.org/wp-content/uploads/2022/11/Mellon-Art-Museum-Staff-Demographic-Survey-11162022.pdf.

Tareq Rajab Museum. n.d. "School and a Scholarship to England." https://trmkt.org/tsr-education/.

Taussig, Karen-Sue, Klaus Hoeyer, and Stefan Helmreich. 2013. "The Anthropology of Potentiality in Biomedicine." *Current Anthropology* 54 (S7): S3–14. https://doi.org/10.1086/671401.

Taylor, Alan. 2017. "The Opening of the Louvre Abu Dhabi." *The Atlantic*, November 8. https://www.theatlantic.com/photo/2017/11/the-opening-of-the-louvre-abu-dhabi/545333.

Tchen, John Kuo Wei. 1992. "Creating a Dialogic Museum: The Chinatown History Museum Experiment." In *Museums and Communities: The Politics of Public Culture*, edited by Ivan Karp, Christine Kreamer, and Steven Lavine. Smithsonian Institution Press.

Toukan, Hanan. 2021. *The Politics of Art: Dissent and Cultural Diplomacy in Lebanon, Palestine, and Jordan*. Stanford University Press.

Tsing, Anna. 2005. *Friction: An Ethnography of Global Connection*. Princeton University Press.

UAE Government. 2016. "National Programme for Happiness and Wellbeing—The Official Portal of the UAE Government." National Programme for Happiness and Wellbeing. https://u.ae/en/about-the-uae/the-uae-government/government-of-future/happiness/national-programme-for-happiness-and-wellbeing.

UNESCO. 1982. "Situation and Trends in Cultural Policy in Arab Member States." Programme and meeting document. World Conference on Cultural Policies (2nd). https://unesdoc.unesco.org/ark:/48223/pf0000049345?posInSet=19&queryId=7017ab78-27df-40d1-90d3-e230d9dac6ab.

UNESCWA. 2015. "The Bahrain Arts Society." United Nations Economic and Social Commission for Western Asia, October 6. https://archive.unescwa.org/bahrain-arts-society.

Unnikrishnan, Deepak. 2017. *Temporary People*. Restless Books.

Velthuis, Olav. 2011. "The Venice Effect." *The Art Newspaper* June: 21–24.

Velthuis, Olav. 2005. *Talking Prices: Symbolic Meanings of Prices on the Market for Contemporary Art*. Princeton University Press.

Velthuis, Olav, and Stefano Baia Curioni, eds. 2015. *Cosmopolitan Canvases: The Globalization of Markets for Contemporary Art*. Oxford University Press.

Velthuis, Olav, and Amanda Brandellero. 2018. "Introduction to Special Issue on Global Art Markets." *Poetics* 71: 1–6. https://doi.org/doi.org/10.1016/j.poetic.2018.11.007.

Verdeil, Eric. 2012. "Michel Ecochard in Lebanon and Syria (1956–1968): The Spread of Modernism, the Building of the Independent States and the Rise of Local Professionals of Planning." *Planning Perspectives* 27 (2): 249–66. https://doi.org/10.1080/02665433.2012.646774.

Voon, Claire. 2017. "Dubai, a City Known for Censorship, Launches Typeface for Self-Expression." *Hyperallergic*, May 2. http://hyperallergic.com/375986/dubai-a-city-known-for-censorship-launches-typeface-for-self-expression/.

Vora, Neha. 2018. *Teach for Arabia: American Universities, Liberalism, and Transnational Qatar*. Stanford University Press.

Vora, Neha. 2015. "Expat/Expert Camps: Redefining 'Labour' Within Gulf Migration." In *Transit States*, edited by Abdulhadi Khalaf, Omar AlShehabi, and Adam Hanieh. Pluto Press.

Vora, Neha. 2013. *Impossible Citizens: Dubai's Indian Diaspora*. Duke University Press.

Vora, Neha, and Natalie Koch. 2015. "Everyday Inclusions: Rethinking Ethnocracy, Kafala, and Belonging in the Arabian Peninsula." *Studies in Ethnicity and Nationalism* 15 (3): 540–52. https://doi.org/10.1111/sena.12158.

Wakefield, Sarina. 2021. *Cultural Heritage, Transnational Narratives and Museum Franchising in Abu Dhabi*. Routledge.

Wakefield, Sarina. 2012. "Falconry as Heritage in the United Arab Emirates." *World Archaeology* 44 (2): 280–90. https://doi.org/10.1080/00438243.2012.669644.

Walsh, Katie. 2012. "Emotion and Migration: British Transnationals in Dubai." *Environment and Planning D: Society and Space* 30 (1): 43–59. https://doi.org/10.1068/d12409.

Walsh, Katie. 2007. "'It Got Very Debauched, Very Dubai!' Heterosexual Intimacy amongst Single British Expatriates." *Social & Cultural Geography* 8 (4): 507–33. https://doi.org/10.1080/14649360701529774.

Wang, Peggy. 2014. "Making and Remaking History: Categorising 'Conceptual Art' in Contemporary Chinese Art." *Journal of Art Historiography* 10: 1–17.

Warehouse421. 2017. "Foreword." In *Bayn: The In-Between*. Maraya Productions.

Watenpaugh, Heghnar Zeitlian. 2004. *The Image of an Ottoman City: Imperial Architecture and Urban Experience in Aleppo in the 16th and 17th Centuries*. Brill.

Weber, Max. 1998. *The Protestant Ethic and the Spirit of Capitalism*. 2nd ed. Roxbury Publishing.

Welland, Sasha Su-Ling. 2018. *Experimental Beijing: Gender and Globalization in Chinese Contemporary Art*. Duke University Press.

White, Arnold. 2018. "Sociable Solitude: The Early Modern Hermitage as Proto-Museum." *Intersections* 56: 405–50.

Williams, Raymond. 1977. *Marxism and Literature*. Oxford University Press.

Willis, John. 2009. "Making Yemen Indian: Rewriting the Boundaries of Imperial Arabia." *International Journal of Middle East Studies* 41 (1): 23–38.

Wilson, Alice. 2023. *Afterlives of Revolution: Everyday Counterhistories in Southern Oman*. Stanford University Press.

Win, Thet Shein. 2014. "Marketing the Entrepreneurial Artist in the Innovation Age: Aesthetic Labor, Artistic Subjectivity, and the Creative Industries." *Anthropology of Work Review* 35 (1): 2–13. https://doi.org/10.1111/awr.12026.

Winegar, Jessica. 2008. "The Humanity Game: Art, Islam, and the War on Terror." *Anthropological Quarterly* 81 (3): 651–81. https://doi.org/10.1353/anq.0.0024.

Winegar, Jessica. 2006. *Creative Reckonings: The Politics of Art and Culture in Contemporary Egypt*. Stanford University Press.

Wolf, Eric. 1982. *Europe and the People Without History*. University of California Press.

Wright, Andrea. 2021. *Between Dreams and Ghosts: Indian Migration and Middle Eastern Oil*. Stanford University Press.

Wu, Chin-Tao. 2009. "Biennials without Borders?" *New Left Review* 57: 107–15.

Wu, Chin-Tao. 2002. *Privatising Culture: Corporate Art Intervention since the 1980s*. Verso.

Yúdice, George. 2003. *The Expediency of Culture: Uses of Culture in the Global Era*. Duke University Press.

Zahlan, Rosemarie Said. 1978. *The Origins of the United Arab Emirates: A Political and Social History of the Trucial States*. Routledge.

Zarobell, John. 2017. *Art and the Global Economy*. University of California Press.

Index

Note: Page numbers followed by *f*, *t*, or *m* refer respectively to a figure, table, or map on that page. Page numbers followed by "n" and another number refer to an endnote on that page.

CULTURE AND ECONOMIC LIFE

Artists at Work: Rethinking Policy for Artistic Careers
Joanna Woronkowicz
2025

Good Kids: Why Children Demand the Right to Work with Dignity
Isabel Jijon
2025

Clawing Back: Redistribution in Precarious Times
Deborah James
2025

Happy Meat: The Sadness and Joy of a Paradoxical Idea
Shyon Baumann, Emily Huddart Kennedy,
Josee Johnston and Merin Oleschuk
2025

*Cosmopolitan Scientists: How a Global Policy of
Commercialization Became Japanese*
Nahoko Kameo
2024

The Indebted Woman: Kinship, Sexuality, and Capitalism
Isabelle Guérin
2023

Traders and Tinkers: Bazaars in the Global Economy
Maitrayee Deka
2023

For a complete listing of titles in this series, visit the
Stanford University Press website, www.sup.org.

The authorized representative in the EU for product safety and compliance is:
Mare Nostrum Group
B.V Doelen 72
4831 GR Breda
The Netherlands

www.ingramcontent.com/pod-product-compliance
Lightning Source LLC
Chambersburg PA
CBHW050439290526
45786CB00006B/2081